The C++ Programmer's Mindset

Learn computational, algorithmic, and systems thinking to become a better C++ programmer

Sam Morley

<packt>

The C++ Programmer's Mindset

Portfolio Director: Kunal Chaudhari

Relationship Lead: Dhruv J. Kataria

Project Manager: K. Loganathan

Content Engineer: Deepayan Bhattacharjee

Technical Editor: Irfa Ansari

Copy Editor: Safis Editing

Indexer: Tejal Soni

Proofreader: Deepayan Bhattacharjee

Production Designer: Ajay Patule

Growth Lead: Mansi Shah

First published: November 2025

Production reference: 1141125

Published by Packt Publishing Ltd.

Grosvenor House

11 St Paul's Square

Birmingham

B3 1RB, UK.

ISBN 978-1-83588-842-1

www.packtpub.com

To Saba

Contributors

About the author

Sam Morley is a research software engineer and mathematician at the University of Oxford, where he works on the DataSig project. He is the lead developer of the RoughPy library for computational rough paths in the data science of streamed data, and several other high-performance accelerator libraries in C++ and CUDA. Sam is a former lecturer in mathematics and author of *Applying Math with Python*. He greatly enjoys logical puzzles and is often found pondering fiendish Sudoku puzzles.

I want to thank my friends and colleagues at the University of Oxford, the broader DataSig team, and my friends from the Alan Turing Institute. I'd also like to thank my family, especially my parents, who've been very supportive throughout.

About the reviewers

Alexei Kondratiev is a mission-critical software and embedded systems engineer with 20+ years of experience in Medical, Automotive, Advanced Driver Assistance Systems (ADAS), and Aerospace, low-latency and high-throughput concurrent and asynchronous C++ software development. He has a solid background in network programming and protocols, distributed systems, system and embedded programming, troubleshooting, integration with open-source projects, performance analysis, and optimization.

He is a C++ software developer at LTA Research, an aerospace research and development company that builds experimental and certified manned airships.

At LTA, he is an owner of the Soft Real-Time Embedded Linux Airship Helium Gas Cells Volume Monitoring System, Soft Real-Time Hardware Simulation System, and Soft Real-Time Dynon Avionics SkyView HDX Emulator of the Glass Cockpit Electronic Flight Instrument System R&D C++ projects.

Julian Faber has more than 30 years' experience of software design and development with C++, working for some of the largest investment banks in the world. Deeply passionate about creativity within software engineering, his focus these days is latency sensitivity on trading systems and enhancing usability. A hallmark of his work is designing systems to be fully testable, as he is a keen advocate for complete testing of software.

Join us on Discord!

To join the Discord community for this book - where you can share feedback, ask questions to the author, and learn about new releases - follow the QR code below:

`https://packt.link/deep-engineering-cpp`

Table of Contents

Preface

Solving problems is a large part of writing code. Sometimes these are small problems that we barely acknowledge and sometimes they are grand challenges that seem insurmountable at first. Whatever domain you work in, and whatever the problem, solving problems is an iterative process with false starts and dead ends until you eventually find the "right" path – this is normal. After solving a few big problems, you'll start to recognize some common features in this process: breaking the problem down into smaller pieces, formulating or finding good abstractions, recognizing patterns that appear in other kinds of problems, and formulating a list of steps to follow to construct solutions to the problem. In computer science, this framework for solving problems is called **computational thinking**.

Of course, formulating abstract solutions and algorithms is only part of actually solving the problem. The other part is actually realizing the solution as software and delivering it, whatever form that might take. This means you must first select the right tool to build this software, which includes selecting the programming language to use. Sometimes this choice is made for you, but other times, the choice depends on many factors. When performance is paramount, C++ is an obvious choice.

Modern C++ is very powerful and comes with a large ecosystem of high-performance libraries. Many substantial updates in the past decade have brought C++ into the modern era of programming languages. More than anything, what C++ provides is control. Other languages can achieve performance in some places, but they often fall down in other areas. Few languages deliver the same performance as C++ without sacrificing control, flexibility, or ease of use.

Being proficient at solving problems in C++, of course, requires you to have a good knowledge of C++ and standard techniques. Delivering the right balance of performance and flexibility often also requires an understanding of the broader context in which the code will run: the operating system, hardware, processor features, and specific accelerator hardware.

Having all this in mind when choosing data structures and designing algorithms can give you the edge. But it's more than that. Understanding these concepts will also help you select good abstractions and identify useful patterns more easily. The connection between C++ and problem-solving is two-way, and that is the topic of this book.

Who this book is for

This book is for people who are already familiar with the basics of C++ programming who are looking to become better at solving complex problems. No background in theoretical computer science is assumed; where this does appear, we keep it light on detail and give references to textbooks that explain it more.

This is not a step-by-step guide for solving problems. Instead, it is a discussion about the interplay between the C++ language, features, and facilities, and the computational thinking framework. We explain the context surrounding working in C++ that you should keep in mind and how this relates to the problem-solving process.

What this book covers

Chapter 1, Thinking Computationally, introduces the computational thinking framework for solving problems. We discuss the different components of computational thinking and how these might manifest in the problem-solving process. We also discuss a few features of modern C++ and good coding practices that will be used throughout the book.

Chapter 2, Abstraction in Detail, goes into more detail about abstraction. Specifically, we look at the abstraction mechanisms in C++ and how these can help us find useful abstractions in the data or methodology of the problem we're solving.

Chapter 3, Algorithmic Thinking and Complexity, talks about the design and analysis of algorithms. We discuss computational complexity and the different kinds of algorithms, and some design characteristics of different kinds of algorithms you can use when designing your own algorithms.

Chapter 4, Understanding the Machine, discusses modern computer hardware and operating systems and how understanding these can help us write code that runs faster (even if we can't reduce the complexity).

Chapter 5, Data Structures, discusses different data structures and their characteristics. We discuss different patterns of memory usage and how these impact performance in practice.

Chapter 6, Reusing Your Code and Modularity, considers the different mechanisms for making your code reusable and modular using the mechanisms in C++: functions, classes, namespaces, and so on. We also discuss packaging entire compiled components as libraries.

Chapter 7, Outlining the Challenge, describes a large challenge that we will solve over the course of the next five chapters. This includes using the principles of computational thinking to find a strategy for how to tackle the challenge as a whole.

Chapter 8, Building a Simple Command-Line Interface, is the first chapter of our big challenge. Here we design a simple command-line interface that will allow us and the end user to interact with our eventual solution to the problem.

Chapter 9, Reading Data from Different Formats, is the second chapter in our big challenge. We discuss the problem of ingesting data from two different common formats and designing the internal interfaces that allow us to hide the implementation details.

Chapter 10, Finding Information in Text, is the third chapter in our big challenge. It covers searching free-form text for specific patterns using regular expressions.

Chapter 11, Clustering Data, is the fourth chapter in our big challenge. We implement a k-means clustering algorithm to reduce our large, messy dataset to a small number of representative points.

Chapter 12, Reflecting on What We Have Built, is the final chapter in our big challenge. We add the finishing touches to the program and run it on some sample data. We look back over what we built in the previous four chapters and reflect on what worked well and what didn't work so well.

Chapter 13, The Problems of Scale, looks at how we might scale up our computations to deal with large, computationally intensive problems that require multiple threads, multiple processes, or even multiple computers.

Chapter 14, Dealing with GPUs and Specialized Hardware, looks at different means of interacting with specialized accelerator hardware for specific tasks. We look at OpenMP device offload, CUDA programming for Nvidia GPUs, and SYCL programming.

Chapter 15, Profiling Your Code, is where we examine our code through a profiler to see where our code is spending its time and how we might use this information to make our code faster.

To get the most out of this book

In this book, we assume that you have at least a basic knowledge of C++ programming and are familiar with the syntax and features of the language, and know how to use the CMake build system generator on your operating system of choice.

Most of the code samples in this book are written in standards-compliant C++, so it should work on any platform that provides a C++ compiler that supports at least C++20 (some chapters also require C++23). Some code fragments will only work on X86(-64) hardware, especially in *Chapter 4*, but the build system will simply not build these targets on other architectures (sorry ARM users).

Software/hardware covered in the book	Operating system requirements
C++20 (and C++23 in some places)	Windows, macOS, or Linux
CMake 3.30+	

Each folder in the GitHub repository for this book has a separate `CMakeLists.txt` file. These are independent of each other. In some of the folders, we need additional dependencies. These are either acquired automatically using the CMake `FetchContent` functions or findable with CMake `find_package`. For these, we also provide a `vcpkg` manifest file to download and build the missing dependencies.

If you are using the digital version of this book, we advise you to type the code yourself or access the code from the book's GitHub repository (a link is available in the next section). Doing so will help you avoid any potential errors related to the copying and pasting of code.

Download the example code files

The code bundle for the book is hosted on GitHub at `https://github.com/PacktPublishing/The-CPP-Programmers-Mindset`. We also have other code bundles from our rich catalog of books and videos available at `https://github.com/PacktPublishing`. Check them out!

Download the color images

We also provide a PDF file that has color images of the screenshots/diagrams used in this book. You can download it here: `https://packt.link/gbp/9781835888421`.

Conventions used

There are a number of text conventions used throughout this book.

`CodeInText`: Indicates code words in text, database table names, folder names, filenames, file extensions, pathnames, dummy URLs, user input, and Twitter/X handles. For example: "This function just calls `std::signal`, as follows."

A block of code is set as follows:

```
void setup_signals() {
    std::signal(SIGINT, &sigint_handler);
}
```

Any command-line input or output is written as follows:

```
cmake -B build -S . -GNinja -DCMAKE_BUILD_TYPE=Release
cmake --build build --config=Release
```

Bold: Indicates a new term, an important word, or words that you see on the screen. For instance, words in menus or dialog boxes appear in the text like this. For example: "Sometimes, **large language model** (**LLM**)-based coding assistants can be a great help."

> Warnings or important notes appear like this.

> Tips and tricks appear like this.

Get in touch

Feedback from our readers is always welcome.

General feedback: If you have questions about any aspect of this book or have any general feedback, please email us at `customercare@packt.com` and mention the book's title in the subject of your message.

Errata: Although we have taken every care to ensure the accuracy of our content, mistakes do happen. If you have found a mistake in this book, we would be grateful if you reported this to us. Please visit `http://www.packt.com/submit-errata`, click **Submit Errata**, and fill in the form.

Piracy: If you come across any illegal copies of our works in any form on the internet, we would be grateful if you would provide us with the location address or website name. Please contact us at `copyright@packt.com` with a link to the material.

If you are interested in becoming an author: If there is a topic that you have expertise in and you are interested in either writing or contributing to a book, please visit `http://authors.packt.com/`.

Share your thoughts

Once you've read *The C++ Programmer's Mindset,* we'd love to hear your thoughts! Scan the QR code below to go straight to the Amazon review page for this book and share your feedback.

`https://packt.link/r/1835888437`

Your review is important to us and the tech community and will help us make sure we're delivering excellent quality content.

Free Benefits with Your Book

This book comes with free benefits to support your learning. Activate them now for instant access (see the "*How to Unlock*" section for instructions).

Here's a quick overview of what you can instantly unlock with your purchase:

PDF and ePub Copies

- Access a DRM-free PDF copy of this book to read anywhere, on any device.
- Use a DRM-free ePub version with your favorite e-reader.

Next-Gen Web-Based Reader

- **Multi-device progress sync**: Pick up where you left off, on any device.
- **Highlighting and notetaking**: Capture ideas and turn reading into lasting knowledge.
- **Bookmarking**: Save and revisit key sections whenever you need them.
- **Dark mode**: Reduce eye strain by switching to dark or sepia themes.

How to Unlock

UNLOCK NOW

Scan the QR code (or go to `packtpub.com/unlock`). Search for this book by name, confirm the edition, and then follow the steps on the page.

***Note:** Keep your invoice handy. Purchases made directly from Packt don't require one.*

1

Thinking Computationally

Solving problems is a central part of being a programmer, as well as a useful skill for everyday life. The methodology is broadly the same wherever you look: identify smaller, more tractable challenges; realize these as instances of a general class of problem; solve the intermediate challenges; and put everything together as a sequence of simple steps to solve the larger problem. In computer science, we call this computational thinking.

This chapter serves as an introduction to the basic components of computational thinking at a high level. The objectives are to lay the foundation for more detailed analysis and in-depth examples later in the book. The first part of the chapter introduces the four components of computational thinking (decomposition, abstraction, pattern recognition, and algorithm design). The second half of the chapter deals with C++ specifically and identifies some aspects of the C++ language and standard library that can not only help implement efficient solutions, but also help you think about the problems themselves.

It is important to remember that the four components of computational thinking are not a step-by-step guide to solving problems. Learning how and when these different components come together to deliver a solution relies on a good knowledge of the tools and methodologies available to you as the solver, and on your past experience. This chapter will help you get started with building the necessary foundations of the theory and set the stage for building out some basic examples to get you started with tackling larger and more complex problems later.

Solving problems is an iterative process. There will be many failed attempts and false starts. This is a necessary part of the process. The last part of the chapter deals with good software practices that will enable you to iterate quickly and easily on your designs and arrive at a correct and usable solution more quickly.

In this chapter, we're going to cover the following main topics:

- The components of computational thinking
- Decomposing problems
- Building abstractions and recognizing common patterns
- Understanding algorithms
- Using modern C++ and good practice

> **Free Benefits with Your Book**
>
> Your purchase includes a free PDF copy of this book along with other exclusive benefits. Check the *Free Benefits with Your Book* section in the Preface to unlock them instantly and maximize your learning experience.

Technical requirements

In this chapter, we discuss the theory and methodology of computational thinking. As such, this chapter doesn't include much code. However, some of the later sections do have some samples of C++ code, and, as with the rest of this book, some familiarity with C++ is expected. Since the latter sections describe good practice for working with code, the `Chapter-01` folder in the GitHub repository for this book (`https://github.com/PacktPublishing/The-CPP-Programmers-Mindset`) includes these samples of code along with unit tests. These tests do not contribute to the content of the chapter.

The components of computational thinking

Solving problems is an iterative process. There are many things to consider at each step. As some challenges are overcome, others will emerge. Computational thinking provides the framework for deciding what step to take next. As with all iterative processes, there will be steps that don't work out because the solutions you arrive at are unsatisfactory or simply don't work, but this is all part of the process.

Before we continue, we need to discuss what we mean by a "problem." *For the purposes of this book, a problem is a specific task with well-defined constraints and parameters.* The actual nature of the task can be relatively simple or highly complex, as long as it is specific. The constraints can also be broad in nature: they can be managerial (time constraints, deadlines), technical (performance), or domain-specific (physical limitations). The parameters describe the data and other information that is provided in order to solve the task.

The four components of computational thinking are as follows:

- Decomposition
- Abstraction
- Pattern recognition
- Algorithm design

Each step in the problem-solving process will involve one or more of these components, but they are not, in themselves, the steps that one must follow. For instance, some steps will fall into a class of well-known problems with "off-the-shelf" solutions that can be implemented with ease. Other steps will be complex and require decomposition into many smaller problems. Moreover, these components cannot be considered in isolation. One cannot decompose a problem without understanding the essential constituents of the problem or recognizing standard patterns among the noise of contextual information that may or may not be relevant. You must consider all the components at once.

It is sometimes easy to miss the bigger picture when you are solving small and nuanced problems – especially how your solution will interface with the larger system. This could be the larger piece of software in which your solution will live, or the way clients interact with your software. These issues are also part of the problem that you would need to solve, using the components of computational thinking to guide you.

As you gain experience, the number of patterns and standard problems that you recognize will grow, and the speed at which you arrive at useful abstractions will increase. In the beginning, these aspects will be the most troublesome. In the remainder of this book, we will look at common techniques and some standard problems that will allow you to get started with problem-solving. Unfortunately, we cannot simply give you a complete catalogue of patterns and abstractions: if all problems were already solved, there would be no need for a framework for solving problems.

Solving problems is not only an iterative process, but also a dynamic process. Some choices will have implications for the rest of the process and possibly even for previous steps. For example, selecting a programming language, such as C++, will have a dramatic effect on the way you go about designing algorithms, selecting abstractions, the standard patterns available, and the way you further decompose problems. For example, if one solves a problem in Python, one might try to lean on the numerous high-performance libraries, which may or may not provide the exact functionality required. However, in C++, you have more freedom to implement your own high-performance primitive operations.

There will be times when you have to undo several steps of the process, especially while you're still building experience. The important thing here is to understand that this is a necessary step in the learning process. You must endeavor to understand why that particular line of investigation failed and how to incorporate this knowledge into the next iteration. Don't be afraid to go back to the beginning (time allowing) and start again. Sometimes this is the only way to make progress.

In the remainder of this chapter, we look in more detail at the four components of computational thinking. For now, we will only discuss the components in general. We will revisit these components in far more detail in later chapters, when we look at real examples and how to apply these concepts using C++.

General advice

Solving problems can be hard, especially when you're fairly new to a particular domain, language, tool, or working environment. Here is some general advice on how to make this easier and more enjoyable.

- Keep a journal of patterns, abstractions, and other information that you can refer back to when new problems appear. As you get more experience, you will internalize many of these, but there will always be some that you forget about that you might need to call on in the future.
- Seek out small problems to hone your skills. Websites such as LeetCode (`https://leetcode.com/`) have huge libraries of small problems that are designed to teach specific patterns and techniques. This can help, especially at the beginning when you don't have your own catalogue to draw upon. The greater the variety of problems that you see, the more you have to draw upon when you're looking for patterns and abstractions when solving entirely new problems; the problems don't need to be identical, just similar enough to provide inspiration.
- Talk to colleagues and friends about problems, where this is appropriate. Sometimes the act of explaining a problem can help make it clearer for you and will sometimes help you to solve the problem directly. If you can find a more senior or experienced colleague who is willing to help, then they can share their own expertise with you, which can sometimes help you arrive at solutions more quickly. If no colleagues or friends are available, even talking the problem through with your rubber duck can help – and they are always willing to listen.

A far too mathematical example

Before we go into detail about the components of computational thinking, we should first look at an example where many of these ideas manifest. The example we will use is solving a specific differential equation from elementary calculus. Don't be put off by the presence of equations in this section. The actual mathematics used here is not the important part; the way that we work through the problem is. Nevertheless, this example is a good choice precisely because of this added complexity; you will sometimes have to operate outside your comfort zone.

A differential equation is an equation that involves one or more derivatives of a function that evolves according to some other variable x. Differential equations are used in many fields to describe how a system evolves depending on various factors. For instance, Newton's theory of mechanics is described using differential equations (he invented calculus in order to describe the world through these equations). The equation we consider here is far simpler; it involves the first and second derivatives of y, denoted y' and y'', whose coefficients are simple constants. The equation is

$$y'' - 3y' + 2y = x^2 + x$$

with some initial conditions $y(0) = y'(0) = 1$. The objective here is to find an expression for the function y, written in terms of x, that when "plugged in" to this equation on the left-hand side, gives the right-hand side. To solve this problem, one has to break it down into smaller parts; it cannot be solved directly as a whole (at least not easily).

The first level of decomposition involves solving two separate problems: first, we find a solution to the simpler equation where the right-hand side is zero; the second is to find an expression that "displaces" the solution to the first sub-problem to obtain the correct right-hand side. This is akin to fitting a straight line to a set of data; first, you find the gradient and then move the line up and down until it fits properly. (In fact, mathematically speaking, it is exactly this.)

Let's focus on the first sub-problem, finding the "general solution." Here, we're asked to find a solution to the simpler equation

$$y'' - 3y' + 2y = 0, y(0) = y'(0) = 1$$

This seems tricky until one realizes that an equation of this kind has solutions that look like $y = e^{mx}$. The derivatives of this are $y' = me^{mx}$ and $y'' = m^2e^{mx}$, so plugging those into the equation gives

$$0 = y'' - 3y' + 2y = m^2y - 3my + 2y = (m^2 - 3m + 2)y$$

There are two ways the far-right expression can be zero. The first is that the function y is constantly zero (which cannot be true, since $y(0) = 1$), or if the quadratic equation $m^2 - 3m + 2 = 0$ holds. We have reduced solving a part of the differential equation to finding the roots of a simple quadratic polynomial – a common pattern often taught in high-school mathematics.

The so-called auxiliary equation $m^2 - 3m + 2$ can be factorized into $(m - 1)(m - 2)$, meaning the two roots (the values of m for which the quadratic equals 0) are $m = 1$ or $m = 2$. The general solution to our simple differential equation is thus given by a linear combination of e^x and e^{2x}, something like

$$y = Ae^x + Be^{2x}$$

To find the values of the two constants A and B, we need to use the two initial conditions. The condition $y(0) = 1$ is straightforward to apply, because we just substitute for x and y in the equation to get

$$1 = y(0) = Ae^0 + Be^{2\times 0} = A + B$$

For the second equation, we need to differentiate, but this is also not too hard:

$$1 = y'(0) = Ae^0 + 2Be^{2\times 0} = A + 2B$$

This is a common pattern in mathematics called a system of **simultaneous equations** (again, often taught in high-school level mathematics). We can solve this by subtracting the former equation from the latter to get $B = 0$, leaving $A = 1$. (Don't worry too much if you haven't seen this before; it isn't important.) This means our general solution is now $y = e^x$.

Now we have a solution that behaves correctly, in shape, but it doesn't solve our original equation. For that, we need to find an "offset" that translates our general solution into the true solution. To do this, we look at the right-hand side of the original equation $x^2 + x$. It's quite reasonable to presume that the factor by which we need to translate our general solution has a similar form to this expression, perhaps something like $ax^2 + bx + c$, where a, b, and c are constants that we need to find.

We need to plug our proposed translation into the differential equation, so we need to differentiate it. The first derivative is $2ax + b$ and the second derivative is just $2a$. (Again, don't worry if you're not following this working; it isn't important.) Thus, we need to solve the new equation

$$2a - 3(2ax + b) + 2(ax^2 + bx + c) = x^2 + x$$

This is yet another common pattern in mathematics called "comparing coefficients" of the left and right. (Two quadratic expressions are equal if and only if each pair of corresponding coefficients is equal.) Let's rearrange the left-hand side to make this more clear:

$$(2a)x^2 + (-6a + 2b)x + (2a - 3b + 2c) = x^2 + x$$

From this, we see that we need each of the equations $2a = 1$, $2b - 6a = 1$, and $2a - 3b + 2c = 0$ (no constant term appears on the right-hand side) to hold. Again, we find ourselves back at solving simultaneous equations. To avoid repeating the process, the solution is $a = 1/2$, $b = 2$, and $c = 5/2$. Putting everything back together now gives the solution

$$y = e^x + \frac{1}{2}x^2 + 2x + \frac{5}{2}$$

Now for the important bit, reflecting on what we have done. In solving this single mathematics problem, we have actually decomposed it into a number of smaller problems, which required far less knowledge of mathematics. We divided the initial problem into two: the simpler problem (general solution) and then the translation problem (specific solution).

- Within the general solution branch, we recognized the form of the equation (pattern recognition). Finding the roots of the auxiliary equation is another sub-problem – one that is completely isolated from the main problem – and then solving the system of equations to obtain the general solution is yet another. This gives us the form of the general solution, which we must then use the two initial conditions to turn into the actual general solution, yet another sub-problem. We differentiate the form of the general solution and apply the initial conditions to obtain a system of equation. We can apply the standard techniques for solving such a system (pattern recognition) to obtain the true general solution.
- Within the particular solution branch of the problem, we recognize that the translation must have a similar form as the right-hand side of the original equation, prompting us to find the derivatives of a general quadratic expression (two sub-problems where the second is dependent on the first). After plugging these derivatives into the equation, we observed that we could compare coefficients (pattern recognition) we obtain another system of equations to solve.

After resolving both branches, we have to put everything back together to obtain the full solution. This is actually a crucial step, and often non-trivial, especially as the division into smaller problems becomes more complex, and where there are interdependencies.

You might be wondering where abstraction and, to a lesser extent, algorithms come into this problem. Mathematical problems are often abstract in nature; they are already an instance of a larger, specific problem in which the crucial components have been extracted. However, this is not to say there is no room for abstraction within this problem. For instance, finding the roots of a quadratic expression and solving systems of linear equations are both well-understood general problems that appear all over the place. We didn't mention this explicitly, but the techniques we used (factorization and Gaussian elimination) are general techniques for solving the respective abstract problem, applied specifically here.

The question of algorithm design is trickier to discuss here. Obviously, solving this kind of problem is a fairly standard "algorithm" in mathematics. Indeed, it is taught in many mathematics courses at various levels. It might not be presented in the usual way that an algorithm is presented in computer science, but it is a set of simple steps that one can repeat to solve exactly this kind of problem. **Gaussian elimination** (the process we used to solve both systems of equations) is a well-known algorithm from numerical linear algebra that is used all over the place. Perhaps you could try and think of a few places where systems of equations like these might appear in your field of work?

Now that we have seen an example of solving a multifaceted problem (albeit from a very different context), we can examine the components of computational thinking in more detail and see how these components work together to derive solutions to new problems.

Decomposing problems

One of the most significant stumbling blocks, particularly when starting out, is breaking down a problem into smaller, more tractable parts. The tendency is to try to tackle the problem as a whole, rather than attempting to decompose it into smaller parts. There are two common reasons for this. The first is that the solver lacks confidence in their skills to correctly decompose. This is common among beginners. The second, which is more common among slightly more experienced solvers, is due to a fear of losing sight of the bigger picture. Obviously, one must keep track of the larger picture; a client would not accept a piece of software that solves one aspect of their problem but not the whole. A balance must be found between finding plausible routes to a solution without losing track of the overall problem.

Ideally, one would break down a problem into a number of isolated sub-problems, but generally this requires many steps of decomposition. Once you have sub-divided the problem several times, this might become the case, but generally, there will be dependencies between these sub-problems. These could be *temporal dependencies* – one problem must be solved before the other – or *technical dependencies* – where the solution to one problem depends on or is otherwise informed by the solution to (not the result of) another sub-problem. As the solver, you need to be wary of these constraints. Sometimes, embracing these interdependencies is key to finding a full solution.

Decomposing can also increase the overall complexity of the problem. Each stage of decomposition increases the number of items that must be incorporated back into the overall solution. This is not to say that these stages should be avoided, but it is something to keep in mind. Aim to decompose a problem as minimally as possible to avoid adding complexity and to make sure you don't get too bogged down in the detail and lose track of the larger problem.

Some problems come with obvious decompositions, but this is not always the case. When this does happen, these easily defined sub-problems are almost always the best way to proceed. As you gain confidence and experience, more problems will start to look like this, and there will be more obvious divisions between parts of even complex problems.

Decomposing a simple thought experiment

Suppose you're planning a dinner. The problem comes with already well-defined parts: the starter, main course, dessert, and drinks. Each of these is a specific problem to be solved, although they do have some weak linkages. (For example, the choice of main course will impact the choice of wine, which is a kind of technical dependency. Dinner is served after the starter, which is a temporal dependency. Both are weak, since one could technically order any wine with any main, and starters could be brought with mains.) If there are no complicating factors, such as specific dietary requirements, then each of these problems can be solved rather easily. In any case, these three parts will always need to be solved in some way or another in order to successfully deliver dinner to the guests.

To solve this problem, one might start by selecting the main course. Then one can select the starters and dessert courses (separately) to complement the mains. Finally, the drinks can be selected to complement each of the other components. In this way, we reduce the likelihood of having to backtrack because of incompatible course choices; the main course is the most important component, so solve this problem first.

General strategies for decomposing problems

Not all problems can be decomposed easily. Sometimes you must formulate an abstraction for a problem before you start trying to decompose it. Other times, the decomposition comes by recognizing that the problem is similar to some well-known class of problems. Usually, it will be a combination of both, along with a lot of trial and error. Over time, this process becomes easier, but it is never easy.

There are some general strategies for how to go about decomposing a problem, but there are often many "correct" decompositions. There is certainly a trade-off between finding the best decomposition versus finding a decomposition that is sufficient to solve the problem; don't let perfect be the enemy of good. Ultimately, the most successful strategy is simple trial and error, taking obvious steps where they present themselves and relying on experience and similarity to other problems otherwise. Sometimes, you need to refine (or create) your abstractions before a pathway to decomposition appears.

A good way to start to collect parts of a problem together into coherent sub-problems is to ask reasonable questions about the problem or parts thereof: what is going to be the most difficult part of this problem; what information do I need for that part; do I need to apply any preprocessing to change the information before I can use it; do I need to apply any postprocessing to results before I return them to the user?

Most coding problems have at least three components. The first is acquiring the data from the user and converting it into a form that can be used. The second is doing the actual work required by the problem. The final step is performing any postprocessing and returning the results to the user. Sometimes this involves abstraction mechanisms made available through the programming language (e.g., classes).

Computing the average annual temperature differences

Let us assume that you have a database of regional temperature readings from around the world at regular intervals over many years. The problem in such a case is to compute the average year-on-year change in temperature in each region for each year. A very simple approach is to simply compute the average temperature of each region over each year, compute the difference from the previous year, and then collect these differences together. However, this does not quite capture the nuance of the problem.

The most difficult aspect of this problem is accounting for seasonal variation that occurs within the yearly cycle. Merely computing the differences between yearly averages would not account for this. A much better approach is to compute the difference between corresponding values within consecutive years and then average these differences over the whole year. However, even this isn't perfect because it doesn't account for short-term variability in temperature. A far better approach, provided we have enough data, is to compute an indicative temperature for a given period within the year. We can compute the average temperature within a short sliding window around the time in question to "smooth out" the volatility in local weather. These smoothed values should be broadly comparable year to year.

Another problem that might appear here, and in many similar problems, is whether all the measurements were taken with the same units: in many places, Celsius is the preferred unit of measurement for temperature, but in some places, Fahrenheit is the preferred unit. Many errors have been caused throughout history by failing to account for units of measurement, sometimes with catastrophic consequences. Ideally, all measurements should be converted to Kelvin (the SI unit for temperature on an absolute scale) before any computations are done.

To formulate a decomposition, we first look at the three high-level components. The first is loading and preprocessing data, which involves applying the conversion to Kelvin and placing the standardized data in a place where we can find it later (either on disk or in RAM, for instance). The second is doing the actual work of computing average differences. This will involve many sub-problems outlined above. The final high-level component is postprocessing the results to return to the user. For this problem, there is little, if any, postprocessing to be done, but sometimes this will be a significant step.

Computing the average regional differences is the main challenge. We have several sub-problems to solve here. A flow chart depicting the order of operations involved here is shown in *Figure 1.1*.

- For each source of data, we need to compute the averages over sliding windows of time over the whole year. None of these computations relies on any of the other computations, so they are a strong candidate for parallelization.
- We need to compute the annual differences between corresponding window averages. This can also be done in parallel.
- Finally, we need to average the window differences over each region for each pair of consecutive years.

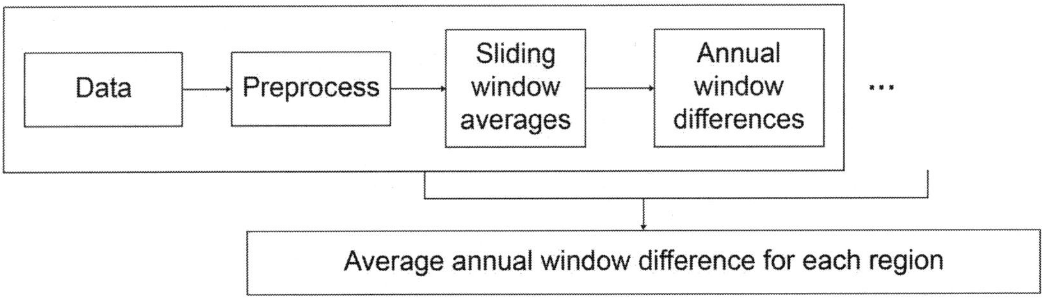

Figure 1.1: Flow chart showing the order of sub-components of a regional weather comparison problem, including where the data has dependencies on previous steps and where solutions can be done in parallel

Now we have a reasonable understanding of the challenges that we will face in order to completely solve this problem. We have not yet made any attempt to actually solve these sub-problems. We don't need to decompose further; each of the sub-problems already seems feasible without further decomposition. However, the option remains open to us should we need it.

Building abstractions and recognizing common patterns

Concrete problems are often messy. They have many components and are generally provided with more information than one needs to actually solve the problem. This extraneous data is often distracting and gets in the way of solving the problem. To get around this, one needs to extract only the essential information, discarding the irrelevant excess, and identify only the general concepts of data and processes. This process is called abstraction.

An abstraction is a generalized view of a concept or data that keeps only the essential information and properties of the concept. A well-designed abstraction allows one to devise simple and elegant solutions to problems that are otherwise complex and opaque. They take time to build, but the payoff can be dramatic. A good abstraction will apply to a large class of problems and will become a useful tool for the future. They can help you realize your problem as a more general class of problem, or invent a new general class of solution that can be used elsewhere.

Aside

The author is a mathematician by training. The process there is exactly the same, although they are known for taking the abstraction step a little further than is perhaps warranted.

Abstraction is not just a tool for reducing problems to something simpler but more general. As a programmer, you use abstractions all the time, such as functions, classes, system memory, and file systems. Abstractions are very important in programming because they allow you to build reusable code that functions in many scenarios, rather than being specific to each problem. The C/C++ runtime libraries provide functions for allocating and freeing memory that can be used for many different things in many different circumstances.

There are several places where abstraction really matters. The first, and probably most immediately useful, is for the initial ingestion and preprocessing of data. When writing software, you will need to decide how your program will obtain the data it needs to solve a problem. Will it be a Unix command-line tool that reads directly from the terminal (`stdin`) or a file on the disk? Will it be a GUI application where the user types the data in directly? Will it be part of a library that exposes an interface that other developers can use? Each of these appears different, but with a well-designed abstraction, you could be flexible enough to answer any of these design objectives.

Another reason to abstract your input data is to make sure it conforms to your requirements. As described above, units of measurement are not standardized around the world, and assuming that all measurements use the same units is dangerous. Using an abstraction on the interface of your application would allow you to work with the data, placed in the correct units, regardless of the input type (assuming that the unit information was provided). We will come back to this idea later too.

Abstractions are also useful when designing algorithms, as we shall see later. For instance, if your data belongs to, or can be easily embedded in, a mathematical structure such as a vector space, then the operations and methodology of that structure can be used to devise an algorithm. This is advantageous for several reasons. Mathematical structures are well studied – perhaps too much so – so these can be used to make strong guarantees about the algorithm. Second, mathematical operations, particularly those concerning vector spaces, are well studied, and there are many optimized implementations of them.

Identifying commonalities in data

Data is an obvious place to look to build abstractions. As described previously, forming abstractions around the source and nature of the data provided can ease the acquisition, validation, and processing of data. However, before we can do this, we need to filter out the information that is not relevant to the problem. Of course, this is a classic "chicken and egg" problem since one sometimes cannot tell what information is relevant before actually solving the problem.

Finding these generalizations starts with asking some basic questions about your data. Is the data numerical in nature? If so, what kind of numbers? Numerical data is likely to fit into some kind of mathematical structure. It has natural orderings, which may or may not be relevant to your problem, and more specifically, there will be "equals comparable" to one another (the operation == is defined for numerical values). It also has arithmetic (+, -, *, /), which has well-defined interactions with the ordering and equality comparisons. Each of these is an abstract property that numbers happen to possess. Any given problem might require that your data be ordered and comparable (such as searching and sorting), or that it has some or all arithmetic operations, but not actually rely on the actual form of the underlying data.

Text data is a great example of an abstract class of data. Text is a sequence of characters taken from a particular "alphabet," such as the ASCII code table or the UTF-8 code table. The actual nature of these characters might well be important. For instance, ASCII characters are represented by a single byte, whereas UTF-8 has multi-byte characters as well as single-byte characters. It is not necessarily important to know what alphabet is used for a particular set of text data, but it is important that you know how to identify individual characters, compare them, or otherwise operate upon them.

Broadly speaking, many problems can be generalized by considering what traits parts of the data must satisfy (having ordered, equality comparable, iterable, etc.). Sometimes it is easy to identify which traits are required up front (searching generally requires iterable and comparable), but other times this isn't possible. Sometimes you need to solve the problem with concrete data to realize that it can be generalized. Sometimes it cannot be generalized at all.

Identifying structure in the problem

Sometimes it's not just the data that can be abstracted. Sometimes the problem itself has a general structure that can be identified and exploited. A typical example of this might be to identify one part of a problem as an instance of a theoretical framework. For instance, if one step of a problem is to find particular patterns within data, which for text is usually accomplished with regular expressions (this is pattern recognition). The abstraction comes by understanding that the computational theory of regular expressions is **deterministic finite automata** (**DFA**), which are the abstraction that we seek. These kinds of abstractions can be difficult to spot but generally lead to high-quality results.

Finding abstractions such as this can give you a theoretical framework in which the solution to the main problem can be found. Finite automata (and finite state machines) are a very powerful pattern that can be used in a great many situations. Once you know that part of the problem involves such a construction, you can start to look for other parts of the problem that also fit this model. This might not be successful, but it does at least give options for where to look and how to proceed.

Having a good understanding of some of these fundamental theories obviously makes identifying these kinds of abstractions and understanding what capabilities they have easier. Topics such as regular expressions are very well understood, even if they are sometimes difficult to use in practice. There are several other similar patterns that you should endeavor to understand; sorting and searching algorithms are another great example. Numerical methods for solving linear systems, constrained optimization, and graph algorithms, such as shortest path, are great examples. Numerical algorithms have a habit of turning up in unexpected places.

A digression into Sudoku

Many common puzzles and games ultimately require the solver or player to recognize patterns within the context of the game. This is especially obvious in Sudoku puzzles. Here, the objective is to place the digits 1-9 in a 9-by-9 grid so that each digit appears once in each row, column, and 3-by-3 box. Simple Sudoku puzzles only require basic techniques such as identifying pairs of digits or other kinds of mutual exclusion within a given row or column. However, harder puzzles require the solver to identify more complex patterns within the grid.

For instance, more difficult Sudoku puzzles require the solver to identify intermediate patterns such as "X-wings." Here, the solver identifies a pair of rows (or columns) and a digit where the only valid position for the digit in each of the rows appears in a pair of columns. Since both rows must contain the digit, and it cannot appear in the same column in both rows, we can deduce that the only valid position for the digit in the two identified columns is within the two given rows, allowing us to eliminate this digit from other positions within the columns. (The same logic applies symmetrically if one started with a pair of columns.) There are many patterns in Sudoku, and being a good solver requires one to be able to identify and exploit the deductions provided by these patterns.

Note

Chess is another example of a game where the ability to recognize patterns of play is crucial for being a good player. This allows the player to quickly identify paths to victory and counterstrategies that can be employed to win the game. Part of learning how to play these games is to learn some of the common patterns that appear and how to use or counter them. Solving problems is no different. Being an effective programmer requires you to learn some of the common patterns, their uses, and how to incorporate them into solutions to problems.

Common functional patterns

There are many functional patterns that you should be familiar with. We've already mentioned a few. Sorting patterns involve placing elements in order according to a sorting predicate. A search is a related problem that uses a condition or predicate to find a specific element or range within a set of data. Other patterns include filtering (and the related random sampling), shuffling, and permutations of a range of data. These are useful patterns that appear frequently in programming, sometimes in their standard form, but often in a less obvious form.

Many problems eventually reduce to solving a numerical problem, such as solving a system of equations, constrained optimizations, or graph algorithms. These tend to require some work to find the correct mathematical formulation of the problem. Again, this is obvious in some cases and not in others. More important patterns come from statistics and probability. Generating high-quality random numbers is a complicated topic. Problems that have a statistical component are usually obvious; any time there is uncertainty in measurements or methodology, statistics will probably be needed.

Combinatorics is the branch of mathematics that deals with the various ways that a (finite) set can be combined – how the elements can be permuted, or paired up, and so on. This branch includes graph theory, which appears frequently in programming problems. Problems that make explicit use of graph theory include dependency resolution (dependencies of a project are usually expressed as a directed graph), scheduling (turns out to be a graph coloring problem), and route planning is either a shortest path or traversal problem depending on the objectives.

Common structural patterns

Recognizing functional patterns is usually an early step in the problem-solving process. Structural patterns usually appear in the final stages, when designing algorithms or finally implementing your solution. Structural patterns include the design patterns and idioms for a particular language that allow you to design interfaces and make your code efficient. (The classic books on design patterns includes "structural patterns" as one of the topics; our usage of the term includes everything described in this book and not just what they describe as structural patterns.) We will use many structural patterns.

For example, the strategy (or policy) pattern is a means of encapsulating a family of different, but interchangeable, methodologies that can be used to obtain a result in different circumstances. For instance, one might define various algorithms for reading data from a file as strategies, and change the strategy based on the file type. We will make use of this pattern several times later in this book.

Other patterns worth mentioning are adapters, facades, flyweights, and proxies. These are all examples of patterns that adapt the interface of a given object or class to allow it to be used in some other context. Another useful pattern is a decorator, where the capabilities of an object are extended by means of a wrapping class.

> **Note**
>
> One pattern that is used heavily in C++ is the "template method" pattern, where the skeleton of an algorithm is described in terms of some generic (placeholder) operations that can be customized by the specific implementation. The C++ standard template library is full of examples of these kinds of patterns, especially in the `algorithm` header. This pattern excels when producing general-purpose and flexible implementations of algorithms that can appear in many different contexts.

Understanding algorithms

An algorithm is a set of instructions for taking data, subject to some conditions called **preconditions**, and producing an output, satisfying some **postconditions**. Being able to formulate, articulate, and understand algorithms is an essential skill for anyone who writes software. Algorithms are generally written in a pseudocode language that describes the steps in a language-agnostic way that should be comprehensible to anyone familiar with basic programming constructions.

Reasoning about algorithms and understanding their computational complexity is a much larger topic that we will return to in *Chapter 3*. In this section, we focus on how to read algorithms and understand what they do.

Before we continue, we need to understand some basic theory of computation. Broadly speaking, there are two (equivalent) models of computation: **sequential** (Turing machine) and **functional** (lambda calculus). In the sequential model, one starts at the beginning and performs one step at a time until the task is complete, whereas in the functional model, one tackles parts of the problem by recursive calls to routines. Most programming languages favor one model or the other, though it is common to take aspects from both models. For instance, C++ is primarily sequential, though C++ templates are functional. On the other hand, **Haskell** is a purely functional language. Regardless of whether you explicitly make use of either model, it is important that you have knowledge of how both models operate.

Discussing algorithms is best done by means of example. We will now look at a very simple algorithm that will serve as a good introduction to the terms, and learn how to read the pseudocode descriptions of the steps of an algorithm.

Finding the maximum value in a list

Suppose you have a list of numbers (for simplicity, let's say these are all integers) and you wish to find the maximum value contained therein. A very simple way to accomplish this is as follows:

1. Take the first element and store this as the current maximum.
2. For each of the remaining elements, compare to the current maximum and replace if it is larger.
3. Return the current maximum, which should now contain the global maximum.

Unless you know more, it is hard to do better than this. To know that you have the maximum value, you must have compared the proposed maximum to all of the elements of the list and checked that no other element exceeds this value.

This is an algorithm, though it is not presented in the pseudocode language mentioned above. To formalize the procedure, we should translate from the plain language above into pseudocode, which is more similar to how it would be written in code. An example of an algorithm that finds the maximum value in a list of numbers is given here.

```
INPUT: L is a list of numbers with at least one element
OUTPUT: Maximum value of L

max <- first element of L
```

```
WHILE not at end of L
  current <- next element of L
  IF current > max
    max <- current
  END
END

RETURN max
```

The uppercase words are *keywords* that denote common operations such as conditionals, loops, inputs, outputs, and return outputs. The `OUTPUT` statement declares the postconditions on the value that is provided by the `RETURN` statement. The `<-` denotes assignment. This is to make it fully distinct from the equality operator =. Notice that this form doesn't make any reference to specific means of accessing the data; that is for the implementation to define based on the form of the data that is provided. Let's see how this translates to standard C++. We can write this as a function template that takes a "container" that has begin, end, and a dependent type called `value_type` that supports <.

```
template <typename Container>
typename Container::value_type max_element(const Container& container) {
    auto begin = container.begin();
    auto end = container.end();

    if (begin == end) {
        throw std::invalid_argument("container must be non-empty");
    }

    auto max = *begin;
    ++begin;

    for (; begin != end; ++begin) {
        const auto& current = *begin;
        if (max < current) {
            max = current;
        }
    }

    return max;
}
```

This is a very general implementation that makes basically no assumptions about the form of the container or the element type that it contains. We throw an exception if the container is empty, which is one "correct" way to handle this. The maximum of an empty collection is ill-defined; the defining condition is vacuously true for any value. Another option would be to change the return type to `optional<...>` and return an empty value in this case. This has the advantage of potentially allowing for `noexcept` to be added to the function declaration, reducing the runtime cost of launching this function. Of course, this implementation is for demonstration only; you should use the constrained algorithm `std::max_element` from the `algorithm` header instead.

Notice that the general structure of the implementation is exactly as set out in the pseudocode. This is by design. You might even want to annotate parts of your code with comments to indicate exactly which part of the algorithm is being implemented. This helps other developers (including your future self) understand how you have implemented the algorithm, and what the specific parts are supposed to do.

We could generalize this implementation further by taking an optional comparison operator to be used instead of >, but this is complicated because there are conditions on orderings for which the maximum is a well-defined and unique value. For instance, in some orderings, not all values are comparable, which would demand special handling in the implementation. This is beyond our capabilities at the moment.

Characteristics of an algorithm

Not all lists of instructions are algorithms. To earn that distinction, they must satisfy some reasonable conditions:

- **Finiteness**: An algorithm must terminate after a finite number of iterations. The actual number of iterations will usually depend on the inputs (and outputs), and the number of iterations might grow rapidly, but it must eventually terminate.
- **Definiteness**: The steps of an algorithm should be described precisely and unambiguously. The objective is to translate an algorithm into computer code, so enough information must be present in order to reasonably do this.
- **Inputs**: An algorithm should have zero or more inputs that belong to well-defined sets (defined by the preconditions mentioned above).
- **Outputs**: An algorithm should have one or more outputs, derived from the inputs using the steps of the algorithm.

- **Effectiveness**: An algorithm should be effective in producing the desired output from the input parameters. The individual steps should be sufficiently basic that the process can be carried out exactly using pen and paper.

One usually turns to the rigor of mathematical proof to show that an algorithm satisfies these properties. For instance, mathematical induction can be used to prove that an algorithm is effective. The number of steps required by an algorithm usually depends on the size and nature of the inputs (and possibly the outputs). This relationship is called the **complexity** of the algorithm, which we shall discuss in more detail later, in *Chapter 3*.

The preconditions on the inputs should usually be checked in a good implementation of the algorithm. This can be done implicitly by means of static types, such as those in C++, or explicitly by conditional statements. There are various ways to do this, of course, depending on how robustly these checks should be performed.

One additional consideration when writing algorithms out is clarity. An algorithm is only useful to you and others if it can be understood and implemented. When presenting the pseudocode for an algorithm, you should make some effort to make sure the steps are clearly presented and easy to follow. The same way that decomposition can help solve problems, it can also help articulate their solutions, especially when the decomposition is "obvious."

Let's examine our algorithm for finding the maximum value of a list of numbers for these properties. The algorithm "visits" each element of the list exactly once, so for a list that contains n elements, the algorithm will terminate after exactly n steps. Thus the finiteness condition is satisfied. The algorithm is written clearly and unambiguously. The actual mode of traversing the list is not specified exactly, but, as we see in the C++ implementation, this is necessary to accommodate the different forms of "list" that might be available in any given programming language. (Not all languages have a `std::vector`, and not all containers support index access.) The only input is a list of numbers, which must satisfy the precondition of being non-empty. The only output is a single number that satisfies the postcondition of being the maximum value from the list. (A number m is the maximum value of a set of numbers S if m is a member of S and if each s taken from S satisfies $s \leq m$.) The final condition is effectiveness. The steps listed do indeed produce the valid maximum value, and each step specifies exactly (though not specifically) one operation that must be performed.

Recursive algorithms

Not all problems have an algorithm that is so easy to write down. Let's look at a more complicated example. Consider a very simple "language" defined by the following grammar.

```
letter ::= 'a' | 'b'
word   ::= letter | '[' word ',' word ']'
```

This language consists of "words," that consist of either a single "letter" (taken from an alphabet of two letters, 'a' and 'b') or a pair of words surrounded by square brackets and separated by a comma. The characters that appear in quotations are *literals* that are exactly as they should appear. The other terms are as defined by the language. For instance, all of the following are valid words in this language.

```
a
 [a,a]
 [a,[a,b]]
 [[a,a],[a,[a,b]]]
```

Notice that this language is recursive in nature. A word might contain a pair of words, so it is natural that algorithms to work with this language might also be recursive in nature.

Suppose that we want to design an algorithm to extract the end of the first valid word from a string. This problem is complicated because we need to make sure that every open bracket is correctly matched with its closing partner. There are ways to do this without recursion (simply counting brackets might be sufficient), but the purpose of this example is to demonstrate recursive algorithms. Here's how this algorithm might be defined.

```
INPUT: String s that starts with a valid word
OUTPUT: the position of the last character of the first valid word

character <- get first character from s

IF character = 'a' or character = 'b'
    RETURN 0
END

position <- 0
# s[0] is a '['
position <- position + 1
```

```
# find the first word after '['
a <- substring of s starting from index position
i <- end index of first word from a
position <- position + i

# s[position+1] is ','
position <- position + 1

# get the end of first word after ','
b <- substring of s starting at index position
j <- end index of first word from b
position <- position + j

# s[position + 1] is a ']' matching s[0]
position <- position + 1

RETURN position
```

The lines prefixed by a # are comments that are there for exposition only. Notice that this algorithm invokes itself twice when there is a word that is not a letter. This is the best way to ensure that one always contains the correct number of matching pairs. This is how we might implement the preceding algorithm in C++.

```
size_t end_of_first_word(std::string_view s) noexcept {

    if (!s.starts_with('['))  {
        return 0;
    }

    size_t position = 0;

    assert(s[position] == '[');

    position += 1;
    auto a = s.substr(position);
    auto i = end_of_first_word(a);
    position += i;
```

```
    position += 1;
    assert(s[position] == ',');
    position += 1;

    auto b = s.substr(position);
    auto j = end_of_first_word(b);
    position += j;

    position += 1;
    assert(s[position] == ']');

    return position;
}
```

This is not an optimal implementation, but that doesn't matter right now. This is an exact translation of the pseudocode set out in the algorithm into C++, including assertions for the comments that describe what should be the case if our algorithm is correct.

We're making use of the `string_view` class from C++17, which is a better way to work with non-owning strings than using raw `const char*` C-style strings. Using `string_view` will help ensure we don't access memory outside of the string, which would be easily done with a C-style string. Moreover, it provides many convenience methods such as `substr` and `starts_with`. An alternative would be to work directly with a pair of iterators defining the range of values, but this is not much better than working with C-style strings.

We haven't included any error checking in this implementation beyond the assertions, and the function is marked `noexecpt`. This means calling this function on a string that doesn't start with a valid word is undefined behavior. The precondition on the string is that the string starts with a valid word, so it is the responsibility of the caller to ensure that this condition holds. This might be necessary on the "hot path" of a program, where checking for invalid strings might be too costly.

Writing out computations recursively is often easier than writing them out in a sequential manner, but one must remember that languages like C++ are not designed to work in this way. Recursive implementations might perform worse than a sequential implementation, since calling functions in C++ can be an expensive operation. Modern optimizing compilers might be able to inline function calls or otherwise reduce the cost of invoking these functions, by tail recursion optimization or otherwise. However, if the number of recursions cannot be known at compile time, the options are limited. Here is an example of how one might implement an algorithm that does not rely on recursion.

```
size_t end_of_first_word(std::string_view s) noexcept {
    size_t position = 0;
    int depth = 0;
    for (const auto& c : s) {
        switch (c) {
            case '[': ++depth; break;
            case ']': --depth;
            default:
                if (depth == 0) {
                    return position;
                }
        }
        ++position;
    }
    return position;
}
```

You may notice that this implementation is more difficult to reason about. Moreover, this implementation cannot so easily be generalized if some other operation needs to be performed, other than simply finding the position of the end of the first valid word.

The trade-off between flexibility and performance is a common dilemma for programmers. It is crucial to understand the properties of your solutions and design algorithms according to what is required by the context. If flexibility is not a concern, then it's fine to optimize further and cut off the pathway to adding capabilities. However, one should never optimize until the performance is measured and the algorithm is known to underperform; measure twice, cut once.

This concludes the four components of computational thinking. Now we can see how modern features of C++ and good software engineering practices can help solve problems too.

Using modern C++ and good practice

There are many reasons to use C++ for solving problems, but the main reason for choosing C++ is that you need to make high-performance solutions. Modern C++ has many features that make it easy to write fast and (relatively) safe code without taking away control of the low-level primitives that the programmer can use to achieve the best possible performance. In this section, we will look at some of the features of modern C++ that can be used to write high-quality code for solving complex problems without compromising performance.

Before we start, we need to make something clear. Just because C++ provides the tools for micro-optimizing your code, that doesn't mean that you should be using them. Modern compilers are far better at producing optimized machine code than even very experienced programmers writing hand-crafted assembly code. Trust the compiler toolchain to optimize your code and only spend time making micro-optimizations if it is absolutely necessary. Remember, you need to keep the bigger picture in mind, and over-optimizing one part of the code probably means that you are neglecting another.

That being said, it is important to understand that not all code is going to produce optimal performance. We have already seen an example where the C++ code is unlikely to achieve maximum performance with the recursive algorithm for parsing strings. But, as we mentioned in the commentary on that algorithm, the first task is to solve the problem and obtain a correct solution. Then, and only then, should you consider whether the algorithm has the desired performance characteristics.

It is a good idea to keep track of the parts of the code where performance will really matter. For example, any tight loops that perform an operation on (potentially) large sets of data are likely to need to be optimized, but a function that obtains records from a database is not, since this will always be constrained by the connection to the database. This allows you to focus on the most important parts when it comes to optimizing your code.

Another thing we need to address early is the issue of memory management. Do not manage your memory by hand with `new` and `delete` – or worse, with `malloc` and `free`. This is a recipe for creating memory leaks and invoking undefined behavior. Use standard containers such as `std::vector`, smart pointers (`std::unique_ptr`, `std::shared_ptr`), and other mechanisms provided by the standard template library (or other high-quality libraries such as Boost and Abseil). This is especially true if you make use of multithreading, where it is essential that your memory management is thread-safe.

Building C++ projects with CMake

This is a good point to discuss how we will configure and build our C++ projects throughout this book. CMake is a cross-platform build-system generator that constructs a set of build files (Makefiles, Ninja configurations, or otherwise) from a source file called `CMakeLists.txt` in the project root. The syntax can be a little frustrating at first, but you will quickly get used to it (if you aren't already).

Modern CMake organizes code and dependencies into targets, which are usually either static or shared libraries or executables. It has a sophisticated mechanism for finding dependencies with its `find_package` function, which can then be linked to our targets, providing the necessary `include` directories and link lines necessary to successfully integrate the functionality of the dependency into our project. CMake also provides various functions for controlling the configuration of the compiler, such as setting the appropriate flags for a particular C++ standard in a portable way. This really takes the pain out of configuring cross-platform builds. A very basic skeleton for a C++ project, `CMakeLists.txt`, is as follows.

```
cmake_minimum_required(VERSION 3.30)

project(MyProject)

set(CMAKE_CXX_STANDARD 20)
set(CMAKE_CXX_STANDARD_REQUIRED ON)

add_executable(MyExecutable main.cpp)
```

The first line specifies the version of CMake that is required to configure the project. (At the time of writing, 3.30 was a fairly recent release of CMake.) The next line declares the project, which is the point at which CMake performs some background tasks such as finding the compiler and checking various settings. The next two lines set the C++ standard and set this standard to be required, which will cause CMake to emit an error if the compiler does not support this standard. Finally, we add an executable, called `MyExecutable`, which has one source file called `main.cpp` attached to it. We can link dependencies, external or other targets we declare in the CMake file, using this line:

```
target_link_libraries(MyExecutable PRIVATE MyDep)
```

Here, `MyDep` is the name of a target (either constructed using `add_library` or via a call to `find_package`) that should be linked. The `PRIVATE` specifier declares that the link information does not need to be propagated along with our target. This is sensible for an executable, which cannot be linked by another target, but it might not be appropriate for library targets.

To configure the build system, one uses the `cmake` executable from the command line or via an integration with your IDE of choice. (CLion has excellent CMake support, and there is a CMake extension of VSCode. Visual Studio also supports CMake projects.) On the command line, one can use the following invocation to configure and build the project in release mode.

```
cmake -B out/Release -S . -DCMAKE_BUILD_TYPE=Release
cmake --build out/Release --config=Release
```

The configured build files are placed in the `out/Release` directory, as specified by the `-B` argument, and the source file is specified with the `-S` argument (using '`.`' for the current working directory). The final argument sets the build type to release settings for the configuration. On most build systems, this is sufficient to build in release mode, but some build systems, such as MSBuild, support multiple configurations, in which case the `--config=Release` argument on the following line becomes necessary.

One of the advantages of CMake is that one can attach several different package managers, such as **vcpkg** or **conan**, to make obtaining, finding, and linking dependencies easier. Moreover, CMake is more feature-complete and easier to use than some of the similar tools that exist, such as Bazel and Meson. The documentation is quite readable, and it is extremely flexible.

Throughout the remainder of this book, and in the corresponding code repository, you'll see many examples of CMake files and how to use them, particularly in *Chapter 7* and *Chapter 12*.

Views, ranges, and algorithms

The C++20 standard brought many features to C++ that had been standard in other languages for many years. These include copy-less memory views (`string_view` and `span`), along with ranges and constrained algorithms. These are great improvements over the iterator-based interfaces that existed before, as they allow for cleaner and safer code.

String views and spans can be thought of as ranges in which the elements are stored contiguously in memory. (All the bytes are stored together and in order in a single block with no gaps between them.) String views are immutable in that the elements in the range cannot be modified. (Modifying strings in-place is dangerous because a new UTF-8 character might require more space than the character that it replaces, forcing a new allocation.) Spans provide mutable or immutable access to the block of elements.

A range is an abstraction on top of the usual iterator access to containers. Loosely speaking, a range is any object that exposes a `begin` and `end` that allow sequential access to the elements of the container; a far better description can be found at `https://en.cppreference.com/w/cpp/ranges`. The power of ranges comes from the fact that they can be composed with views, which provide modifications to the underlying iterator range. For example, the `enumerate` view modifies the range to return a pair of index and value. Combined with a range-based loop, these make for some very simple and easy-to-read code. For example, we could rewrite the more optimized version of the word-finding function from before using this mechanism as follows.

```
size_t end_of_first_word(string_view s) noexcept {
    int depth = 0;
    for (const auto [position, char] : std::views::enumerate(s)) {
        switch (char) {
            case '[': ++depth; break;
            case ']': --depth;
            default:
                if (depth == 0) {
                    return position;
                }
        }
    }
}
```

This isn't substantially different from the previous implementation, but it does make the intent clearer. Now it is very obvious that the `position` variable should be tracking the current index of iteration. Moreover, this has the added benefit of decontaminating the surrounding scope, since the position is initialized inside the context of the range-based `for` loop. This is not a problem, but it does help keep code clean.

Templates and concepts

Templates are arguably one of the best features of C++, and also one of the most difficult and frustrating; anyone who has had to debug a template metaprogram bug will understand. The reason they are so powerful is that they allow the coder to write a single piece of code that can apply to many types on demand, without requiring a new implementation for each combination of types that is needed in a given program. There are some downsides to this: template instantiation is expensive for the compiler and very complex, and errors are very difficult to find and debug.

Templates actually form a complete programming language in themselves. They can be used to compute values at compile time, reducing the runtime cost of using those values to effectively zero. A template (class, function, or value) is *instantiated* by the compiler for each combination of types with which it is used, meaning that the compiler takes the body of the template and replaces the template parameters with the specific types that were provided by the code. For instance, our `max_element` template function could be instantiated by the following snippet of code. This instantiation is performed recursively, and if at any point in this process the compiler encounters an expression that is not valid, it raises a compiler error. These errors can be very difficult to diagnose because the error could have been caused far away from the first place where it is detected.

Concepts are an extension of the template mechanism that allows the user to declare the exact set of requirements for a template requirement up front. This means the compiler does not need to recursively instantiate the template to find out whether it is valid or not; it just checks whether the concept is valid for the type and emits an error if this is not the case. This leads to better error messages for the coder and potentially improves the speed of compilation. The basic concept for our `max_element` function might be defined as follows.

```
template <typename T>
concept OrderableContainer = requires(const T& t) {
    // Has a dependent type called "value_type", which is orderd by <
    std::totally_ordered<T::value_type>;
    // Has a begin and end methods valid on Const T&
    t.begin();
    t.end();
};
```

This is not a complete description because we do not specify that the `begin` and `end` methods should return iterators. Moreover, we don't check that the `value_type` is copy constructible. Fortunately, we don't need to reinvent the wheel here; we can just extend the `forward_range` concept from the standard library, as shown here.

```
template <typename T>
concept OrderableContainer = std::input_range<const T>
    && std::totally_ordered<std::range_value_t<const T>>
    && std::copy_constructible<std::range_value_t<const T>>;
```

This implementation checks that `const T` is an `input_range`, meaning that it has `begin` and `end` that return iterators that can read values in a forward iteration pattern, and that the value in this input range is ordered. This is actually significantly more general than the one we defined because ranges might be declared in other ways besides having an iterator to the first element and one past the last element. To account for this generalization, we really should make use of the `range` library rather than using the `begin` and `end` methods directly. This has the added benefit of creating cleaner code, as follows.

```
template <OrderableContainer Container>
std::range_value_t<Container> max_element(const Container& container) {
    auto begin = std::ranges::begin(container);
    const auto end = std::ranges::end(container);

    if (begin == end) {
        throw std::invalid_argument("Container must be non-empty");
    }

    auto max = *begin;
    ++begin;

    for (; begin != end; ++begin) {
        if (max < *begin) {
            max = *begin;
        }
    }

    return max;
}
```

Notice that we still have to check that the container is not empty. This can only be tested at runtime, whereas concepts are a compile-time construction. The only real difference is using the `ranges::begin` and `ranges::end` functions to get the iterators. This is probably overkill for such a simple function, but thinking in terms of concepts can be a great help as you try to formulate abstractions of your problem. Moreover, the more concepts you use, the better experience you will have debugging large, complex bodies of templated code. This covers how to handle data flexibly and efficiently. The next section shows how to handle cases where things go wrong.

Handling errors in C++

You should always account for things that might go wrong when implementing solutions to problems. There are always things that can go wrong: preconditions might be violated, the algorithm might fail to produce an outcome (for instance, if a numerical method fails to converge), data might be ill-formed or in a format that is not supported, there might be imposed limits that are reached (such as limiting the amount of time that can be spent on a single computation). Your implementation should have a mechanism for gracefully handling these kinds of errors that can occur.

It's worth pointing out the difference between a *failure* and an *error*. For instance, if we implement a search algorithm, then this might reasonably fail to find an entry that satisfies the condition. This is a failure, but not an error. An error occurs when the program enters an invalid state or encounters a problem that it cannot handle. Failures should be handled as a routine problem using constructions such as `std::optional` or returning the end iterator for a failed search. Errors should be propagated to a point where they can be handled gracefully or terminate the application.

For a long time, there were two ways to handle errors in C++.

- We can use the built-in exception mechanism, which has the advantage of being global and, unless an in-flight exception is explicitly caught by a try-except block, will terminate the whole application with a meaningful error message. This is desirable in some cases, but sometimes not. The exception mechanism has benefits, but it is also a fairly expensive way to handle errors. It also causes the compiler to add a large amount of error-handling code around function calls and so on. Exceptions are particularly problematic on API boundaries or when working with remote procedure calls.
- Alternatively, we can use C-style errors, where functions return an integer that is 0 if no errors occurred and a non-zero error code if an error did occur. This is extremely lightweight and makes sense in many applications where a failure should not cause a program to terminate. The disadvantage is that the amount of information that can be conveyed by this mechanism is extremely limited.

Ideally, there should be an alternative that is lightweight, like the C-style error codes, but expressive and flexible, like the exception model. In C++23, the `expected` template was added to the C++ standard library, which allows one to return a single object that can either contain the valid result of a function call or an unexpected (error) value and is never empty. This has the advantage of permitting a very lightweight error handling mechanism that remains local (unless explicitly propagated), which provides a great deal of flexibility, especially on interface boundaries.

> **Note**
>
> If C++23 is not an option, Abseil has the `Status` template class, which serves a similar function, and Boost has the Leaf library, which has a similar `result` template class.

Besides errors, you might also consider adding logging capabilities to your code (though not in places where performance is critical). This can be extremely helpful when tracking down bugs or unexpected behavior once the code leaves the development environment. Remember that any code that is "shipped" or incorporated into a package needs to be maintained by somebody (including future you). Any time you can spend to make this process less arduous is time well spent. Adding logging using a standard logging library such as `spdlog` or equivalent is a low-effort way of providing a wealth of debugging information to users who cannot simply launch a debugger to see what is going on inside the library.

Testing your code

Even very simple software projects should have tests. Every new feature should add new tests. Every reported bug should be confirmed by adding tests. This is the only way to know that your code is "correct" and performs appropriately. There are several layers of tests that you should include: **unit tests**, **integration tests**, and **end-to-end tests**. A complete suite of tests should contain all three kinds of tests that cover as much of the package as feasibly possible.

1. The first layer contains unit tests, which test small, isolated units of functionality such as single functions and algorithms or a class interface. These are used to provide very fine-grained diagnostics on small parts of the software, aimed at identifying particular components that are not implemented correctly and making sure they run without causing unexpected errors or crashes. These tests tend to be small, quick to run, and relatively numerous. The suite of unit tests is run regularly as part of the development process, as well as when preparing for deployments.
2. The second layer contains integration tests that exercise larger groups of functionality that operate together, such as a collection of algorithms that work in tandem to solve a particular problem (or part thereof). These tend to be larger in scale than unit tests, but still operate on a relatively small scale. These tend to be larger tests that each exercise several different parts of the package together. These tests might take a little more time than unit tests and won't be run quite as frequently – perhaps only once a new feature is complete, before and as part of the deployment process.

3. The final layer contains end-to-end tests, which test the entire lifetime of a piece of software, and tend to be larger and take longer than unit tests and integration tests. These might only be run when preparing to make a new release of the project, rather than as part of the development cycle. Generally, there are a small number of end-to-end tests that cover the main workflows of the software.

There are several testing harnesses available in C++. Two of the most common are **GoogleTest** and **Catch2**. GoogleTest is a very flexible library, is quite easy to set up and use, and is very extensible. Catch2 is a simpler library that is less flexible but easier to set up and use. Catch2 is a header-only library that does not require linking to external runtimes, whereas GoogleTest requires linking to the `gtest.(so|dll)` library. The tests included with the code for this book use GoogleTest.

Version control

Git (and **GitHub**) is the de facto standard for maintaining control of source code versions and managing a code base. It is a very effective tool for this task. Even relatively simple software projects should be kept in version control – which doesn't have to be public or even stored on a server somewhere. This is for a number of reasons. The first is that, at some point, you might need to revert some code to what it was at some point in the past because of mistakes or performance regressions. The second reason, which might not be an issue for very small projects, is sharing your code with a larger team of developers (or even just between your own personal computers).

Services such as GitHub and GitLab provide the ability to run continuous integration testing that can help identify any changes that break existing functionality or otherwise find problems. This also helps to make sure that your code runs on all the different platforms that you support (Windows, Linux, macOS, and various different architectures). No single computer can test all of these configurations on its own. Continuous integration tools make this easy.

Summary

This chapter introduced the four components of computational thinking, which form a framework for solving large, complex programming problems. This is just the foundation. To be effective at solving problems, one needs to understand the theory and have a wealth of examples to draw upon. In the following chapters, we will deepen our theoretical knowledge and start to form bridges between the theory of solving problems and the facilities provided by the C++ language. This will help us understand the kinds of patterns and abstractions to look for in our problem-solving. We also discussed some good practices that will speed up the iteration of solutions and allow us to develop correct and efficient solutions to difficult problems quickly. In the next chapter, we will go into more detail about building abstractions in problems and the mechanisms available to us in C++ to facilitate abstract thinking.

2

Abstraction in Detail

Abstraction is a term that is used in many different contexts, even within this book. In *Chapter 1*, we talked about formulating abstractions within the problem domain, such as data abstractions and structural abstractions. The programming language one uses to implement solutions also has abstraction mechanisms, which are obviously related to the abstractions in the problem. The purpose of this chapter is to understand abstractions as they relate specifically to C++.

C++ provides many abstraction mechanisms to make writing complex code easier, but these mechanisms can also teach us how to think about the problem. In this chapter, we will look at the abstraction mechanisms from C++ and how they can help guide us to find useful abstractions in new problems. After all, features of the language and the functionality in the standard library are there to facilitate exactly this. We will focus on four facilities in C++: the algorithms from the standard library, functions, classes, and templates.

The purpose of this discussion is to understand the possible directions that one might aim for when decomposing problems or formulating abstractions. It always helps to understand roughly where a solution might be heading so you can be on the lookout for the features and standard patterns that might occur along this route. This is what we'll try to do here. This chapter also serves as a reminder of some of the powerful features at your disposal in C++ and what can be accomplished with them.

In this chapter, we're going to cover the following main topics:

- Common categories of problems
- Understanding standard algorithms
- When to use functions
- When to use classes
- Using templates

Technical requirements

The focus of this chapter is on establishing a link between the languages and library features of modern C++. Some familiarity with C++ is assumed, but we try to explain more modern features that you might not have encountered before. There are some exercises associated with this chapter found in the `Chapter-02` folder of the GitHub repository for this book: `https://github.com/PacktPublishing/The-CPP-Programmers-Mindset`. Some snippets of code also have tests in this repository.

Common categories of problems

Before we start, we need to have some understanding of the different categories of problems. This is important because it forms part of the context in which we formulate our abstractions and thus guides our choices of how to implement solutions. All problems can be broken down into a set of basic problems via a sequence of reductions. These basic problems are those that you probably already know how to solve – for instance, using classic data structures and algorithms. As you gain experience, fewer reductions will be needed in most cases, and you will recognize problems that are of increasing complexity and know how to solve these. Very broadly, basic problems fall into one of four domains, at least for the purposes of this discussion, each with numerous subcategories and some overlapping concepts:

- Combinatorial problems, including sorting and searching
- **Input-output** (**IO**) problems, and interacting with the host system
- Numerical problems, including generating random numbers
- Interface problems, including interacting with users

Combinatorial problems are those that involve counting, sorting (or otherwise rearranging), searching (for a single value or a range of values), otherwise combining elements in a range, and graph problems. This describes a very large and generally well-understood branch of computer science, encompassing most classic data structures and algorithm courses. There are excellent algorithms for identifying common substrings or finding instances of a particular pattern within a string (regular expressions). This also includes tasks such as route finding (or graph traversal). Most of the simple examples of problems in this category include finding or sorting simple linear data – data that can be naturally placed in a line without losing contextual information. However, it also covers problems that are not so simple. Finding a route in two- or three-dimensional space, navigating around obstacles in the environment, is one such example (using the A* algorithm, for example).

Input-output problems are those that involve finding and loading data to be processed, such as locating the file on a disk and loading it into a sequence of bytes within the program's address space, where it can be accessed directly, or the reverse. Most (if not all) operating systems include a sophisticated file system, which allows users and programs operating in user space on the computer to locate data on disk. (This is itself a great example of how abstractions can be used.) Files provide an interface that allows the program to obtain the data. Data might not be located on disk; it could be located on another device reached by a network connection, or it might not exist anywhere (for instance, a sensor that is constantly transmitting readings). Obtaining data from these sources can be trickier, especially if it is ephemeral. Once the program has finished its processing of the input data, it will need to store or otherwise display the results. This category also includes problems involving moving data between devices on the same system, such as moving data to a GPU and initiating a computation (though the nature of the computation is very likely to be of the next category).

Numerical problems are those that are inherently mathematical: performing calculations directly on data; encoding/decoding (or encrypting/decrypting) data; solving optimization problems; statistical analysis or inference; and many others. These problems appear everywhere – have you ever wondered how video streaming services derive suggestions for you? It can be quite tricky to identify numerical problems "in the wild." This is primarily because of the breadth of this category, and because there is usually some additional work to be done to understand a problem within this general category. It takes some thinking to turn a recommendation problem into a problem of linear algebra. Recognizing the numerical aspects of a problem and identifying the requirements within the data and the feasibility of the final results are part of this process.

Interface problems are slightly different, somewhat related to the IO problems, although far different in purpose. This category concerns how other users or programs will interact with your solution. Is this a simple command-line application? Is it a programmatic interface (API)? Is it a website? Each of these involves a set of (related) challenges. This is an essential component of all programming-related problems; if nobody can interact with your solution to the problem, then it doesn't really exist. Sometimes this challenge is obscured because you're adding new functionality to software that already has a well-defined interface, but it is still there and demands attention. A poorly implemented interface can mean the program is unusable, will break frequently, or will become difficult to maintain.

Abstraction is the primary mechanism for enabling one to realize a complex problem as one or more basic problems. The nature of the abstraction depends on the problem and the basic categories that it intersects with. For instance, for categorical problems, we might typically look for abstractions in the data and operations. The algorithm for sorting is identical, regardless of whether the ordering is done by less-than or greater-than. For IO-type problems, the abstractions typically arise around the interface between the program and the operating system of the computer, and potentially around the form and format of the data. For numerical problems, the data and methodology are the likely abstraction pathways, possibly involving some transformation of input and outputs so that they can be operated upon numerically. (For instance, large language models operate on integer tokens and not strings containing words or letters.) For interface problems, the mechanism for interacting with the consumer is the abstraction. The functions and classes that make up the user interface hide the details of the actual implementation.

Connecting problems with C++ abstraction mechanisms

The C++ language and standard library contain many useful tools for delivering abstractions. The tricky part is understanding when and how to use these to solve problems; in essence, this is the topic of this book. The first step is, of course, to try and identify the broad categories outlined above that exist in the context of your problem. It's safe to say that at least interfaces will be involved, and IO is also likely to be a component. Unless your problem is specifically an IO problem, it will almost surely involve at least one other category. (Identifying the different categories involved is, of course, a good way to start to decompose your problem into smaller parts.)

The C++ language provides several mechanisms for encapsulating and abstracting specific aspects of a program. For instance, it allows us to abstract a chain of operations used to transform input data into output data. They are themselves an encapsulation of this chain of operations, allowing a higher-level user to make use of the function to transform inputs to outputs without understanding the actual implementation.

This is a common pattern among language features; many of these are designed to encapsulate certain functionality so it can be reused or hidden from the user for other reasons (such as intellectual property protection). These mechanisms are primarily applicable for designing interfaces and interacting with libraries that implement solutions to some general problems (such as LAPACK for linear algebra).

Also included in the language are the powerful template and concept features. These mechanisms allow us to write a single piece of code that can be used for multiple C++ types. The compiler fills in the correct code at compile time for these types. Most of the C++ standard library is built around templates, so it can be used flexibly without requiring the library itself to contain compiled versions of the code for each possible combination of types. (Even this would not begin to approximate the flexibility of templates.) Concepts are the extension of the template system to allow the programmer to specify precisely the requirements of types passed into a template, primarily to aid debugging template code. Concepts are a great way to think about data and functionality. Each time you see a new problem, try to understand, from a conceptual point of view, what the requirements are. This is part of formulating an abstraction for your data (see the discussion in *Chapter 1*).

The C++ standard library is a collection of standard abstractions for specific tasks: working with the file system and interaction with files; storing data in various forms; working with basic mathematical operations (`exp`, `log`, etc.); working with text, strings, and regular expressions; standard algorithms; and many more. These are building blocks that help us interact with the system, the user, and with standard algorithms that appear commonly in programming problems. We already introduced the `algorithm` header in the previous chapter, and we will discuss it again in the next section. This contains implementations of many combinatorial algorithms (sorting and searching are the major ones). These function templates are extremely flexible and can be used anywhere these problems appear.

Input and output with C++

Most of the remainder of this chapter will be dedicated to using the C++ language and libraries to define, implement, and interface with solutions to some of the categories of problems. However, there is one aspect that is worth discussing before we dive into these details. This is the facility for loading (or otherwise "inputting") data and saving, storing, or printing results. Most IO in C++ is handled using the "streams" interface, encapsulated in various headers such as `iostream`. Fundamentally, an (input) stream is some kind of object that allows the user to read one or more bytes in a structured or unstructured manner. (There are other requirements of an `istream` object, but these broadly support the `read` functionality.)

This interface is quite flexible and works very well for reading from files on disk (`ifstream`) or from the terminal (`cin`). It allows one to read raw bytes from the file, or to read structured data such as integers or floating-point numbers using the stream in `operator >>`. For example, the following block of code reads bytes from `cin` to construct a double.

```
double value;
std::cin >> value;
```

This makes the assumption that the current sequence of bytes defines a valid double value in the format we are expecting. (In this case, a sequence of digits exactly as we would have written in the code itself.) If this assumption fails, such as the byte pattern contains a letter 'a', then an error state is set (either by failbit or an exception, depending on the stream configuration). Of course, there are many ways that a double could be stored as a sequence of raw bytes – a textual representation is just one example. This topic is called **serialization**.

Serialization is the process of taking a value and producing a representation that can be stored, independent of the internal state of the program, can be loaded later, and "exactly" recover the value as it was. There are many different means of doing this; JSON, XML, and Protocol Buffers are all examples of formats for serializing complex objects into text or raw bytes that can be transmitted or stored and then loaded elsewhere. The stream interface of the standard library is far more primitive than this – most serialization libraries are built on top of this interface.

The reason for this diversion into IO is partly to explain how we can address those challenges when writing our code, but it is also a perfect demonstration of how stacking relatively simple abstractions can build very powerful tools for solving complicated problems. This is a concept that will appear many times within this book.

Using standard algorithms

Algorithms are the bread and butter of programming and are a topic that we will describe in great detail in the next chapter. The standard `algorithm` headers are not algorithms as such, but instead are implementations of common (families of) algorithms for solving common abstract problems. (These mostly cover problems from classic data structure and algorithm courses from classic computer science.) They are surprisingly useful and turn up in lots of places. The power of these functions comes from their use of templates for every aspect of the operation: different search predicates, different comparisons and orderings, indirection, and projection.

As we have seen before, the real trick is finding places where these functions can be used, with simple operations or something more bespoke. Sometimes it can appear as if none of these functions are appropriate, until you frame the problem (via abstraction) in the correct way. This part of the standard library contains functions covering several categories of algorithms. The main ones are listed here.

- **Search operation**: Find an item in a range that satisfies some condition
- **Copying operations**: Copying or moving data around
- **Transformation operations**: Transforming the items in one range to another
- **Permutations**: Changing the order of items in a range
- **Sorting and partitioning**: Ordering items by a predicate and splitting a sorted range
- **Binary searching**: Searching but done faster using ordering
- **Generating operations**: Filling a range in various ways

The kind of reasoning required to put these functions to use effectively is very specific to the problem at hand. Sometimes this involves finding a means of (efficiently) iterating through your problem space or finding a proxy for the problem space that achieves this goal. Alternatively, it could mean finding the right predicate or ordering. This is best illustrated by example.

Iterating through the problem domain

Suppose you are tasked with designing a system to find the closest positive signal to a given position in a grid. The signal is defined by an intensity score that can be located using the grid position. For simplicity, let's say the grid is a 5 × 5 grid and the observer is in the center position. One approach is to search the entire grid, row by row, starting at the top left, and find all positive signals. Then we can perform a second step to find the signal that is closest to the start position. This will work quite well for modest-sized grids. However, if the grid is very large and the start position is not at the top left of the grid, then this is very wasteful. The code for this is as follows:

```
int dim_x = 5;
int dim_y = 5;

double compute_signal_intensity(int x, int y);
double detection_intensity = 5.0;

// A simple abstraction of a grid position
struct Pos {
    int x;
```

```
    int y;
};

std::vector<Pos> signals;
signals.reserve(dim_x*dim_y);
for (int y = 0; y < dim_y; ++y) {
    for (int x = 0; x < dim_x; ++x) {
        if (compute_signal_intensity(x, y) > detection_intensity) {
            signals.emplace_back(x, y);
        }
    }
}
```

Once we've found all the positive signals, we can use `std::min_element` with a custom ordering to find the closest signal to the start position.

```
Pos start {2, 2}; // middle of the grid

auto dist_to_start = [&start](const Pos& pos) {
    return std::max(std::abs(pos.x - start.x),
                    std::abs(pos.y - start.y));

auto ordering = [&dist_to_start](const Pos& a, const Pos& b) {
    // a simple distance metric that will work nicely
    return dist_to_start(a) < dist_to_start(b);
}

auto closest_pos = std::min_element(signals, ordering);
```

This is a rather brute-force approach, and we're not making use of any explicit abstraction, which leads to a functional but not efficient solution. The crucial information that we are forgetting is that the search is not global over the whole grid – we don't care about signals that appear far away from the starting position unless there are none closer. Injecting a little abstraction and using a more appropriate algorithm will yield a better, more efficient, and more flexible approach that we can modify later.

Our goal is to make use of std::find, which is a much more appropriate algorithm, to find the first signal (which should be the closest one) and then terminate. We need to find a means of iterating outwards from the starting position. Let's suppose that we have a range object that describes such an iteration, call it ExpandingSearchRange, and then we can find the closest position using the following very simple code.

```
auto predicate = [detection_intensity](int x, int y) {
    return compute_signal_intensity(x, y) > detection_intensity;
}

ExpandingSearchRange range(pos_x, pos_y);
auto closest_pos = std::ranges::find(range, predicate);
```

Assuming ExpandingSearchRange behaves as expected, this is guaranteed to find the closest signal position to the start (pos_x, pos_y). Since this terminates when it finds the first position at which the predicate function returns true, the expected number of evaluations of compute_signal_intensity is dramatically smaller than the dim_x*dim_y guaranteed evaluations from our first attempt. Moreover, should our objectives change or if additional constraints are imposed, we can simply swap ExpandingSearchRange with a modified version that meets the updated criteria.

We won't implement ExpandingSearchRange here, but you should think about how this might be implemented. In the next section, we'll look in more detail at how best to use functions (and function-like objects) both to segregate parts of the algorithm and as part of the abstraction itself.

When to use functions

Functions encapsulate a unit of computation and are most often used to allow that unit of computation to be used in many places. In their pure form, they operate on one or more input values to produce one or more output values. (Of course, C++ functions can only have a single return value, but we'll come back to this.) The term "pure" means that the function itself is independent of the global program state; only the input data has any effect on the outputs. Non-pure functions have their uses too, but are far less easy to reason about. For this reason, we shall mostly restrict our attention to pure functions here.

Pure functions are a mathematical concept, defined as a relation between two sets under which each member of the "input" set is related to exactly one element of the "output" set (the codomain). That is, any given configuration of inputs should always produce the same output. This is obviously a very general concept, but keeping this in mind is a good reminder of how these should be used. A function should represent a single computation, which might be a numerical calculation or something more general, and return its result.

As we mentioned, C++ functions can only return a single value, but this does not mean that multiple values cannot be returned. For instance, we could make use of aggregate objects such as `std::pair` or `std::tuple` to package multiple values into a single object that can be returned, or we could adopt a more C-like approach in which the result is written to one or more addresses passed as pointer arguments. Both approaches have their uses. C++ functions are also unlike their mathematical inspiration because they might fail to complete their calculation for various reasons. In mathematics, the domain of a function can be limited by any number of constraints, whereas C++ can only limit function arguments by type; checking values must be done at runtime, leading to errors.

A function can also be thought of as a means of hiding actual implementation details from the wider program. They are a very low-cost (especially if inlined) means of abstracting particular details such as a distance function between points, an ordering or other comparison, or a predicate function for searching. Functions should be used to logically structure implementations and as a means of providing flexibility for the problem domain. For instance, in the previous section, `compute_signal_intensity` might have several possible implementations that would yield different search characteristics.

Creating interfaces based on functions

One of the most important uses of functions is as the main interface for your code for external users (library consumers or directly via a GUI or other interface). The advantage of a function is that it is a simple concept that transfers well across boundaries. For instance, C++ functions can be made to use C calling conventions, making them usable from other languages that know how to call C-style functions. (Many languages have the capability to link against libraries compiled in C and use the functions.) Once inside the interface function, you're free to make use of any of the mechanisms at your disposal to actually implement your solution.

Functions are a good way to define your interface because they are simple and easy to understand, but are still quite expressive. If one needs more complex functionality, one can make use of a more complex configuration object. This can be set with sensible defaults (depending on the problem, of course), so users who just need the basic functionality don't need to spend a long time configuring. This is a remarkably flexible approach that has relatively small overheads in terms of runtime cost and overhead for the programmer.

Consider the following example. Suppose the problem is to load data from a selection of sources, provided by the user, and then produce a set of summary statistics (mean, standard deviation, min, max, etc.). A very simple interface might include a simple `struct` that contains the summary statistics, a single function that takes the sources as a sequence of strings describing where to find the data (using uniform resource identifiers, for example), and a configuration that allows the user to customize the actual set of summary statistics produced. (We can't omit these from the return `struct`, but we can simply not calculate them.) This could be defined as follows:

```
struct SummaryStatistics; // definition omitted, not really important

class Configuration {
    bool b_include_mean = true;
    bool b_include_std = true;
    // more fields with sensible defaults
public:
    bool include_mean() const noexcept { return b_include_mean; }
    void include_mean(bool setting) noexcept {
        b_include_mean = setting;
    }
    // functions that the user can use to customize
};

std::vector<SummaryStatistics>
compute_statistics(const Configuration& config, std::span<const
std::string> sources);
```

Notice that the `Configuration` object is entirely inline, but it is still part of the interface of the program. Indeed, if this class changes (by adding new settings, for instance), then the function would have to be recompiled and would likely break backwards compatibility.

There is a good argument for making your programming interface as minimal as possible, making use of inline functions or very simple classes to adapt more complex driver routines rather than exporting everything. (This might be ideal, but it will not always be feasible.)

Sometimes, functions will not be completely sufficient for describing the interface you need. In this case, you might have to turn to using a class-based interface. This has some advantages in terms of flexibility, but it does expose some additional details about the implementation that one might want to keep private (to maintain intellectual property, for instance). There are ways around this, but none of these are as simple as a function-based interface.

Functions as building blocks

Functions are very useful for solving combinatorial or numerical problems. Typically, these kinds of problems have several moving parts. At the outer level, there is typically some kind of driving operation that performs an iteration over the problem domain. Inside this driver is a computation aspect and a decision aspect. In a sorting problem, the computation involves comparing pairs of elements, and the decision is whether to swap the positions of the two elements. The same holds true in many numerical algorithms that involve collections of data. (Obviously, computations that operate on single numbers or small collections of numbers do not usually require such complexity.) Functions are ideal for isolating these aspects and making the final solution easier to understand.

For example, suppose we want to find the value of a real number t at which some unknown (continuous) function f obtains the value zero. One approach would be to use repeated bisection. This problem requires three pieces of information. The first is the (continuous) function itself, which takes a single argument and returns a single number; the second is a point in the domain at which the function takes a positive value; and the third is a value at which the function takes a negative value. We can implement the algorithm as follows:

```
#include <cmath>
// definitions of helper functions omitted
template <typename Function, typename Real>
Real find_root_bisect(Function&& function, Real pos, Real neg, Real tol)
{
    auto fpos = function(pos);

    // Driving Loop
    while (compare_reals_equal(pos, neg)) {
        auto m = midpoint(pos, neg); // computes the midpoint (pos +
neg)/2
```

```
        auto fm = function(m);

        // Quit early if the function is already (almost) 0.
        if (std::abs(fm) < tol) { return m; }

        // The decision logic to find the next point to check
        if (std::signbit(fm) == std::signbit(fpos)) {
            pos = m;
            fpos = fm;
        } else {
            neg = m;
        }
    }

    return fpos;
}
```

There are two "building block" functions in this implementation. The first (`compare_reals_equal`) is a function to determine whether two real numbers are distinguishable from one another – remember that C++ doubles only have a precision of approximately 15 decimal places (at best). The second function (`midpoint`) is used to compute the midpoint of the two given values. This isn't strictly necessary here because computing the midpoint is so simple, but other similar algorithms use more complicated logic to determine which point should be checked next. Both of these building blocks could be replaced by more nuanced implementations that could change the characteristics of the iterative method. Keeping these as functions allows us to replace them more easily later (abstracting the algorithm), perhaps using additional template arguments and function-like objects (see the next section). At the very least, using functions here allows us to remain flexible as to the `Real` type. For instance, we might use a type that does not overload `operator+` but works in the algorithm.

Let's take a moment to understand the requirements of this algorithm. The first constraint is the mathematical requirements of the function. We require that the function takes a single real number, returns a single real number, is continuous – if one were to plot this function, the line would have no jumps – and that it has at least one positive value and at least one negative value. We cannot check that the function is continuous in the code.

The function will still run if this is not the case, but might not produce a meaningful answer (garbage in, garbage out); this is quite typical of numerical algorithms. The other conditions can be checked. For instance, we can check that the function is positive at one value and negative at the other rather simply, but we omit these checks in the preceding code to save space.

Function-like objects

In C++, we can define classes that have an `operator()` member function, which allows instances of the classes to be called like functions. These are surprisingly useful because they interact better with the template mechanism. (Function pointers cannot be meaningfully default-constructed, but function-like objects can.) The standard library contains several function-like objects in the `functional` header, including `std::less` and `std::hash`. These objects are used as default template parameters for containers such as `std::map` and `std::unordered_map`, and also in algorithms.

Function-like objects also include lambda functions, which are really syntactic sugar that the compiler turns into a class definition during compilation. Captured variables are just data members of this class that are injected into the call function body. Lambdas are a very useful means of declaring function-like objects. Our previous examples illustrate this perfectly.

More generally, callable classes can be used to represent functions that carry internal state (non-pure functions). A good example of where this is useful is if your function has some implicit random state. The class can maintain the random generator (e.g., `std::mt19937`) that is used to inject random state whenever the function is called. Here is an example.

```
#include <random>

class FunctionWithNoise {
    std::mt19937 m_rng;
    std::normal_distribution<double> m_dist;
public:

    double operator()(double arg) noexcept {
        auto noise = m_dist(m_rng);
        return 2.*arg + 1 + noise;
    }
};
```

Such a function would be useful in simulating data, where we need to generate large amounts of data that follows a known trend, but includes some randomly generated noise. For instance, this class could be useful for testing the performance of an inference pipeline.

Functions are very useful, but they are limited by the fact that they cannot usually hold state. Function objects can carry state, but this is a very poor reflection of the flexibility and power of fully object-oriented programming. In the next section, we will see how to make use of all the features of classes and inheritance to build truly flexible systems.

When to use classes

Classes are an encapsulation of data and behavior and should be used in one of two ways. The first is as a structured container that maintains some invariant property that can be used in and queried in algorithms using its methods (for example, `std::vector<...>`). The second use is as an abstract interface that hides the details, in a similar way to how functions can be used to hide implementation details. This allows you to write code against the abstract interface and use any object that implements it – for example, the IO stream interface in the C++ standard library. Both are examples of abstractions, but go about it in (somewhat) different ways.

When we talk about class-based abstract interfaces, we usually mean **dynamic polymorphism** (although that is not always the case). **Polymorphism** (literally translated as "many forms") is a means by which a class (the interface) can be used in place of any class that implements its interface (the implementations). In C++, this is achieved with virtual functions; the pointers to the method implementations are placed in a lookup table that is queried at runtime to find the correct implementation to use. (Virtual functions are a very deep topic with decades of development and optimization, of which this barely scratches the surface. For more information, see `https://en.wikipedia.org/wiki/Virtual_function` and the references contained therein.) This has a small performance cost, but is very powerful.

Polymorphism, as described above, carries a performance cost at runtime. For this reason, we should avoid using polymorphic objects in the performance-critical portions of code where the added time to call a virtual function will accumulate quickly. On the other hand, using polymorphic objects on an interface boundary, especially those between a program and the user or with IO, can effectively hide the added cost of the function lookup. This makes polymorphic objects ideal for interacting with external concerns where the latency of the operation itself is the greatest cost.

Using classes to provide behavior for raw data

One of the basic ways to use a class is to encapsulate a structured set of data and behavior. The idea is that, in order to make use of some tools (such as `std::find`), the data must have some kind of standard interface (such as equality testable or equality comparable). For example, suppose that our problem is to examine an address book to find entries within a specific area. A basic entry in the address book might be as follows:

```
struct AddressBookRecord {
    size_t id;
    int house_number;
    std::string street_address;
    std::string city_and_state;
    int zip_code;
    // Other data fields that aren't relevant to the problem
};
```

Here, we use a `struct` so all these fields are visible to externally defined functions, but in practice, one would probably want to write accessor methods to hide these details from external users and prevent (or facilitate) modification. The `id` field is a unique identifier; every record must differ from every other by `id`. The other fields do not enjoy this property. This means we can write a very simple equality operator for these records as follows:

```
inline bool
operator==(const AddressBookRecord& lhs, const AddressBookRecord& rhs)
noexcept
{
    return lhs.id == rhs.id;
}
```

Whilst `id` can be used to uniquely identify, it does not provide a useful ordering of the records. For this, one would need to look at the other listed fields. There are many different orderings to choose from. A reasonable choice is to order in reverse, starting with `zip_code`, then `city_and_state`, and so on, in dictionary-like ordering. (The implementation is quite long, so it is left as an exercise for you.) Of course, this might not be the specific ordering that you need for a given problem, and you might have to define others.

Unfortunately, operator< can only be implemented once, but anyway, naming these operators will help make the code more readable.

```
bool compare_house_humber(const AddressBookRecord&, const
AddressBookRecord&);
bool compare_zip_code(const AddressBookRecord&, const AddressBookRecord&);
```

In this example, the class contains a copy of all the data, but this won't always be desirable. Moving data around is expensive, so use lightweight views that contain a reference, which can be an actual reference (&), a pointer to the original (*), or a selection of views into certain fields of the data (e.g., string_view). All of these have their uses, but with the slight cost of a pointer indirection, at least in the first two cases. This can be used to implement a new interface on top of the raw data cheaply:

```
class RecordView {
    const AddressBookRecord* p_data;
public:
    size_t id() const noexcept { return p_data->id; }
    // constructors and other methods
}

inline bool operator==(const RecordView& lhs, const RecordView& rhs)
noexcept
{
    return lhs.id() == rhs.id();
}
```

This approach has the added benefit that one can simply change the view type if different behavior is required. For instance, the interface can be changed if a different data ordering is required. The type system in C++ makes this slightly awkward, but it is sometimes useful.

Classes that represent physical objects

The other place that classes appear frequently is in object-oriented programming. Here, we use a combination of abstract interfaces that describe precisely the methods that must be provided, and implementations that give concrete realizations of one or more of these interfaces (we called this polymorphism in the introduction to this section). In this setup, consumers of the interfaces of the classes also have no need to know exactly how these interfaces are realized, only that they are. Interfaces can be stacked and combined, with some caveats that we won't discuss here, to provide a rich ecosystem on which we can build functionality.

These hierarchies of classes and objects are often best utilized to describe physical objects (things that exist in the real world) or objects that live on the computer system (desktop windows, storage devices and files, etc.). Using polymorphism through class hierarchies has a real runtime cost, which makes them inefficient for working with raw data.

Physical objects, as described, all have far greater runtime costs that are much larger than the cost of the abstraction. For instance, a desktop window is redrawn each time the display refreshes, which might occur at 60Hz (60 times per second). This means the logic that is used to determine how a redraw should occur needs to take less than approximately 16 milliseconds, which is far greater than the cost of a virtual method lookup (at worst, a few microseconds).

Suppose our problem is to monitor a system of temperature sensors monitoring some equipment and raise an error. The temperature sensors might interact with the computer in different ways, or report temperatures in different formats. From our perspective, we need a raw temperature, in the form of a single float representing the temperature measurement in Kelvin (the SI unit for temperature). We will probably also need some kind of ID so we can provide some useful information to the user. Here's what the interface might look like.

```
class TempSensor {
public:
    virtual ~TempSensor() = default;
    virtual std::string_view id() const noexcept = 0;
    virtual float temperature_kelvin() const noexcept = 0;
};
```

The two methods are pure virtual, so the implementation must provide both. To be explicit, and to help avoid confusion, use the name of the temperature function, including the units of measurement. This is a reminder to the programmer that, when adding new implementations, they should return Kelvin and not Fahrenheit or Celsius. The function that checks the sensors can be written easily in terms of this interface:

```
#include <format>
#include <span>
#include <stdexcept>

void check_sensors(std::span<const TempSensor*> sensors, float threshold)
{
    for (const auto& sensor : sensors) {
        auto temp = sensor->temperature_kelvin();
```

```
        if (temp > threshold) {
            throw std::runtime_error(
                std::format("Sensor {} reports temperature {}",
                            sensor->id(), temp)
            );
        }
    }
}
```

This abstract interface makes the function very simple, and allows us to write code that doesn't make use of information that we don't need. (We only call the `id` method in the case that the temperature is above the threshold.) Interfaces should generally be sufficient and minimal to achieve the goals that they address. `TempSensor` satisfies both conditions; it does not require anything that isn't used or provide anything that isn't strictly necessary.

Classes and dynamic polymorphism come at the cost of runtime performance. This might not matter in some contexts, but in performance-critical sections, this extra overhead can be devastating. In the next section, see how we can make use of templates and concepts to perform static polymorphism that shifts the overhead to the compiler.

Using templates

Templates are one of C++'s most powerful features, at least until C++26 brings first-class support for reflection. This mechanism allows the user to write code that uses placeholder types that are resolved during instantiation when the compiler sees a use of the template. As we described before, the template mechanism uses *try first and unwind on failure.* (This mechanism is often referred to as **SFINAE** or **substitution failure is not an error** – see `https://en.cppreference.com/w/cpp/language/sfinae.html` or [1].) Concepts work in a slightly different way. Here, the requirements should be listed up front and checked before the template is instantiated (at least in theory).

More importantly, templates and concepts are powerful abstraction mechanisms, allowing us to write code that works with many kinds of data or different algorithms, provided they broadly behave in the correct way (by exposing the correct methods, etc.). It's quite rare that one starts writing code to solve a problem by writing template code, but thinking in terms of templates can sometimes help to find the correct formulation of an abstraction.

The right questions to ask are those such as: what methods need to exist, and what do I expect them to do? These are precisely the questions one should ask when extracting the relevant parts of a problem. We've seen an example of this already when we discussed standard algorithms. For example, `std::find` works for any "data" exposing a "forward range" interface, whose values can be evaluated by the predicate (such as to compare to a given value). We can look to similar properties in our data and in new problems.

Concepts force us to think about these properties up front. We can design our algorithms better if we put in the work up front to understand what the minimal set of requirements is to obtain the objectives. The main thing to understand is how one takes a problem from the problem domain and uses the features in C++ – in this context, templates and concepts – to realize these abstractions. We've already seen some examples of how functions from the `algorithms` header address structure in the problem itself.

Concepts for basic data

At the most basic level, a problem will involve some kind of basic unit of data. This might be something very simple, such as a single grid coordinate, or something more complex, such as a specific record in a database. Concepts allow us to create granular checks on the interface provided by a type at compile time, allowing us to more easily write generic algorithms.

For instance, let's consider the `Pos` structure that we defined earlier. The `x` and `y` coordinates are integers because they describe a position in a grid. From the point of view of the algorithm, it only mattered that `Pos` had these two members, so we could write a concept to check that this condition was satisfied.

```
#include <concepts>
#include <type_traits>

template <typename T>
concept GridPosition = requires(T t) {
    std::is_same_v<decltype(t.x), int>;
    std::is_same_v<decltype(t.x), int>;
};
```

This concept will be satisfied whenever a type `T` has two members `x` and `y` that are both of type `int`. The code we wrote earlier could be replaced with generic code that uses this concept but operates in exactly the same way. This might be a little restrictive, because an `int` might not be large enough to contain the full extent of the grid. This is just a toy example to show what kind of checks are possible and is not intended to be practical.

More broadly, concepts can be used to check that types satisfy high-level requirements such as being ordered (see the `std::totally_ordered` concept), which would be a requirement for sorting algorithms, or being copyable or movable.

We can also check function-like objects to see whether they have the correct form. For instance, `std::predicate` tests whether the type is function-like and returns something convertible to a `bool`. There are also specific requirements, such as `std::input_range`, which we described in *Chapter 1*, and the related `std::input_iterator`.

When presented with a problem, it inevitably comes with some kind of data. This data might be something provided via some other part of the program (passed in a `std::span`, for instance), it could be something that you have to obtain from disk or elsewhere, or it could be something that is less well-defined. If it is a collection of data – such as records from a database – one has many concepts to think about. The first is the form of the collection, which one would hope is something range-like so one can iterate over it. (Different database drivers may provide different interfaces that do not require copying data several times.) Then we have to consider the individual records. In this situation, writing generic code with concepts might make your code easier to maintain later, if you decide to change the database driver, for instance.

Using traits to adapt behavior

We can also use templates to standardize or expand an interface without making extra additions to the type of an object itself. The standard library contains many examples of this. For instance, `std::iterator_traits` is a template that provides information about an iterator type, abstracting away the actual nature of the iterator itself. This allows us to implement algorithms that accept any iterator and make use of the `traits` object to query the provided type, rather than requiring a completely different template function for each kind of iterator. That being said, one might want to specialize for certain kinds of iterator for performance reasons. This mechanism can be thought of as the compile-time equivalent of abstract interface classes. They don't incur a runtime-performance cost but instead take longer to compile.

Traits are obviously somewhat related to concepts. You might think of concepts as a subset of traits. Concepts are an extension of the template and type systems of C++. Traits are more complex since they generally are used to extend or modify the capabilities of a class based on a smaller interface or external factors.

This kind of facade can be used as a very lightweight means of interacting with plain data types such as the preceding `AddressBookRecord`. This is useful if different parts of the algorithm require that the data be interpreted in different ways (that are known at compile time) without requiring any explicit copy or conversion operations.

The more common use, however, is to act as a bridge between a fixed interface, which involves some set of types and functionality, and generic types that can be made to satisfy this interface. A generic interface for converting between types exactly is a good example here.

Suppose you are implementing a framework for performing exact conversions between numerical types. A 32-bit integer can be represented exactly as a double, since a double has 53 binary bits of precision, but a 64-bit integer cannot. The reverse is obviously never true. The C++ language allows for conversions between these types through simple static casts, but it makes no guarantees about exactness. Obviously, we can't change the built-in types to implement safe conversions, so we can instead define a trait.

This trait takes the source and destination types as template arguments and implements the conversion only if it can be done exactly, and otherwise throws an exception. We might define the interface as follows:

```
template <typename From, typename To, typename=void>
struct ExactConversionTraits {
    using from_ref = const From&;
    using to_ref = To&;

    static void convert(to_ref to, from_ref from)
    {
        throw std::runtime_error("invalid exact conversion")
    }
};
```

The final template argument is to allow us to perform compile-time checks using the template parameters. For instance, we can implement conversion for integer types with a partial specialization of this template. Here, we use the `std::intgeral` concept to check whether both inputs are integers, but we could have used `std::enable_if_t` and `std::is_integral_v` in the final template argument to achieve the same effect (pre-C++20).

```
#include <concepts>
#include <limits>

template <std::integral From, std::integral To>
struct ExactConversionTraits<From, To>
{
    using from_ref = const From&;
    using to_ref = To&;

    static void convert(to_ref to, from_ref from) {
        if (from <= std::numeric_limits<To>::max
            && from >= std::numeric_limits<To>::min) {
            throw std::runtime_error("invalid exact conversion");
        }
        to = static_cast<To>(from);
    }
};
```

We can actually make this code much better by performing compile-time checks to remove unnecessary bounds checks at runtime. This will mean that the runtime cost of using this trait is zero if `From` is a 32-bit signed integer and `To` is a 64-bit signed integer, where the latter is guaranteed to exactly represent the former. We leave it as an exercise to specialize this trait for floating-point numbers.

The astute reader will have noticed that we seem to be doing something rather interesting with the signature of the `convert` function. Instead of taking a `const From&` argument and returning an instance of `To`, we instead take two reference arguments that are defined by member types in the trait. This is to accommodate types that might not be easily constructed, such as those that must be hidden behind a pointer. A concrete example of this is a **GNU multi-precision (GMP)** rational number `mpq_t` that is usually passed as a pointer, since it is implemented in C. Using this setup allows for greater flexibility than otherwise would be possible. Of course, there is nothing to stop you from extending the trait to include these other functions.

Summary

In this chapter, we examined the various abstraction mechanisms and standard algorithms that are provided by the C++ language and standard library. These serve two purposes in our pursuit of solutions to complex problems. The first is to help guide the way we formulate abstractions within the problem itself, such as identifying the critical properties and supported operations of the data. The second is to provide the possible routes that we might take and expose patterns and abstractions, and algorithms too, that we might look for in our problems. This accelerates the process of solving problems using computational thinking.

The standard library algorithms provide numerous high-quality and high-performance implementations of many combinatorial and numerical algorithms. These are generally encapsulated in template functions that make them extremely flexible and provide a very simple interface. Functions and classes form the basic building blocks of encapsulation and abstraction that can be used to tackle almost any problem. Templates and concepts increase these capabilities greatly and shift work to the compiler, further increasing runtime performance.

Now that we have a good understanding of abstraction mechanisms and how they can be applied in various situations, we can move on to understand more about algorithms and how to reason about them.

Reference

1. Vandevoorde, D., Josuttis, N.M. and Gregor, D. 2018. *C++ templates: the complete guide*. Boston, MA: Addison-Wesley.

3

Algorithmic Thinking and Complexity

Algorithms are step-by-step instructions for how to transform inputs into outputs. This is the bridge between a theoretical solution to a problem and an actual implementation in code. Writing out an algorithm formally allows us to analyze it mathematically to understand how the algorithm will run. The main characteristic that we look for is the *complexity* of the algorithm, which gives a measure of how long it would take to execute the algorithm to obtain the solution based on the size of the inputs and outputs.

Algorithms are a language-agnostic description of what needs to be done to solve a particular problem. This is important because it might not be easy to translate from one language to another, but an abstract description means a new programmer does not need to unpick language-specific details. Being able to read, analyze, and implement algorithms is an important skill for every programmer. The ability to formulate your own algorithms is also an important skill.

There are two parts to developing an algorithm. The first is designing a first algorithm to solve a particular problem. This first attempt is not usually an optimal solution, but it is a necessary step. The second step is to chase down performance bottlenecks, which demands a far greater understanding of the problem and its context. This chapter aims to give some hints about how to design algorithms and things to keep in mind when chasing performance, but it is not a comprehensive guide. The latter sections of this chapter describe, at a high level, some of the general patterns for designing algorithms and some of the special considerations for how to find extra performance in your algorithms.

In this chapter, we're going to cover the following main topics:

- Understanding algorithms
- Computing complexity
- Designing your own algorithms
- Requirements and considerations

Technical requirements

The focus of this chapter is on developing some theory and techniques for designing and analyzing algorithms. Some familiarity with C++ is assumed, but we try to explain more modern features that you might not have encountered before. This chapter contains several exercises, possible solutions to which can be found in the `Chapter-03` folder of the GitHub repository for this book (`https://github.com/PacktPublishing/The-CPP-Programmers-Mindset`), along with a system of tests so you can test your own solutions. Some snippets of code also have tests in this repository.

Understanding algorithms

In *Chapter 1*, we gave a definition of an algorithm and listed the essential properties. In this section, we will discuss how we go about verifying those properties and reasoning formally about an algorithm. This topic is, as you might suspect, an extensive field of study that is the subject of many books; *Introduction to Algorithms* by Cormen et al. is a classic book on the subject [1], and *The Art of Computer Programming* by Donald Knuth [2] is another. This section is intended to give just enough information to inform the rest of this chapter, and not a thorough treatment of the theory.

Recall from *Chapter 1* that an algorithm must be finite, definite, effective, and have clear inputs and outputs. When developing new algorithms, the first thing one should check is correctness: does the algorithm actually deliver what it says it does? For this, one should ideally endeavor to prove mathematically that the algorithm is sound. For simple statements that don't operate on data of varying size, we can prove the algorithm directly. For algorithms that operate on data that has a varying size, we need to use something like mathematical induction.

A direct proof is a sequence of logical statements, with each statement having a logical consequence of previous statements or external statements that have been proven true themselves. (The latter are called **theorems**.) There are other methods of proof, but those aren't so relevant here.

Proof by induction

Induction is a technique for proving statements depending on a size parameter (a positive integer). Suppose we have some predicate $P(n)$ that is either true or false for some non-negative integer n. If we can show that the following conditions hold, then we can deduce that $P(n)$ holds for all values of n. These conditions are as follows:

1. $P(0)$ is true.
2. If $P(k)$ is true for an arbitrary value of $k \geq 0$, then $P(k + 1)$ is also true.

What happens here is that the first condition tells us that $P(0)$ is true. The second condition then tells us that $P(0)$ being true implies that $P(1)$ is also true. Then $P(1)$ being true implies that $P(2)$ is true, and so on for every n. The first condition is sometimes called the **base case**. The second is the **inductive step**. The assumption that $P(k)$ is true for some k is often called the **inductive hypothesis**. Often, the base case will be that the predicate holds at 0, but it doesn't have to be. For instance, it could start at 1 or 2. The corresponding statement is then proven for all values greater than or equal to the base case. Here is a classic example of how induction can be used to prove mathematical statements.

Example

Consider the following statement. The sum of the first n positive integers can be calculated as follows:

$$\sum_{i=1}^{n} i = \frac{n(n+1)}{2}.$$

We can prove this statement holds for all $n \geq 1$ using induction.

First, consider the base case $n = 1$. In this case, the sum on the left-hand side is 1. On the right-hand side, the expression is $1\,(1 + 1)/2 = 1$. These two are clearly equal, so the base case is proven.

Next, assume that for some $k \geq 1$, the statement is true for $n = k$; that is,

$$\sum_{i=1}^{k} i = \frac{k(k+1)}{2}.$$

This statement is the inductive hypothesis. Now, the task is to show that the result holds for $n = k + 1$ using this fact. Here, we can start with the left-hand side. Well, we have the following:

$$\sum_{i=1}^{k+1} i = (k + 1) + \sum_{i=1}^{k} i$$

Applying the inductive hypothesis, we obtain the following:

$$\sum_{i=1}^{k+1} i = (k+1) + \frac{k(k+1)}{2}.$$

We can rearrange the previous right-hand expression to obtain the following:

$$(k+1) + \frac{k(k+1)}{2} = \frac{2(k+1)+k(k+1)}{2} = \frac{(k+2)(k+1)}{2}.$$

This is precisely the statement required for $P(k+1)$ to be true (after a little reordering of the terms). Thus, the $P(k)$ being true implies that $P(k+1)$ is also true and, by induction, we have shown that the statement holds for all values of $n \geq 1$.

In our case, the predicate is usually the statement that the algorithm produces correct outputs for inputs of length n. The inductive step involves assuming that the algorithm produces correct results for a sequence of length n and then proving, using this assumption, that the algorithm produces correct results for a sequence of length $n+1$. Let's look at another very simple algorithm.

Example

Suppose our problem is to find a specific value in a list of n elements, if it exists, returning the position on success. The basic algorithm for doing this is a sequential search, iterating through all elements until the target value is found, or until the end is reached and the element is not found. It might seem rather obvious that this algorithm does exactly what it claims to, but it is a nice introduction nonetheless.

Our base case is that the algorithm works when there is a single element in the sequence. Following the algorithm, we need only check whether the single element in the list is the target value or not. Either way, the correct value is returned.

Next, assume the algorithm works for some $k \geq 1$. To check a sequence of length $k+1$, one first checks the first k terms, and then the final $(k+1)$ term. This amounts to running the algorithm on a sequence of length k. By the hypothesis, we know the algorithm either has already found the target value, and returned already (in which case we're done), or the value has not been found. In this case, check the final value. If it matches the target, return $k+1$, or return not found. The algorithm has successfully completed.

This example is rather trivial, but sometimes the details need to be written down. When learning a new technique, it is best to start by writing down simple examples before diving into more complex examples.

Sometimes, a slightly different formulation is needed, where one assumes (in the inductive hypothesis) that the algorithm works for all sequences of length $k \leq n$ and then proves that this implies that it holds for $n + 1$. This is especially useful for recursive algorithms.

Computing complexity

Computational or algorithmic complexity is a measure of how the running time of an algorithm grows depending on the size of the inputs. This is a theoretical computation that is independent of the specific hardware or implementation. Computational complexity is the primary means of comparing the efficiency of different algorithms (for achieving the same aim). The analysis of algorithmic complexity can be rather tricky, so we won't go into too much detail here.

Complexity is usually recorded in "big-oh" notation, such as $O(1)$, $O(\log n)$, $O(n)$, and $O(n^2)$. The number that appears here is the term that dominates the theoretical execution time for large enough n. Here, $O(1)$represents constant complexity, where the operation takes a constant amount of time regardless of the size of the input; $O(n)$ means the running time is related to the size of the inputs in a linear manner. Quadratic complexity $O(n^2)$ means that the theoretical running time is dominated by the square of the size of the input parameters.

Examples

Index-based lookup into an array of memory has constant complexity $O(1)$. The amount of time required to access the array doesn't depend on the size of the array itself. (This is the ideal; it's actually not physically possible to achieve this complexity, at least with current technology.)

A linear search, such as the *find* algorithm described in the previous section, has linear complexity $O(n)$. To search through the entire sequence, we must (at worst) visit every element in the sequence. Each visit has constant complexity, so the overall complexity depends only on the number of elements in the sequence.

A binary search into an ordered sequence to find any particular element has logarithmic complexity $O(\log n)$, which is better than the $O(n)$ complexity. Here, we can make use of the ordering of the data to decide whether the element lies in the first half of the sequence or the latter. Repeating this process results in $logn$ splits to find the element (or determine that it is not present).

The best sorting algorithms have complexity $O(n \log n)$ in the worst case; some perform better in the best case scenario (we won't describe what this means here), but $O(n \log n)$ is the best that can be achieved. A simple insertion sort algorithm has $O(n^2)$ complexity

Formally, an algorithm $A(n)$ (depending on n) has complexity $O\big(g(n)\big)$, for some function $g(n)$, if there exists a constant $c > 0$ and a positive integer n_0 such that the running time $T\big(A(n)\big)$ satisfies $T\big(A(n)\big) \leq cg(n)$ whenever $n > n_0$. This is a very technical definition, so let's break down the parts. Firstly, note that we only care about large (positive) integers; $O\big(g(n)\big)$ is a statement about the **asymptotic behavior** of the algorithm, not the behavior for small values of n. (The behavior for small values of n is often obscured by other time costs of the algorithm.) Secondly, we allow ourselves an arbitrary constant of flexibility. In practice, this constant can be quite large, but it doesn't matter for large values of n. This is an upper bound for the running time, indicating the worst-case scenario. Many algorithms have a lower average complexity or best-case complexity.

Computing the complexity of an algorithm (at least informally) simply requires examining the steps and adding up the number of operations. This works well if the steps are sufficiently simple and involve operations of known complexity. However, one must be careful. It can be easy to miss a source of complexity, or the aggregation of complexity can be more complicated. Formally proving the complexity of an algorithm needs induction, and can be rather involved. Cormen et al. [1] give a very readable and thorough discussion of how to go about proving that an algorithm has a given complexity.

Another important note is that the complexity (the function that appears in the brackets after O) only needs to report the largest power or most dominant term. For instance, $O(n^2 + n)$ and $O(n^2)$ describe precisely the same complexity. If the algorithm has two input size parameters, it is not uncommon to see complexity as a function of both input sizes. Computing the average of a sequence consisting of n vectors, each with k components, has complexity $O(nk)$ since we must visit each of the k coordinates of each of the n vectors exactly once. However, if the size of the points is unimportant for the purpose of the discussion, then the dependence on k is consumed by the constant.

Relationships between complexity

Clearly, there is an inherent ordering between the different complexity classes. For instance, linear complexity $O(n)$ is surely better than quadratic complexity $O(n^2)$, but where does logarithmic complexity factor in? The lowest possible complexity is constant complexity $O(1)$. This indicates that the algorithm does not depend at all on the size of the inputs. We already noted that element lookup in a linear array has constant complexity (at least theoretically). Logarithmic complexity comes next (such as a binary search), as it sits between constant and linear complexity $O(n)$. Polynomial complexity $O(n^r)$ increases with degree r. The largest class of complexity that appears, even somewhat regularly, is exponential complexity 2^n. However, these algorithms have running times that grow so rapidly that they tend to be impractical.

To illustrate, the differences between a selection of representative complexities, plotted on a logarithmic axis scale, are shown in *Figure 3.1*.

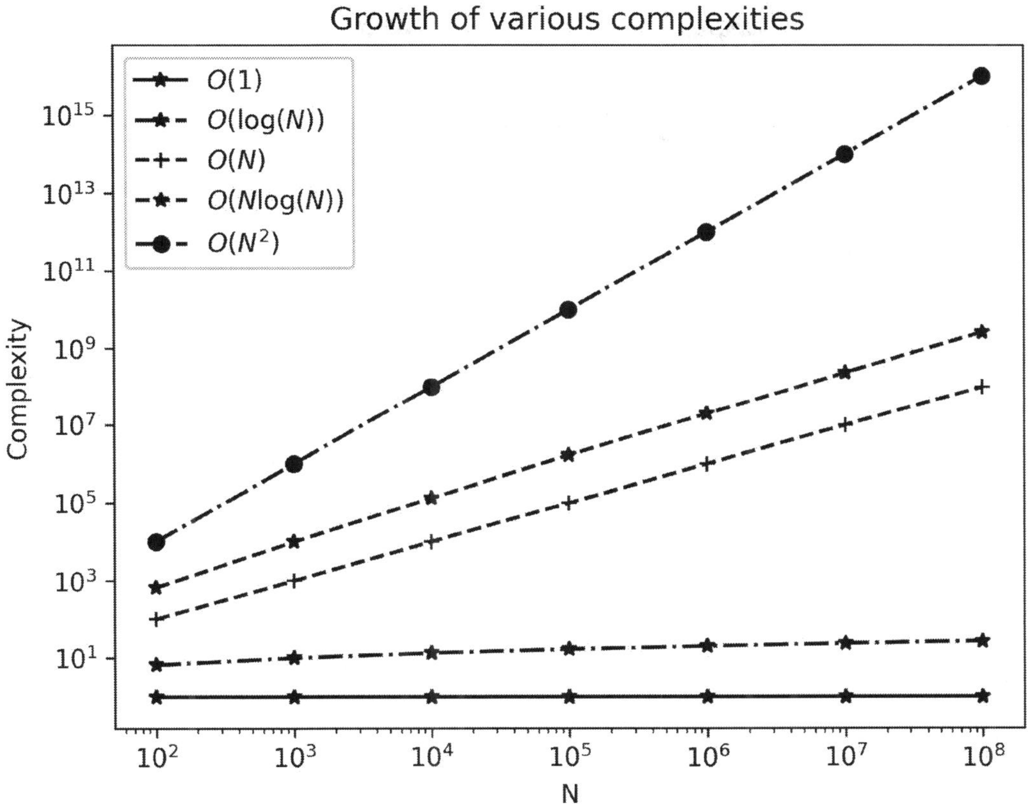

Figure 3.1: Plot of the growth of different algorithmic complexities ranging from constant complexity to quadratic complexity, presented on a logarithmic scale

Amortized complexity

Sometimes, the algorithms are not uniform in their complexity. There may be cases where a very expensive operation is triggered on a semi-regular basis during the execution of the algorithm. The big-oh complexity reflects the worst-case cost of using an algorithm, which will usually be the aggregation of the spikes and not the usual average case.

For example, consider the complexity of the `push_back` operation on `std::vector`. Most of the time, an insertion at the end of the vector has $O(1)$ complexity; this is simply the cost of incrementing the pointer to the end of the active buffer and constructing the new value. However, if there is no remaining allocated space, then the vector must reallocate and copy/move all data from the old buffer to the new buffer, which is allocated (usually) twice the size of the old one. This reallocation and moving of data has linear complexity, since each element must be touched once. However, because the vector buffer doubles in size each time, these reallocations occur less frequently as the number of elements grows. In this case, we might say that the cost of a `push_back` operation is an **amortized constant.**

We can be a little more precise here. The cost c_i of the ith insertion into a vector is i if i is a power of 2, and 1 otherwise. Thus, the cost of the first n insertions is n plus the contribution of all the reallocations that have been done after n insertions. Because of the growth strategy, the number of reallocations is the greatest integer less than the (base 2) logarithm of n, written as $[\log_2 n]$. The cost of the j reallocation is 2^j. (Allocations occur at the i insertion if i is a power of 2, that is, when $i = 2^j$.) Adding these up, we obtain the following equation:

$$\sum_{i=1}^{n} c_i = n + \sum_{j=0}^{[\log_2 n]} 2^j = n + \frac{2^{[\log_2 n]+1} - 1}{2 - 1} < 3n$$

Thus, the total cost of the first n insertion is $3n$, meaning the amortized cost is $3\,n/n = 3$, a constant!

Now that we have a basic understanding of the properties and analysis of algorithms, we can look at how we might start to design our own algorithms, which is the content of the next section.

Designing your own algorithms

Designing algorithms is not always a complicated task. Most problems are relatively simple, at least once you factor out the components that one can recognize as standard problems (with standard solutions). Building on top of well-known algorithms and piecing together a solution from several such algorithms is definitely the preferred method from both a time and efficiency perspective. We dedicated a significant portion of the two previous chapters to recognizing these standard problems in various ways. The reason is simple: don't reinvent the wheel. Chasing performance and algorithmic efficiency often requires a departure from basic patterns and specific knowledge of the problem and the technology. To design basic algorithms, one needs to understand some basic design patterns for algorithms. Algorithm design goes hand in hand with data structures, but we won't cover this until *Chapter 5*.

Unfortunately, not all new problems are really instances or combinations of well-known problems. Thus, it will always be important that programmers can develop their own algorithms for these new problems. We might not be able to give a standard algorithm to use in this case, but we can give some suggestions of general classes of algorithms and techniques you can use to construct your own. This is the topic of this section. Again, it's important to remember that algorithm design and data structures go hand in hand. Keep this in mind as we discuss some of the general concepts for constructing algorithms.

Often, while developing an algorithm as part of solving a problem, the other aspects of problem solving (decomposition, abstraction, and standard patterns) make developing an algorithm a fairly "obvious" procedure – if it is not obvious, that is perhaps an indication that you have not found a good abstraction yet – and the algorithm almost writes itself. Developing a new algorithm that has better complexity than an existing algorithm is a complicated affair, and certainly not the topic of this chapter. Mathematicians believed for a long time that the best algorithm for computing the product of square $n \times n$ matrices had $O(n^3)$ complexity. That, of course, was until Strassen's divide and conquer recursive algorithm became known with a complexity of approximately $O(n^{2.8})$. This was the product of many years of study, and resulted in a relatively modest improvement. The real gains come from ensuring one works with the hardware to improve the efficiency (but not complexity) of the algorithm. We cover some of these considerations in the next section.

Iterative algorithms

A very simple way of traversing the inputs is to process each item of input in sequence, one after the other. (We use the term *item* here rather loosely because the input might not be a sequence of elements.) This process describes an iterative algorithm. For example, the `std::min_element` and `std::max_element` functions from the standard library are examples of iterative algorithms. The advantage of this approach is that it is very simple, but it does have consequences for the complexity. Even assuming each processing step only has constant complexity, an iterative algorithm will have at least linear complexity.

That being said, writing down a simple iterative algorithm is an obvious place to start when developing a new algorithm. Like solving a problem, developing an algorithm is itself an iterative process that will involve multiple attempts before you arrive at a solution that can be considered acceptable for the task. There is another reason to write down the simplest iterative algorithm, and this is for testing purposes. A simple algorithm is likely to be easier to prove correct and implement in code, and thus can serve as a means of testing that future implementations are correct.

An iterative algorithm revolves around a loop. Within the loop, we perform a set of operations that, when the iteration terminates, will mean our data satisfies the postcondition of the algorithm. To do this, we establish an invariant that must be maintained through each iteration. This invariant is the ingredient that allows us to prove the validity of our algorithm. For instance, in our algorithm for finding the maximum element in *Chapter 1*, we used an iterative pattern to find the maximum element. We started by setting the maximum element to the first element in the sequence, which we labeled m. From there, we iterated through the remaining elements in the sequence. The invariant here is that m is greater than or equal to all the elements we have seen so far. The operation of swapping m with the maximum of m and the current element maintains this invariant. Thus, by the time we finish, m is equal to the largest element in the sequence.

Choosing the correct invariant is not always simple, but thinking in terms of invariants will make designing algorithms easier and proving that they actually work possible. The invariant must be present, even if it seems trivial. This forms the crucial ingredient for proving that the algorithm is valid (by induction). Thinking about invariants is like abstraction. Once you find the "right" invariant for your problem, it makes writing the algorithm substantially easier.

Recursive algorithms

A recursive algorithm has two parts. The first handles the indivisible "base case" for the recursion. This is the part of the algorithm that can be handled without recursing further. In the preceding example, this is where the exponent is 0 or 1. The second part is separating the problem into two and recursing into each. This recursion may be trivial if it is already one of those indivisible cases that we have already dealt with, or it could be a recursion into two or more equally sized parts (or something else).

Many problems can be expressed more easily recursively; the solution of an input depends on a solution to a previous input (such as an input of a smaller size). This general approach to designing algorithms has some advantages, too. In the most basic implementation, a recursive algorithm simply mimics the iterative pattern, solving by recursing onto the $(n - 1)$st case, solving the n case individually, and then putting the two together. Theoretically, this is exactly the same as performing the simple iteration. However, thinking in terms of recursion opens up alternative means of splitting the data that can lead to more efficient algorithms.

Example

Writing an algorithm to compute the integer power of a number has a very obvious iterative solution. To compute x^n for some x (not zero, for the sake of simplicity) and some positive integer n, we can use a very simple loop:

```
template <typename T>
T power(T x, unsigned n) {
    if (n == 0) { return T(1); }
    T result = x;
    while (--n > 0) {
        result *= x;
    }
    return result;
}
```

This has linear complexity (but it is very simple). Using a relatively simple recursive algorithm, one can achieve logarithmic complexity. This is an example of the **divide and conquer** type algorithm, which we will discuss in the next section. The implementation is as follows:

```
template <typename T>
T power(T x, unsigned n) {
    if (n == 0) { return T(1); }
    if (n == 1) { return x; }
    const auto pow2 = power(x, n / 2);
    T result = (n % 2) == 0 ? T(1) : x;
    return result * pow2 * pow2;
}
```

This is definitely not as simple as the iterative solution since we have to deal with the end cases (where $n = 0$ or $n = 1$). We also have to distinguish between odd and even powers. However, since we divide the power argument by two each time, we need to invoke this function $log_2(n)$ times to compute x^n. Each call in this chain requires at most three multiplications (and some conditionals) that have constant complexity.

Specifically for C++, one can make use of recursive algorithms to compute values at compile time using `constexpr` functions or even more primitive template methods. In C++11, one could only make use of recursion in `constexpr` functions, but more modern standards have extended this to include loops and other constructs. However, efficiency is still important here because inefficient compile-time computations increase the build time of your code substantially.

Recursive algorithms may be a very convenient means of expressing a computation, but they have some drawbacks when it comes to implementation in C++. In C++, a recursive function might benefit from tail recursion optimization, which is essentially the compiler unwinding the recursive call stack into efficient assembly code. This can only be applied in certain situations. When the compiler cannot do this, the usual rules of function calls apply. Each time a function is called, a new stack frame is added to the stack. The cost of adding a new frame to the stack is not large but is not zero, so large recursions can have a real impact on runtime performance. In extreme cases, the space required for a large number of stack frames can lead to other problems, such as stack overflows.

Divide and conquer algorithms

Many problems involve computing over some kind of domain defined by the input data. When the different parts of the search domain are independent of one another, we can divide the domain into smaller instances of the same problem and work on these smaller instances in isolation. This is the divide and conquer technique. In our example in the previous section, we gained efficiency by the fact that the two smaller instances were identical computations, thus eliminating half the work at each step. The finiteness of a divide and conquer type algorithm is guaranteed by the fact that we make the problem smaller each time; decreasing sequences of positive integers terminate after a finite number of steps. Examples of divide and conquer from the standard library include binary search functions such as `std::upper_bound` and `std::lower_bound`.

Divide and conquer algorithms have three basic steps: divide, process, and combine. As the name suggests, it divides the space into smaller instances of the same problem. The second step processes (conquers) each of the smaller problems (using recursion). Finally, once all the smaller problems are solved, we combine the solutions at the highest level to complete the problem. The combination step might be as simple as multiplying results from the smaller instances together, or it could be far more complex. However, if we divide our work intelligently, we can avoid needing to invoke these combinations too often.

The analysis of divide and conquer algorithms can also be rather simple because of the "master method." The execution time of a divide and conquer type algorithm can be expressed as a recurrence relation. Here, the running time of the nth sized problem is expressed as some expression involving the kth sized problem, where k is smaller than n, say $k = n/2$. The master theorem deals with recurrences as follows, given constants $a > 0$ and $b > 1$:

$$T(n) = aT(n/b) + f(n).$$

Such recurrence relations are common in divide and conquer methods. The theorem itself, see *section 4.5* of *Introduction to Algorithms* [1], gives expressions for the complexity in three different cases. We won't state the theorem here to avoid the technicalities. Broadly speaking, the complexity of such a recurrence is determined by that of $f(n)$. A special case is when $f(n)$ is comparable to $n^{\log_b(a)}$, then $T(n)$ is comparable to $n^{\log_b(a)}\log_2(n)$. In our multiplication example, where $a = 1$ and $b = 2$ and $f(n)$ is constant, it gives the overall complexity as $O(\log_2(n))$.

A classic example of a divide and conquer algorithm is the **quicksort** algorithm. Here, a sequence is sorted by first partitioning the sequence around a pivot element. Then, apply quicksort to the data left of the pivot and to the right. The quicksort algorithm is very simple, but there are choices for how to partition the code. Here is a basic implementation in C++:

```
template <typename T>
std::ptrdiff_t partition(std::span<T> data)
{
    auto& pivot_value = data.back();
    std::ptrdiff_t pivot_pos = 0;
    for (auto j=0; j<data.size() - 1; ++j) {
        if (data[j] <= pivot_value) {
            std::swap(data[pivot_value], data[j]);
            ++pivot_pos;
        }
    }
    std::swap(data[pivot_pos], pivot_value);
    return pivot_pos;
}

template <typename T>
void quicksort(std::span<T> data)
{
    if (data.empty()) { return; }
    auto pivot = partition(data);

    quicksort(data.subspan(0, pivot));
    quicksort(data.subspan(pivot+1));
}
```

In this algorithm, there is no combination step. Once both of the conquer steps have been completed, there is no further work to be done. Most of the work in this algorithm is done in the divide step. This step not only finds the position at which the division should occur, but also performs a rudimentary sorting into values below and above the pivot value. In this implementation, we choose the last element as the pivot. One could select any other element (or even select one at random) without changing the characteristics of the algorithm.

Graphs and graph algorithms

A **graph** G is a pair consisting of a set of **vertices** V and a set of **edges** E that connect two vertices to one another (including possibly one vertex to itself). In some literature, vertices are also called **nodes**. Graphs appear quite naturally in computer science and programming because they describe connections between concepts, structures, and operations in a way that allows for concrete analysis. It is no surprise then that there are many algorithms for computing with graphs, including finding the shortest path from one vertex to another or splitting a graph into smaller pieces.

Before we go any further, we should introduce some of the terminology connected with graphs. In a graph G, a **path** is a sequence of edges that connect one vertex to another. A **cycle** is a path that starts and ends at the same vertex. Many graph algorithms require a graph to be **acyclic**, meaning that it does not contain any cycles. An acyclic graph in which every vertex is connected by a path is called a **tree**.

Graph vertices and edges can carry additional information. Perhaps the most common way of annotating the edges in a graph is to assign them a direction or weight (or both). These weights can represent many different things, such as distances, traffic capacity, costs, and so on. Finding the shortest path between two nodes in a graph (including those with weights) is a classical problem from graph theory and computer science, which is solved by Dijkstra's algorithm.

The algorithm itself isn't so important for this particular discussion, but the general strategies for working with graphs are. Many graph algorithms are so-called **greedy algorithms**, whereby one selects vertices or edges according to some associated numerical quantity. For instance, one might select nodes starting with those with the largest degree (the degree of a vertex is the number of edges that start or end at that vertex). This includes algorithms such as Dijkstra's algorithm.

Searching a graph can be done in one of two different ways. The first is **breadth-first**, where one searches all adjacent vertices before picking one direction and then repeating. In contrast, a **depth-first** search follows each path to its fullest extent before backtracking and selecting the next. The different strategies have different uses, depending on the needs of the problem.

Graphs can also be used to reason about algorithms. Many processes can be modeled as a computation tree of some kind, which allows us to reason about the process mathematically. For instance, our implementation of `power` comes about by constructing the computation tree for computing the power of a number, and rebalancing so that each branch of the tree carries more of the "foliage." Trees also appear heavily in data structures (e.g., B-trees). Combined with a heuristic, we can potentially cut entire branches from a work tree if we can determine that it will never lead to a solution (or is unlikely to).

Optimization algorithms

Optimization is a problem that appears in many domains, but is primarily a numerical problem. The goal of this kind of problem is to maximize or minimize an objective function, which may be a proxy for all kinds of things, such as cost or rate of return. Broadly, the field is split into two classes: linear and non-linear. Linear optimization involves finding the solution to a system of linear constraints. Here, the objective function is linear – that is, of the form $f(x_1, \dots, x_n) = a_1x_1 + \cdots + a_nx_n$ for some constants $a_1, \dots, a_n$ – and is accompanied by one or more constraints (e.g., $x_1 > 0$).

The basic method for solving a constrained linear optimization is the (linear) **simplex method**. The set of linear inequalities in the problem defines a feasible region in the ambient space, in which we seek to maximize the objective function. The shape of this region is a simplex – an intersection of a number of half-planes (defined by the linear inequalities) – which gives the method its name. Since the objective function is linear, the optimal solution lies at one of the vertices.

The other class of the optimization problem involves non-linear systems. Here, the objective function is non-linear (and usually quite complicated). These problems can be rather more complicated than linear optimizations; linear functions are extremely simple. If the derivative is known, one can use a **gradient descent** method to find the minimum. If the derivative of the objective function is not known (or is known to not exist), other methods do exist. The Nelder-Mead algorithm is one such algorithm and is a derivative-free optimization. Of course, the price of not using the derivative is that the algorithm is less efficient at finding the optimal value.

Optimization over a tree can often make use of **branch and bound** algorithms, in which one makes use of a **heuristic** to determine which branch is most likely to contain the optimal solution and prune the search space. This reduces the complexity, effectively shrinking the search space.

Gradient descent

Gradient descent methods are very popular because of their computational efficiency and flexibility. If the gradient of the objective function can be computed, then one can very easily minimize the function itself. However, not all functions are differentiable, and those that are can still exhibit odd behavior. A common drawback of gradient descent methods is that they can "get stuck" at **local minima** (think of this as a bowl in the graph of the function) and thus not find the global minimum of the function. There are some ways to mitigate the risk of this.

The central premise of gradient descent is that one can quickly find where the objective function achieves its minimal value by moving downhill (relative to the function) in the direction that is steepest. Mathematically, the steepest descent is determined by the negative of the gradient. The size of the step in this steepest descent is sometimes called the **learning rate**. To make this clearer, let's look at a simple example.

Example

Consider the function given by $f(x, y) = x^2 + y^2$. This function is very simple and it is quite easy to see that it achieves its minimum value at (0,0), where it obtains the value 0. (Everywhere else, the function is strictly positive.) Now, suppose that we pick a starting point (1,2), and a maximum step size of $1/4$. We can perform gradient descent to "walk" toward the minimum value.

The first thing we need is the gradient, which, in this case, can be computed quite easily as $\nabla f = (2x, 2y)$. Thus, the steps we should take should be in the direction $-\nabla f = (-2x, -2y)$. Since we start at (1,2), our first step should be in the direction $(-2, -4)$ with a step size of $1/4$, meaning our new position is $(1 - 1/2, 2 - 1) = (1/2, 1)$. Repeating the process once more, we calculate the negative gradient at $(1/2, 1)$ as $(-1, -2)$ and make a step of size $1/4$ in that direction to land at the position $(1/4, 1/2)$. This process never actually reaches (0,0), but the sequence of iterations does converge to it. (After a moderately large number of iterations, the point is essentially indistinguishable from (0,0).) This is typical; it's not usual that a gradient descent eventually lands on the minimum value.

When the gradient of a function is not known in an explicit form, such as this, one can estimate the derivative data in various ways. One method that is common in the machine learning ecosystem involves computing the derivative by tagging data and tracking the basic operations that are applied. This information can be used to compute the gradient. This is a fairly complex topic, so we won't cover it here.

Dynamic programming

Dynamic programming, like computational thinking itself, solves problems by decomposing a problem into smaller parts. The difference here is that the subproblems in dynamic programming overlap (and generally have the same form as the main problem itself). The advantage comes when one remembers (**memoizes**) the solutions to smaller subproblems to be used when solving the larger subproblems that depend upon them. (Yes, the subproblems form a graph, with arrows denoting dependencies between subproblems.)

Not all problems lend themselves to dynamic programming solutions; finding the shortest path between vertices in a graph can be solved using dynamic programming, but finding the longest path might not. Obviously, the problem must be decomposable into smaller subproblems. In addition, the problem must also satisfy additional constraints in order for a dynamic programming approach to be effective. The first is that the optimal solution to the problem should be an aggregate of the optimal solutions of the subproblems it involves. This is referred to as **optimal substructure** in *Introduction to Algorithms* [1]. The second is that the subproblems should overlap. The more the subproblems overlap, the more benefit there is to memoizing solutions to these subproblems, and thus the greater the reduction in the running time.

The final step of solving a problem using a dynamic programming approach is to reconstruct the final (optimal) solution by considering all the constituent subproblems. This step might be relatively simple. In the shortest path problem, one considers the subproblems of finding the shortest path from each vertex connected to the original start in the graph obtained by deleting the original start. In this case, the real shortest path is the shortest of these paths when taking into account the cost of traversing the edge from the original start to the start of each path. It is not always true that the shortest overall path will be the shortest subpath, since the cost of adding the new initial edge may change the total to make a different choice more optimal.

Randomized algorithms

Randomness is a powerful tool. If we understand the distribution of data provided to an algorithm, we can compute the average complexity of the algorithm. Our measure of complexity represents the worst-case scenario, but these are relatively uncommon in many cases. For instance, when sorting a sequence, the worst-case scenario is where the elements are in reverse order. However, this is one configuration from a very large number ($n!$) of possible configurations. Thus, any random sequence of data will likely have better performance than the worst-case scenario. We can perform this analysis because we know the distribution of such arrangements of sequences of a given size.

This is not the only use of randomness when working with algorithms. We can sometimes inject randomness into a problem to hide some of the complexity or otherwise improve the performance of the algorithm. For instance, stochastic gradient descent makes use of the randomness, whether that is randomness intrinsic to the problem or randomness that is somehow injected, to improve the convergence or properties of the descent. This **stochastic gradient descent** is very popular in machine learning.

Requirements and considerations

When designing algorithms for performance-critical parts of problems, it is important to understand the factors that can help or hinder the performance. To that end, we will discuss the architecture of modern processors, memory, and other aspects of modern computers that have implications for performance in the following chapter. This section serves to highlight some of the ways in which we can avoid bottlenecks when designing algorithms.

One of the most important things to remember is to make use of standard tools (including those outside the C++ language or standard library) that are heavily optimized and will almost always perform better than a hand-crafted solution. This really is part of the abstraction and pattern recognition before writing the algorithm, but realizing parts of your problem as instances of well-understood problems, such as linear algebra, means you can use library functions instead of having to write these parts by hand.

When implementing recursive algorithms, remember that C++ is not a functional-first programming language. Recursive function calls carry a fairly substantial overhead (setting up the stack, etc.). The compiler can sometimes recognize when a function is part of a recursive call chain and optimize away the overhead – this is called **tail-call optimization** – but this does not always apply. The other thing that can help here is for the recursive function to be inlined. Sometimes, we can rely on the fact that the recursing function will only be called a relatively small number of times compared to the total amount of work to be done, as is the case in divide and conquer type algorithms, so that the function call overhead is amortized. However, this is something you should keep in mind when implementing your algorithms.

Cache-aware algorithms

Modern CPUs are very fast, so fast that quite a lot of time can be spent simply waiting for data to arrive from memory on which computation can be performed. The cache sits between the CPU and main memory, much closer to the CPU, where data can be accessed much faster and with much lower latency. Typically, the processor (and the operating system or the program itself) will make predictions about the data that will be needed and pre-fetch this data to the cache, ready to be used. Making algorithms that access data in a predictable way can help facilitate this pre-fetching.

Matrix multiplication is a fundamental operation in many real-world operations. (It really does appear everywhere!) The problem here is that data is stored in a linear block of memory, where the data for the second row is stored after all the data for the first, and so on. This means that accessing the elements of the matrix column-wise involves long jumps in the block of memory. This is devastating for cache performance, at least if it is implemented without taking this into account. The optimal solution is to ensure that data is loaded from main memory as little as possible, so we make use of each element as much as possible before it is evicted from the cache. The reason why modern implementations of the **Basic Linear Algebra Subsystem** (**BLAS**) contain fast implementations of matrix multiplication is that they make use of these "blocked" algorithms that are more friendly to the cache (among many other things).

Vectorized operations and SIMD

Designers of CPUs know that many operations that operate on numbers (integers or floats) quite often operate not on a single number but instead over a moderately-sized array of numbers. For this reason, processors have specialized hardware that can operate on multiple numbers all at the same time. This specialized hardware is accessed through the so-called **Single Instruction Multiple Data** (**SIMD**) instructions and extensions. These instructions perform the same operation on 2, 4, 8, 16, or even 32 numbers all at once, which can dramatically improve the throughput of the processor (assuming the memory can keep up with this appetite for chewing data).

SIMD has been around for quite some time, and all modern 64-bit x86 processors implement at least the SSE2 instruction set, which provides instructions that can operate on "vectors" up to 128 bits (two `double` or four `float` types). Many compilers will assume that this is the case and automatically vectorize appropriate loops to make use of these instructions. However, most processors have far more capabilities than just SSE2; many implement AVX2 or even AVX512 instruction sets, which can operate on "vectors" up to 256 bits or 512 bits, respectively (double or quadruple the throughput).

This chapter is about designing algorithms, so the question now is how to design algorithms that can be vectorized when the capability exists. Like with cache-friendly algorithms, the key comes from organizing data before the operation so that the compiler can perform the vectorization. Generally, this simply means making sure the data that is to be operated on is stored in contiguous memory and accessed in order (starting at index `0`). Some compilers are better at identifying these scenarios than others. Even using the iterators of `std::vector` can be enough to prevent vectorization. Using `std::ptrdiff_t` integers as indices and accessing data directly (using something such as `std::span`) is generally the best way to ensure that the compiler recognizes the opportunity.

Another consideration for using SIMD is that one must ensure that the data does not alias. Aliasing occurs when two references or pointers reference overlapping objects in memory. For instance, this might occur if one buffer contains the other. The compiler cannot aggressively optimize operations on data that might alias, because it cannot guarantee that the ordering of operations will be maintained. Helping the compiler to understand that the data does not alias is not particularly easy – at present, the C++ standard does not provide a mechanism for this. The `restrict` keyword can be used in C, but this does not exist in C++. This does not mean it is impossible. For instance, (basic) data stored in two different vectors cannot alias, because the vectors manage their own internal storage, so spans taken for two such vectors cannot alias. However, care must be taken to make such chains of reasoning simple enough that the compiler can make this deduction (or one can make use of compiler attributes and intrinsic functions).

Branch prediction and speculative execution

Some of the performance of modern CPUs comes from their sophisticated branch prediction and speculative execution. With branch prediction, the processor attempts to determine which of the execution paths will be taken, to obtain data from memory, and the instructions associated with that pathway. Speculative execution goes slightly further and executes both alternative paths simultaneously, while the computation determines which of the two results to take and which to discard.

Understanding speculative execution can lead to some interesting opportunities to improve performance, but it also presents a fairly potent risk. The speculative execution mechanisms were the source of severe vulnerabilities a few years ago. These features are very powerful, but if you are working with security-sensitive components, make sure you are mitigating the risks presented by speculative execution. However, this is beyond the scope of this book.

In the non-performance-critical parts of the code, conditionals are commonplace, necessary, and generally have no impact on performance. Where this matters is the so-called "tight loops" of performance-critical sections. A **tight loop** is a small piece of code that is executed on large blocks of data, usually some kind of numerical calculation, that needs to execute as fast as possible. Here, every nanosecond counts, so the accumulated cost of many branching instructions will have a large cumulative effect. However, sometimes such conditionals can't be avoided. In this case, speculative execution can help mitigate the cost, but only if each branch is sufficiently simple.

Summary

This chapter was all about algorithms. An algorithm is a set of instructions that tells a programmer, in a language-agnostic way, how to solve a particular problem. Algorithms have complexity, which is a description of how long the algorithm takes to complete its task based on the size of the inputs. For instance, an algorithm with linear complexity $O(n)$ has a running time proportional to the size of the argument, whereas an algorithm with constant complexity takes the same amount of time regardless of the size of the inputs. Designing efficient algorithms is one way to make your solutions faster. (Of course, reality is far more nuanced than this.)

Sometimes you won't be able to find an algorithm with a lower complexity, but you might be able to change the design of the algorithm to make it more amenable to the hardware. Designing cache-aware algorithms minimizes the number of loads and stores to memory or arranges them so that these loads can have a dramatic impact on performance, even if the complexity is unchanged. (Constructing algorithms with lower complexity is a significant investment of time, and sometimes not necessary.) In the next chapter, we will explore the design of modern computer architecture and how we can make this work to our advantage when solving problems.

References

1. Cormen, Thomas H., Leiserson, Charles E., Rivest, Ronald L., Stein, Clifford. 2001. *Introduction To Algorithms*. 4th ed. Cambridge, MA: MIT Press.
2. Knuth, Donald E. 1997. *The Art of Computer Programming*. 3rd ed. Boston, MA: Addison-Wesley.

4

Understanding the Machine

Modern hardware is extremely complicated and possesses a large number of facilities for making code run more quickly and efficiently. It is important that a programmer understands all the tools at their disposal when solving problems, particularly when chasing performance, and this certainly includes the hardware of the computer and the operating system that works closely with the hardware.

In this chapter, we take a brief look at some of the crucial pieces of hardware, including the various parts of the processor, such as cache memory and **single instruction multiple data (SIMD)** extensions, and the main memory. We will see some examples of how we can design algorithms that make use of the cache memory on the processor and make use of SIMD instructions to greatly improve the throughput of the processor. We will look at higher-level parallelism through multithreading with OpenMP and making use of operating system facilities to make sure the application is adequately supported in its operation. We will also look at some of the more complicated aspects of the processor, such as branch prediction and speculative execution, to see how this can have unexpected impacts on performance.

We can only include so much detail in this chapter. There are numerous resources provided by hardware manufacturers (e.g., Intel or AMD) for specific hardware. A very comprehensive treatise on hardware and its implications for performance by Agner Fog is available at `https://www.agner.org/optimize/`. This is a great resource for understanding how to use the hardware to maximize performance.

In this chapter, we're going to cover the following main topics:

- Understanding modern processor design
- The storage spectrum
- SIMD
- Branch prediction and speculative execution
- The operating system

Technical requirements

This chapter focuses on the features of modern hardware and how we should incorporate this knowledge of these features into our code. There are many code samples in this chapter that focus mostly on features of x86 (64-bit) architectures. Much of the discussion applies to other architectures too (such as ARM), but some of the mechanisms we use (e.g., the `cpuid` instruction) are not as accessible and might require interacting with the kernel. To keep the code simple, we limit ourselves to code that runs on x86 and generic code that will run anywhere.

The code for this chapter can be found in the `Chapter-04` folder of the code repository for this book: `https://github.com/PacktPublishing/The-CPP-Programmers-Mindset`.

Understanding modern processor design

In the early days of computing, processors were relatively simple circuits. They could perform a single operation in exactly the order as provided by the programmer. Modern processors are an entirely different kind of beast. They have multiple cores, each running multiple threads, with instructions that perform multiple operations at once, with some instructions operating on multiple data at once. Moreover, they achieve this with incredible speed; even a relatively pedestrian 3GHz gives a single clock cycle of less than half a nanosecond (10^{-9}). With all this power at their disposal, modern processors can complete tasks with incredible speed.

Of course, being C++ programmers, we want to make sure that we use as much of this power as possible to complete our tasks as quickly as possible. Understanding the features of the processor and designing algorithms that are amenable to the processor will greatly accelerate your code. However, remember that optimizing your code is a tricky, time-consuming task that should only be done when and where necessary.

In this section, we will examine the basic parts of the processor and give a short overview of how these work together to complete tasks. We start with the basic components of the processor.

Basic components

The basic components of a processor have not really changed since the early days of computing. A simplified block diagram of a processor is shown in *Figure 4.1*, which illustrates approximately where in the processor these components are located and how they relate to one another. The core part of the processor is the **arithmetic and logic unit** (**ALU**), which performs basic logic operations and integer arithmetic. It operates on data stored in one of a number of **registers**. The registers have to obtain data from memory, which is handled by the **memory management unit** (**MMU**). The instructions to be performed are also read from memory via an **instruction decoder** circuit.

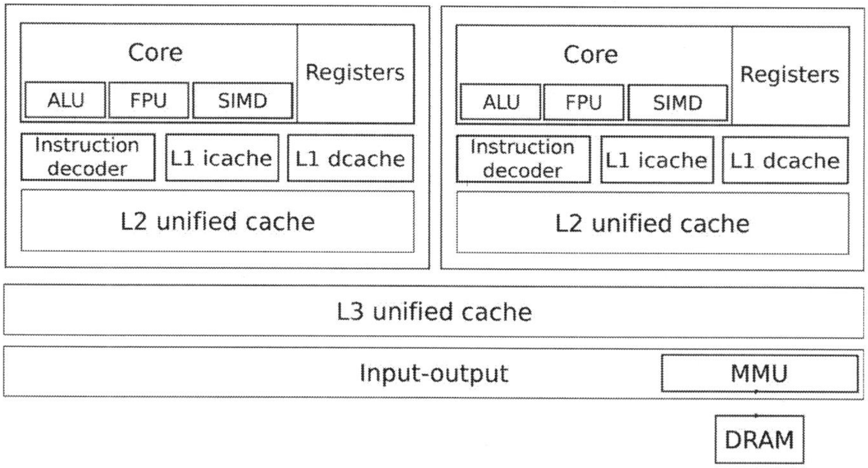

Figure 4.1: A simplified block diagram showing the major components of a modern processor with two cores. The cache layouts may vary between different processors; for instance, the L2 cache may be shared rather than per core

Between the core itself and the MMU lie multiple layers of cache memory. These are small banks of very fast memory, which can be filled with data that the processor will need to bypass the need to go to main memory to retrieve data or instructions. Caches come in three flavors: data, instruction, and unified. As the name suggests, the data and instruction caches exclusively handle data and instructions, respectively. Unified caches handle both data and instructions together. It's fairly typical that only the lowest-level cache is split into separate data and instruction caches, with higher-level caches being unified.

Sitting alongside the ALU is the **floating point unit** (**FPU**). These are a separate set of circuits for performing computations on floating-point numbers. Modern implementations of this make use of **vector registers** that can hold numerous floating-point values to be operated on in parallel (these are SIMD registers). The ALU and FPU (and some other components that we won't discuss here) are referred to as the **backend** of the processor (the part that does the actual work).

The instruction decoder is part of the processor **frontend**. The main job of the instruction decoder is to keep the processor fed with operations to perform. This is no small feat when the processor is potentially performing two or more operations in a single nanosecond. However, this too is a gross simplification. Many processors perform more than one operation at once, and not necessarily in the order given by the programmer. This is called **pipelining**. The processor contains several parallel execution channels and multiple identical sets of registers. The instruction decoder determines dependencies between individual operations and data and puts the instructions into the processor channels. In this way, independent load operations or store operations can be performed in parallel. In this way, the processor can stack up instructions in a way that minimizes the time the processor is stalled waiting for data.

The final important part of the processor is the input-output controller, which communicates with other devices in the larger system, such as storage devices, network interfaces, and **graphics processing units** (**GPUs**). Many of these devices are attached to the processor by the **Peripheral Component Interface Express** (**PCIe**) bus. This is a flexible communication mechanism that allows for high-speed communication with other peripheral devices (such as those mentioned previously) that form the larger computer system. We won't discuss these much, except in our broad discussion of computer storage in the next section and our discussion of GPU programming in *Chapter 14*.

Instruction architectures

Processors come in different flavors. The operations that are supported by a processor are described by the **instruction set architecture** (**ISA**). Many desktop processors implement the x86 instruction set or its 64-bit sibling (x86-64 or AMD64). Mobile devices typically use the **ARM** architecture, which is part of the **reduced instruction set architecture** (**RISC**) family. Recently, ARM-based processors have also been working their way into desktops and data centers, most notably by Apple. There are other RISC instruction sets, such as **RISC-V**, but these are often specialized application-specific hardware rather than general-purpose processors.

Unlike ARM and other RISC instruction sets, a single x86 instruction can perform multiple different operations within the CPU. This has some benefits in that the number of instructions required for complex tasks is reduced, which is important where memory is a premium, like in the early days of computing, but it does lead to more complex, power-hungry processors. That being said, x86-based processors have the benefit of many decades of optimization and other development, which makes them extremely fast, if not the most efficient. In contrast, RISC instructions are far more limited in both number and complexity.

Most instruction sets consist of a core set of basic instructions and a sequence of optional extensions. For instance, the SIMD capabilities (such as AVX instructions) common with x86 are optional extensions to the core architecture, although most processor models implement these extensions. ARM-based processors have similar capabilities via their **NEON** family of extensions. Most ISAs provide an extension specifically for performing cryptographic computations, such as the **SHA** family of hashing algorithms and **AES** symmetric encryption/decryption algorithms, which are essential in many communications applications. Desktop and data center processors generally also have extensions for virtualization, which allow multiple virtual machines to run on a single computer.

There are two mechanisms to determine which extensions to the core architecture are available for a particular processor. The first is during compilation, where one can instruct the compiler to generate instructions assuming a specific extension or even CPU model. (The three major compiler toolchains maintain a database of current CPUs and what extensions they support for exactly this purpose.) In GCC, this is accomplished using the `-m` command-line flag or the `-march=` flag. For instance, adding the `-march="arrowlake"` flag generates instructions that are valid for Intel's 15th-generation Core processors. The alternative is to query the processor at runtime to find out whether a particular extension is supported. On x86, this is achieved using the `cpuid` instruction. In the *SIMD* section, we will show how this can be used to select the fastest implementation at runtime.

CPUID

Most processors provide a means of querying the capabilities of the processor at runtime. On x86 and x86-64, this is achieved by using the `cpuid` instruction, which returns different information based on the leaf identifier (an integer) passed in the `eax` register and the subleaf passed in the `ecx` register. Based on the combination of leaf and subleaf, the `cpuid` instruction populates the `eax`, `ebx`, `ecx`, and `edx` registers with the requested information. Decoding the output requires reading through the instruction documentation, for example, on the Wikipedia page at `https://en.wikipedia.org/wiki/CPUID`. On ARM, there is a collection of system registers that one can query using the `mrs` instruction, but we won't go into detail here.

The major compilers offer intrinsic functions for interacting with the `cpuid` instructions, since there are some nuances that have to be handled carefully. Frustratingly, the interface provided by these compilers is different, so we've put together a rudimentary wrapper to handle these inconsistencies.

The contents of my_cpuid.h, minus the include guards, are as follows:

```
#if defined(__X86__) || defined(__x86_64__) || defined(_M_IX86) ||
defined(_M_X64)

#if defined(__MSVC__)
#  include <intrin.h>
#  define my_cpuid(i, j, regs) \
     __cpuidx(reinterpret_cast<int*>(regs), i, j)
#elif defined(__GNUC__) || defined(__clang__)
#  include <cpuid.h>
#  define my_cpuid(i, j, regs) __cpuid_count(i, j, \
       regs[0], regs[1], regs[2], regs[3])
#endif

#else

#  define my_cpuid(i, j, regs) static_assert(false, "Not implemented")

#endif
```

We're actually using the second version of the cpuid wrapper, which specifies both the leaf and subleaf, because there is a small bug that means the ecx register must be cleared before a second use, leading to invalid responses. This macro-based solution is obviously not optimal, but it is sufficient for what we need here.

Warning

We strongly advise that, should you need this functionality, you make use of higher-level utilities where available. For instance, on Android, one can use the utilities from the cpu-features.h header. On Windows, the GetLogicalProcessorInformation system call can provide some of the same functionality. On Linux, the sysconf system call can provide some information about the hardware. The hwloc library (https://www.open-mpi.org/projects/hwloc/) is a portable means of determining information about the processor and the wider system. Facebook's Folly library contains an implementation of cpuid that is somewhat more robust than what we propose here.

Processor threads

Most modern processors have multiple physical cores, each capable of running independently of the others. Moreover, each physical core is sometimes capable of two threads simultaneously (using Hyper-Threading on Intel processors, for instance), which means that the CPU is capable of running many computations in parallel. To perform large computations, one can divide up the task between all the available cores to maximize throughput. **OpenMP** is a compiler extension and accompanying runtime library that makes writing multithreaded code easier than ever.

OpenMP uses compiler directives (`pragma` statements) to transform blocks of code into multithreaded code that is executed in a thread pool. This allows us to write simple C++ code that can distribute work over a large number of cores without having to write complicated scheduling code or otherwise control the launching and joining of threads by hand. Let's see a very simple example in the form of computing the distance between nearest neighbors within a set of points:

```
namespace ct {
struct Point2D {
    float x;
    float y;
};

// Function that does something non-trivial
float distance(const Point2D& left, const Point2D& right) noexcept {
    return std::hypot(left.x - right.x, left.y - right.y);
}

float nearest_neighbor_distance_omp(std::span<const Point2D> points) {
    const auto size = points.size();
    auto min_distance = std::numeric_limits<float>::infinity();

#pragma omp parallel for reduction(min:min_distance)
    for (size_t i=0; i<size; ++i) {
        for (size_t j=i+1; j<size; ++j) {
            auto dist = distance(points[i], points[j]);
            if (dist < min_distance) {
                dist = new_distance;
            }
        }
```

```
    }

    return min_distance;
}

} // namespace ct
```

In order to compile and run this code, one must link it to an OpenMP runtime library that will take care of organizing and running all the threaded code that makes this work. This is usually accomplished by adding one additional compiler flag to the compiler command line. Fortunately, we can let CMake do this additional work by finding the `OpenMP` package and linking the `OpenMP::OpenMP_CXX` target as follows:

```
set(OpenMP_RUNTIME_MSVC experimental) # needed to use OpenMP > 2.0
find_package(OpenMP REQUIRED COMPONENTS CXX)
add_executable(open_mp_demo open_mp_demo.cpp)
target_link_libraries(open_mp_demo PRIVATE OpenMP::OpenMP_CXX)
```

The compiler will now automatically generate the multithreaded code rather than the simple `for` loop that we wrote in the code sample, and, at runtime, the code will be executed on multiple threads (by default, the same number as there are logical processors on the computer). Note that launching a pool of threads has a definite cost, and using this in places where only small amounts of data are processed might actually hurt performance.

There are probably better implementations of the nearest neighbor algorithm shown here, also parallelizing the inner loop. However, this implementation is sufficient to demonstrate the technique. Benchmarking against the sequential code on 65,536 points yields a 4x improvement in running time when using 8 threads (4,797 ms for the sequential code, and 1,161 ms for the OpenMP code). This code only works to find the distance between nearest neighbors, but cannot give the nearest neighbors themselves. (The reduction variable would not update the two points that gave the distance too.)

Since C++17, one can also cheaply access multithreaded algorithms by using the parallel execution policy on standard algorithms. This doesn't have the same flexibility as OpenMP, but it does avoid needing the additional linkage step (though it would still require linking the threading support with `-pthread` or similar). Unfortunately, it's rather difficult to translate the nearest neighbor algorithm into the language of standard algorithms, at least as they currently stand.

OpenMP is not always available. For instance, Apple Clang disables OpenMP support, although there is a workaround (for the time being). There are, of course, many third-party threading libraries that can be used in place of OpenMP, but none provide the same level of compiler support as OpenMP, so they will require some amount of boilerplate code to set up and dispatch calculations to the runtime (this is the code that `#pragma omp` generates automatically). Depending on the specific scenario, you might want more control over the initialization and finalization of thread pools, in which case the OpenMP interface might prove to be too simplistic. Intel's **thread building blocks** (**TBBs**) are a good alternative if more control is needed, though this too has limitations.

The storage spectrum

Computers store data and instructions in various media, depending on the amount of time it will be stored and how quickly it needs to be accessed. You're probably familiar with disk storage, where your documents and programs are stored long-term, and **random access memory** (**RAM**, or simply *memory*). The processor itself contains registers and the cache, which are very fast but small in size. In this section, we look at the various layers of storage for active programs (not long-term disk storage in general). We start with registers and work our way up through the layers from fastest to slowest, and conclude the section with an example of cache-friendly matrix multiplication.

We can see (most of) the various layers of the storage spectrum in *Figure 4.1*. Here, we see the register page that is part of each CPU core, the L1–L3 caches, and the system RAM (connected via the MMU). What isn't shown in the figure explicitly are the long-term storage (hard disks) and the network, though these are both connected via the input-output component of the CPU.

Registers

A **register** is a different kind of storage than cache memory or RAM; it holds a single integer (including pointers) or floating-point value (ignoring vector registers for now) that is to be operated upon during an instruction. Each core of the CPU has a page of registers; on x86-64, each page has 16 64-bit registers that can be used as operands to instructions. Some of these registers have special purposes, but others are for general use.

Actually, each core could have several multiples of the register page, where each register name can refer to any one of a set of physical registers. The processor will assign the logical name to the physical register in a process called **register renaming** during the instruction decoding stage of execution. This allows the processor to perform multiple operations in parallel, such as in branched execution (see the *Branch prediction and speculative execution* section).

The SIMD extensions of an instruction set generally come with additional registers, such as the `ymm` family of registers for AVX instructions. The exact SIMD extension determines how wide these registers are: SSE registers are 128 bits wide, AVX(2) registers are 256 bits wide, and AVX512 registers are 512 bits wide. In most cases, just as for the standard register pages, the lower half of the wider register forms is the corresponding smaller register. (The lower 128 bits of the `ymm0` register are the `xmm0` register). This allows backward compatibility without requiring duplication of registers.

Cache memory

The processor itself contains data storage in various layers of the cache. These are small banks of RAM stored physically on the CPU die and are very fast to access. A cache is usually layered, with each layer larger but slower than the previous, and is either dedicated or unified. (We described the basics of cache layout in the *Understanding modern processor design* section.) The processor accesses data through each layer cache in sequence, with recently accessed or soon-to-be-accessed data moved into the cache and old data being evicted once it is no longer in use. The programmer has very little control over this process, except in making data accesses "obvious" to the CPU and possibly making use of prefetch instructions.

The first-level cache is typically split into a data cache (`L1d`) and an instruction cache (`L1i`). A typical desktop processor will have around 32 KiB of each type, although some have more. (Enterprise hardware has more still!) This is the fastest level of cache, and accessing data that is stored in the L1 cache can take a few as 1–5 clock cycles or 0–2 nanoseconds. Ideally, one would always like to have cache hits in the L1 cache, since this would give us the best memory throughput. However, this speed limits the size of the cache, meaning that, eventually, we will look for something that isn't in the L1 cache, and we have to go one step further to the L2 cache.

The second-layer cache is usually substantially larger than the L1 cache and is unified—it stores data and instructions together. This cache can vary in size, but usually it has around 1 MiB of capacity, and accessing data that is stored in the L2 cache can take between 5 and 10 cycles or 2–5 nanoseconds. (These numbers are more indicative rather than precise measurements. The actual time depends on the exact processor model and various other factors.) This cache can be owned by a single core or shared between a small number of cores. The slow speed of the L2 cache is balanced with the larger size, meaning a smaller cache miss rate. This means that, on average, the number of misses in both the L1 and L2 cache is quite small compared to having only a L1 cache. Of course, when the requested data is not present in either the L1 or L2 cache, we have to look in the L3 cache.

Not all processors have an L3 cache, but many common desktop processors do. The pattern is exactly as before. This is a larger, but slower cache that cuts down the likelihood of needing to query main memory further still. The L3 cache can be very large, usually ranging between 8 MiB and 200 MiB. (A Ryzen 7900X desktop processor has two 32 MiB unified L3 caches. This is over 1,000 times larger than the L1 cache.) This size comes at a cost, with the latency to access a value from the L3 cache usually taking around 10–40 cycles or 5–20 nanoseconds. As before, this is balanced by further reducing the chance of a cache miss and requiring access to main memory. The L3 cache is generally shared between multiple cores. This has the advantage of easing the migration of a process from one core to another.

One might ask why stop at three layers of cache. The answer is cost. The space on a CPU die is extremely limited and thus expensive. Every square nanometer occupied by cache is space that cannot be used for some other functionality. The other factor is the diminishing returns. Each additional layer of cache would have to be substantially larger than the previous in order to continue to have performance benefits; thus, simply adding more cache is not practical. The same argument also tells us why the size of the L1 and L2 caches has not really grown larger in many years. The latency requirements give a definite limit on the physical size of the memory bank, and we're approaching the limits of how densely we can pack the circuitry into this amount of space.

Cache lines

Each entry in the processor cache is not a single byte, word (4 bytes), or quad-word (8 bytes). Typically, the entries are a larger block of data called a **cache line**. The size can vary, but typically, a cache line is 64 bytes. This means that accessing multiple values that are physically stored in the same cache line does not incur any additional penalty compared with accessing a single value. This means that data that is physically stored together is cheaper to access than data that is far apart. Combining this with the processor's ability to "predict" (see the *Branch prediction and speculative execution* section) what data will be accessed next means that accessing sequentially stored data is very efficient compared to accessing data that is scattered. This is the basis for why using a structure containing vectors of data is generally more performant than using a single vector containing a complex struct of data. (This idiom is common in the computer games industry, for example.)

Querying the processor for the cache size

Cache size does vary from processor to processor, and sometimes it is useful to know how big each level of cache is, so one can tune implementations to fit into the cache better. We can use `my_cpuid` on x86-64-based systems to get information about the cache layout of the processor at runtime and thus allow us to tune our use of cache memory, maximizing performance on whatever hardware. The process of getting cache information is rather involved, so we're going to work through this code slowly.

There is a slight complication in that the `cpuid` leaf one uses to access the cache information varies depending on the manufacturer of the CPU. For Intel CPUs, the `0x04` leaf is used, but on AMD CPUs, the leaf is instead `0x8000001D`. To check which manufacturer is used, we have to check the manufacturer ID string from leaf `0`. Conveniently, we need to query this leaf anyway to check whether the cache query operation is available. Leaf `0` puts the maximum supported leaf in `eax`, the 12-byte manufacturer ID string into the `ebx`, `edx`, and `ecx` registers (in that order). To ease the use of the `cpuid` instruction, we're going to use the `my_cpuid` macro defined in the *Understanding modern processor design* section earlier in this chapter. Thus, the first part of our code is as follows:

```
unsigned cpuid_registers[4];

my_cpuid(0, 0, cpuid_registers);
unsigned max_supported_function = cpuid_registers[0];

if (max_supported_function < 4) {
    return 1;
}

std::string vendor;
vendor.reserve(12);
vendor.append(reinterpret_cast<const char *>(cpuid_registers + 1), 4);
vendor.append(reinterpret_cast<const char *>(cpuid_registers + 3), 4);
vendor.append(reinterpret_cast<const char *>(cpuid_registers + 2), 4);
```

With the manufacturer ID stored in the `vendor` string, we can set the leaf that we should use to retrieve the cache information. At the same time, we set up an array holding the string names of the various types of cache. The ID for Intel processors is `GenuineIntel`, and the ID string for AMD processors is `AuthenticAMD`. We only need to know whether the string is equal to the latter and update the leaf in this case, as shown in the next code block:

```
unsigned cache_leaf = 0x04;
if (vendor == "AuthenticAMD") {
    cache_leaf = 0x8000'001D;
}

constexpr std::array<std::string_view, 4> cache_types = {
    "Null", "Data", "Instruction", "Unified"
};
```

Now, we can use the specified leaf to obtain information about each level of cache. The leaf must be queried multiple times with increasing subleaf indices to obtain all the cache information. For each level, various bits of the eax, ebx, and ecx registers give information about the cache, such as the level, type, associativity, number of sets, and line size. All of this information is required to compute the size. The loop is given here:

```
for (unsigned i = 0; i < 6; ++i) {
    my_cpuid(cache_leaf, i, cpuid_registers);

    // EAX
    // Bits 4:0 (0 = Null, 1 = Data, 2 = Instruction, 3 = Unified)
    unsigned type = cpuid_registers[0] & 0x1F;
    // If the type is zero, there are no more cache entries
    if (type == 0) break;

    // Bits 7:5 - Cache Level
    unsigned level = (cpuid_registers[0] >> 5) & 0x7;

    // EBX
    // Bits 11:0 - Line size - 1
    unsigned line_size = (cpuid_registers[1] & 0xFFF) + 1;
    // Bits 21:12 - Partitions - 1
    unsigned partitions = ((cpuid_registers[1] >> 12) & 0x3FF) + 1;
    // Bits 31:22 - Ways of associativity - 1
    unsigned associativity = ((cpuid_registers[1] >> 22) & 0x3FF) + 1;

    // ECX
    // Number of sets - 1
    unsigned sets = cpuid_registers[2] + 1;
```

```
    // Cache size in bytes = line size × partitions × associativity × sets
    unsigned size = line_size * partitions * associativity * sets;

    std::cout << "L" << level << " " << cache_types[type]
              << ": " << size / 1024 << " KiB" << std::endl;
}
```

The loop up to index `6` is somewhat arbitrary; it is the number of caches if the cache has three layers split into data and instruction, which is almost surely never the case. The loop will always break when `cpuid` returns a cache type of `0` anyway, so this will never overrun. This implementation prints the cache size to the console, but it is only for demonstration purposes. In practice, one would probably store this information in a static variable somewhere so it can be accessed without the overhead of calling the `cpuid` instruction again.

The full code for this example can be found in the `Chapter-04` folder of the code repository for this book, inside the `cache_information.cpp` file.

Main memory

Main memory or RAM is where the computer stores data that is "active" and ready to be used by the processor. Before any application can be run, the code must be loaded into memory, along with all its external dependencies. RAM is relatively slow compared to the high-speed cache, although RAM is generally considered to be very fast compared with long-term storage media such as disks. For the processor to obtain data from RAM, the latency is generally around 60–100 CPU cycles, or about 20–30 nanoseconds. However, RAM speed is not limited in size to the same extent as cache memory.

In the desktop world, RAM is provided in the form of **dual in-line memory modules** (**DIMMs**). These modules hold several memory chips and have a fixed amount of capacity (for instance, 1–2 GiB). These are connected, possibly via a controller circuit, to a bus that connects the memory to the CPU. The transfer speed and other attributes of these memory modules are determined by a standard, the most recent of which is DDR5. (DDR stands for **double data rate**, since two bursts of data are sent on each clock cycle.) The memory modules also have several timings associated with them, one of which is CAS latency.

The **CAS latency** (**CL**) determines the number of cycles between sending the address request and the start of the data response. In other words, this is the latency to access a particular data entry from memory. For DDR5, a CL of 40 cycles is fairly normal. Of course, this does not take into account the transmission time, since larger blocks of data will take longer to transmit. This also doesn't take into account the contention between the multiple cores that could be accessing memory simultaneously.

In other settings besides desktop, the RAM modules might be incorporated into the main board of the system – this is common in thin-and-light laptops and single board computers such as Raspberry Pi – or the RAM can be part of the processor itself, which is usually the case for **system on chip** (**SoC**) setups. Other kinds of RAM modules exist, too, but they generally operate in much the same way.

Matrix multiplication with cache in mind

Matrix multiplication is a fundamental operation for many applications, especially in machine learning and AI. The memory access pattern for this operation is quite interesting, and keeping the cache in mind when writing code dramatically improves performance. A **matrix** is a rectangular array of values. A matrix with m rows and n columns is called an $m \times n$ (m by n) matrix. By convention, if A is a matrix, the entry in row i and column j is denoted by a_{ij}. (In keeping with the C++ zero-based indexing, we will index the rows from 0 to $m - 1$ rather than the more traditional 1 to m.) In the remainder of this section, we will show two implementations of matrix multiplication. Before we can do this, we need to explain the mathematics briefly.

Matrix multiplication combines two matrices to produce a third. More specifically, the product of an $m \times l$ matrix A and an $l \times n$ matrix B is an $m \times n$ matrix C whose elements are defined by the equation

$$c_{ij} = \sum_{k=0}^{l-1} a_{ik}\, b_{kj}$$

Notice that the "inner" dimensions of the matrices A and B match. This is required in order for matrix multiplication to be defined. The resulting matrix always has the shape given by the "outer" dimensions of A and B, in this case, m and n. The `Chapter-04` folder of the code repository for this book contains `MatrixView` and `Matrix` classes that will help us implement matrix-related operations. We won't show the full code here to save space, but you could probably guess what they might look like.

In computer memory, the data for a matrix is stored in a contiguous block of size mn, where the first n elements forms the first row, the second set of n elements forms the second row, and so on. We call this layout **row major** ordering, because the rows are the major blocks of data. There is an alternative **column major** format, where the smaller blocks form the columns of the matrix. In row major format, the element a_{ij} is the element at index $in + j$ in the flat array of data constituting the matrix. Knowing this fact, we can write out a slightly generalized algorithm for computing the matrix as follows:

```
#include "matrix_view.h"
namespace ct {

void dgemm_basic(MatrixView<double> C, MatrixView<const double> A,
        MatrixView<const double> B, double alpha, double beta)
{
    check_dimensions(A, B, C);

    assert(A.is_row_major());
    assert(B.is_row_major());
    assert(C.is_row_major());

    for (ptrdiff_t i = 0; i < A.rows(); ++i) {
        for (ptrdiff_t j = 0; j < A.cols(); ++j) {
            double tmp = 0;

            for (ptrdiff_t k = 0; k < B.cols(); ++k) {
                auto &a_val = A.data()[i * A.cols() + k];
                auto &b_val = B.data()[k * B.cols() + j];
                tmp += a_val * b_val;
            }

            auto &c_elt = C.data()[i * C.cols() + j];
            c_elt = beta * c_elt + alpha * tmp;
        }
    }
}

} // namespace ct
```

The innermost loop contains the sum, and also shows us why this memory access pattern for matrix multiplication is complicated. The innermost loop is accessing data that is far apart (n elements, to be precise) in memory. CPUs like accessing data that is contiguous, not data that is spread out in memory. When n is large, these accesses are indeed very spread out.

We can improve the efficiency of our memory accesses by making small blocks of accesses together. In this way, we can limit our memory accesses to places that are relatively closer together at any one time. This quite simple change almost doubles the throughput. The modified algorithm is as follows:

```
namespace ct {
void dgemm_blocked(MatrixView<const double> A, MatrixView<const double> B,
        MatrixView<double> C, double alpha, double beta, ptrdiff_t block_
size) {
    check_dimensions(A, B, C);

    // For simplicity, only consider block sizes that are powers of 2
    assert((block_size & (block_size - 1)) == 0);

    assert(a.is_row_major());
    assert(b.is_row_major());
    assert(c.is_row_major());

    Matrix<double> tile(block_size, block_size);

    for (ptrdiff_t i_block = 0; i_block < C.rows(); i_block += block_size)
{
        auto i_bound = std::min(C.rows() - i_block, block_size);

        for (ptrdiff_t j_block = 0; j_block < C.cols(); j_block += block_
size) {
            auto j_bound = std::min(C.cols() - j_block, block_size);
            std::fill_n(tile.data(), tile.size(), 0.0);

            for (ptrdiff_t k_block = 0; k_block < B.cols(); k_block +=
block_size) {
                auto k_bound = std::min(B.cols() - k_block, block_size);
```

```
            for (ptrdiff_t i = 0; i < i_bound; ++i) {
                auto i_index = i_block + i;
                for (ptrdiff_t j = 0; j < j_bound; ++j) {
                    auto j_index = j_block + j;
                    for (ptrdiff_t k = 0; k < k_bound; ++k) {
                        auto k_index = k_block + k;
                        auto& a_val = A.data()[i_index * A.cols() +
k_index];
                        auto& b_val = B.data()[k_index * B.cols() +
j_index];
                        auto& t_val = tile.data()[i * block_size + j];
                        t_val += a_val*b_val;
                    }
                }
            }
        }

            for (ptrdiff_t i = 0; i < i_bound; ++i) {
                auto i_index = i_block + i;
                for (ptrdiff_t j = 0; j < j_bound; ++j) {
                    auto j_index = j_block + j;
                    auto& c_elt = C.data()[i_index*C.cols() + j_index];
                    auto& t_val = tile.data()[i * block_size + j];
                    c_elt = beta * c_elt + alpha * t_val;
                }
            }
        }
    }
}
} // namespace ct
```

In this implementation, the temporary value that we use to store the sums in the matrix is now a matrix instead of a single matrix. The `tile` matrix is responsible for storing these values, and is simply erased at each outer loop iteration. This tile can be made small enough to fit in low-level cache memory (for example, using a block size of 32 gives a tile size of 8 KiB, which comfortably sits in the cache used for benchmarking). This means that while the accesses within the tile are somewhat spread, the whole thing is done in the cache and is thus very fast.

The innermost loop is also accessing smaller blocks, the same size as the tile, for simplicity. This probably doesn't have such a dramatic effect, but it will help cache hits slightly, since data in subsequent loop iterations is more likely to be in the cache than the previous algorithm.

Running some rudimentary benchmarks on 1,000 × 1,000 matrices gives the following results. The basic algorithm takes (on average over 39 iterations) 547 ms to complete a single calculation. The blocked algorithm, using a block size of 32, on average over 73 iterations, takes 289 ms to complete a single calculation. This is a near 50% improvement, and this is by no means optimal. Running the same benchmark again with OpenBLAS gives an average time of 24.1 ms for a single execution over 874 iterations. Clearly, there is a lot of headroom in this algorithm for improvement.

Now that we have seen how the cache can dramatically improve the speed at which we can access memory, we turn our attention to using SIMD instructions to accelerate computations.

SIMD

Many processors have extensions that provide instructions that operate on several values at once. These are the SIMD extensions. These instructions can dramatically reduce the number of instructions necessary to perform a calculation on large arrays of data, increasing the throughput of the processor (providing the memory can keep up). We've already mentioned that the compiler can generate these vector instructions where appropriate and where the necessary features are enabled. This process is called **auto-vectorization**.

Auto-vectorization does not always produce the desired effect. For instance, the compiler might fail to vectorize loops that involve seemingly complicated logic, even if this logic does resolve to something very simple. There are no hard rules here, but the best results are usually observed in loops that simply use pointers (or very simple iterators) and indexing with integers. If auto-vectorization does not yield the desired instruction sequence, you might need to use compiler intrinsics, or the C++ SIMD currently in the experimental phase and slated for inclusion in the C++26 standard. In order to show the various means, we need a suitable piece of code on which to experiment. For this, we use the saxpy routine from the **basic linear algebra subprograms** (**BLAS**), which performs the vector operator $y = y + ax$, where x and y are vectors and a is a constant. The prototype function is as follows:

```
#include <cassert>
#include <ranges>
#include <span>

namespace ct {
```

```
void saxpy(float a, std::span<const float> x, std::span<float> y) {
    assert(x.size() == y.size());

    for (auto&& [xv, yv] : std::views::zip(x, y)) {
        yv += a*xv;
    }
}
} // namespace ct
```

Compiling this code with GCC with the -O3 flag yields the following assembly code. We only include the body of the loop here for simplicity. At first glance, it appears that this loop has been vectorized, but in fact, it has not:

```
        movss   xmm1, DWORD PTR [rdi]
        add     rdx, 4
        add     rdi, 4
        mulss   xmm1, xmm0
        addss   xmm1, DWORD PTR [rdx-4]
        movss   DWORD PTR [rdx-4], xmm1
```

Notice that the rdx and rdi indexing registers are incremented by 4 each time, which happens to be the number of bytes of a float. The Microsoft compiler does a slightly better job, but it still isn't perfect. In any case, a simple change to instead use an index-based for loop, as follows, yields better vectorization:

```
namespace ct {
void saxpy(float a, std::span<const float> x, std::span<float> y) {
    assert(x.size() == y.size());

    for (size_t i=0; i<y.size(); ++i) {
        y[i] += a*x[i];
    }
}
} // namespace ct
```

Compiling this with the same compiler options yields the following assembly code. Again, we have extracted the critical part; the full assembly code for the loop obviously contains instructions to handle the edge cases:

```
        movups  xmm1, XMMWORD PTR [rdi+rax]
        movups  xmm3, XMMWORD PTR [rdx+rax]
        mulps   xmm1, xmm2
        addps   xmm1, xmm3
        movups  XMMWORD PTR [rdx+rax], xmm1
        add     rax, 16
```

As expected, GCC has only generated instructions that use the SSE2 extension, and not the more advanced SIMD instructions that are available. One way to get the compiler to generate the more advanced instructions is with compiler flags, as we have mentioned. For instance, for GCC or Clang, we could add the `-mavx2` flag to cause the compiler to generate instructions that use the AVX2 instruction set with 256-bit wide vector registers. However, one might not want to compile the whole file with this flag, and in this case, we might want something more targeted.

If we only want to apply these optimizations to a specific function, we can use **function multiversioning** to generate multiple different versions of the function, each compiled with different instructions. In GCC and Clang, this is made very easy with the `target_clones` attribute. Using `target_clones` is very easy; one just applies it to the function definition as an attribute, and the compiler will generate a dispatching function and several implementations using the different extensions requested. For instance, we could request SSE4.2 and AVX2 versions of our test function as follows:

```
namespace ct {
[[gnu::target_clones("sse4.2,avx2,default")]]
void saxpy(float a, std::span<const float> x, std::span<float> y) {
    assert(x.size() == y.size());

    for (size_t i=0; i<y.size(); ++i) {
        y[i] += a*x[i];
    }
}
} //namespace ct
```

At runtime, the dispatcher function will query the processor to decide what instruction sets are available and dispatch to the most relevant clone. The `default` target is required as a fall-back for when none of the other instruction sets are available. This is a very low-effort means of creating the desired function clones, but it won't work in all circumstances. For instance, one might wish to take control of the dispatching process for some reason or if your compiler doesn't support multiversioning in this manner.

Warning

It is almost always better to let the compiler auto-vectorize a loop rather than doing this by hand using compiler intrinsics or, worse, inline assembly code. The latter are prone to errors that the compiler cannot save you from, and in many cases, the compiler will generate better code than you can write by hand. That being said, we will show you how to do it in case a real need ever arises.

To implement the target clones functionality ourselves, we first need to generate a dispatcher and the function prototypes for each of the clones, as follows. For this, we need to use the `cpuid` instruction (on x86(-64)) or `mrs` together with the appropriate system register name on ARM64. We're only going to demonstrate the technique on x86-64 since this is actually more complicated. (For ARM, especially on Android, one can use the operating system utilities to retrieve this information painlessly.) The following code is to be placed in the `saxpy.h` header file:

```
namespace ct {

// function clones
void saxpy_default(float a, std::span<const float> x, std::span<float> y);
void saxpy_sse42(float a, std::span<const float> x, std::span<float> y);
void saxpy_avx2(float a, std::span<const float> x, std::span<float> y);
void saxpy_avx512f(float a, std::span<const float> x, std::span<float> y);

// dispatcher
void saxpy(float a, std::span<const float> x, std::span<float> y);
}
```

Now, we need to fill in the details of the dispatcher function. Rather than interacting with the assembly code directly, we're going to make use of the `my-cpuid` macro we defined earlier in this chapter. The following is a simplified implementation of a function that gets the widest vectorization instructions available:

```
#include "my_cpuid.h"

namespace ct {

enum class SIMDInstructions {
    Default,
    SSE42,
    AVX2,
    AVX512F
};

inline
SIMDInstructions get_best_instructions() {
    unsigned cpuid_registers[4];
    my_cpuid(0, 0, cpuid_registers);  // Query highest CPUID function
supported
    if (cpuid_registers[0] >= 7) {  // Check for extended features
        my_cpuid(7, 0, cpuid_registers);
        if (cpuid_registers[1] & (1 << 16)) {  // AVX512F support (bit 16
of EBX)
            return SIMDInstructions::AVX512F;
        }
        if (cpuid_registers[1] & (1 << 5)) {  // AVX2 support (bit 5 of
EBX)
            return SIMDInstructions::AVX2;
        }
    }
    my_cpuid(1, 0, cpuid_registers);  // Basic features (EAX=1)
    if (cpuid_registers[2] & (1 << 19)) {  // SSE4.1 support (bit 19 of
ECX)
        return SIMDInstructions::SSE42;
    }
    return SIMDInstructions::Default;
}
} // namespace ct
```

Note that this function is far from optimal; there is no reason to query the processor for its features every time we call a dispatching function. Why don't you try to write a function or class that can retrieve this information and cache the information in a static member? With this function, or some variant thereof, we can write the dispatcher relatively easily, as follows:

```
#include "saxpy.h"
void saxpy(float a, std::span<const float> x, std::span<float> y)
{
    // the dispatcher is also the perfect place for error checking
    assert(x.size() == y.size());

    switch (get_best_instructions()) {
        case SIMDInstructions::AVX512F:
            saxpy_avx512f(a, x, y); break;
        case SIMDInstructions::AVX2:
            saxpy_avx2(a, x, y); break;
        case SIMDInstructions::SSE42:
            saxpy_sse42(a, x, y); break;
        default:
            saxpy_default(a, x, y);
    }
}
```

Each of the actual implementations has exactly the same C++ code; we're still relying on the compiler to auto-vectorize using the correct instruction set. If you're only compiling on GCC or Clang, you can use the `target` attribute and place all these implementations in the same cpp file. (This works in a similar way to the `target_clones` attribute.) However, this won't work if you're using a different compiler, so we'll show a slightly more general method here using CMake to generate multiple versions. First, we're going to write a template for the function stored in `saxpy.cpp.in`. The contents of this file are as follows:

```
#include "saxpy.h"
void ct::saxpy_@INST@(float a, std::span<const float> x, std::span<float>
y) {
    for (size_t i=0; i<y.size(); ++i) {
        y[i] += a*x[i];
    }
}
```

Here, @INST@ is a placeholder for the SIMD instruction set to be used, which will be filled in by CMake. Next, we need to write a bit of CMake code to generate the various files, set the necessary compiler flags, and add the source to the saxpy target. This is accomplished with the following CMake loop:

```
add_library(saxpy STATIC saxpy.cpp saxpy.h)
# omitted lines

if(MSVC)
    set(ARCH_FLAG "/arch:")
else()
    set(ARCH_FLAG "-m")
endif()
# more omitted lines

set(INST default)
configure_file(saxpy.cpp.in saxpy_${INST}.cpp @ONLY)
target_sources(saxpy PRIVATE ${CMAKE_CURRENT_BINARY_DIR}/saxpy_${INST}.
cpp)
foreach(ARCH IN ITEMS sse4.2 avx2 avx512f)
    string(REPLACE "." "" INST ${ARCH})
    configure_file(saxpy.cpp.in saxpy_${INST}.cpp @ONLY)
    set_property(SOURCE "${CMAKE_CURRENT_BINARY_DIR}/saxpy_${INST}.cpp"
            APPEND PROPERTY COMPILE_OPTIONS "${ARCH_FLAG}${ARCH}")
    target_sources(saxpy PRIVATE
        ${CMAKE_CURRENT_BINARY_DIR}/saxpy_${INST}.cpp)
endforeach()
```

Now, the compiler will generate the bodies of the clone functions declared in the saxpy.h header, implemented with instructions from the corresponding SIMD extension. The dispatcher function can dynamically choose the appropriate clone based on the enum variant returned by the get_best_instructions function we defined earlier. As mentioned in a comment, the dispatcher function is a perfect place to perform runtime checks to make sure the function arguments are valid. We could also check whether additional optimizations can be applied. For instance, we could check that the x and y vectors do not overlap or that the memory is aligned on particular boundaries.

If auto-vectorization fails to produce the instructions required, you can use compiler intrinsics that translate directly to SIMD instructions to implement the functions by hand. This is dangerous, though, since it can be quite easy to produce code that is incorrect. Wherever possible, one should lean on the compiler to do this work. That being said, in the following code, we will implement one more function that uses the AVX2 instructions to implement `saxpy_hand` (a declaration of which appears in `saxpy.h`):

```
#include <immintrin.h>

void ct::saxpy_hand(float a, std::span<const float> x, std::span<float> y)
{
    constexpr auto vec_size = sizeof(__m256) / sizeof(float);
    const auto ymm0 = _mm256_set1_ps(a);

    size_t size = y.size();
    size_t pos = 0;
    const auto* x_data = x.data();
    auto* y_data = y.data();

    for (; pos + vec_size <= size; pos += vec_size) {
        auto ymm1 = _mm256_loadu_ps(x_data);
        auto ymm3 = _mm256_loadu_ps(y_data);
        ymm1 = _mm256_mul_ps(ymm0, ymm1);
        ymm3 = _mm256_add_ps(ymm3, ymm1);
        _mm256_storeu_ps(y_data, ymm3);
        x_data += vec_size;
        y_data += vec_size;
    }

    // Clear up the < vec_size terms that remain
    const size_t remainder = size - pos;
    for (size_t i=0; i < remainder; ++i) {
        y_data[i] += a * x_data[i];
    }
}
```

This `immintrin.h` header contains the intrinsics for AVX and AVX2 instructions, such as the ones we used here. The functions prefixed with `_mm256` indicate the AVX vector instructions with 256-bit wide vector registers. The `_ps` suffix indicates that the operation is for packed `float` values. (Here, as in other places, `s` stands for single-precision floats and `d` stands for double-precision floats.) The first function we encounter, `_mm256_set1_ps`, sets each of the values in the registers to be the `float` argument. Then, `_mm256_loadu_ps` loads eight packed values from an unaligned memory address argument (more on this shortly), returning the value in a vector "register" value, `ymm1` and `ymm3` in the preceding example. The `_mm256_storeu_ps` function stores the values from a vector back into memory. The remaining functions perform multiplication and addition, as labeled.

We've prefixed the temporary values here as `ymm` to draw a parallel with the AVX `ymm` registers, although the translation is not exact, since some of these temporaries may still be optimized away. This implementation is rather basic, and during testing, it didn't achieve the same speed as the auto-vectorized equivalent. If you're chasing performance, hand-coding the SIMD instructions might not be the best way to proceed. There are other reasons to use SIMD instructions, though.

Unsurprisingly, when we run some rudimentary benchmarks using our various implementations of the `saxpy` routine, we see an improvement in performance each time we move to a more advanced instruction set. Using a vector size of `5120`, the default and `sse4.2` implementations perform the worst on average (329 ns and 330 ns, respectively), followed by our hand-crafted implementation (298 ns), then the `avx2` implementation (259 ns), and finally, the `avx512f` implementation (243 ns). For comparison, the `saxpy` routine from OpenBLAS managed 278 ns on average. (It's worth mentioning that this is a small problem, and likely the overhead of the OpenBLAS implementation is distorting the reading here.)

For those who are writing code that needs to cross different architecture boundaries, such as from x86 to ARM, you might consider checking out a high-level abstraction layer around SIMD instructions such as the SIMD-everywhere project (`https://github.com/simd-everywhere/simde`) or the Highway library (`https://github.com/google/highway`). These libraries will make writing vectorized code somewhat easier.

Memory alignment

SIMD instructions work best when they access data from addresses that are multiples of the vector size, as such loads are **aligned**. Unaligned access incurs a small performance hit by comparison, since the data to be loaded might be split over different cache lines, for instance. For the best results, one might try to ensure that all data is appropriately aligned for the computations to be done.

You might have noticed that in our matrix example, we made sure that all data was allocated on 64-byte boundaries. In a more optimized implementation, we might first copy the data into aligned storage so that we can make use of the aligned load and store functions in the critical parts of the computation. This makes more sense in the `gemm` routine than in the `saxpy` routine, since copying the data is expensive compared to the computation. This cost is amortized in the matrix multiplication routine.

Since C++17, the `operator::new` and `operator::new[]` allocator functions support an overload taking an additional alignment argument. This allows the programmer to allocate heap memory with a greater than normal alignment, such as 64-byte aligned, as in our matrix multiplication example. This is achieved by the addition of an alignment argument such as `std::align_val_t`, which must be a power of 2. Stack data can also be aligned by making use of the `alignas` operator that was added in C++11. For instance, we can provide an array of floats aligned on 32-byte boundaries on the stack by using the following line of code:

```
alignas(32) std::array<float, 32> aligned_array;
```

The `alignas` operator can also be applied to class types so that all instances of a class are aligned on specific boundaries. This can be accomplished by placing `alignas` between the `class` keyword and the name of the class:

```
class alignas(64) LineAlignedData {
    // contents
};
```

This syntax might cause some problems with other attributes applied to the class definitions, since they should appear in a specific order. (Pre-declarations might help with this.) Some compilers also provide attributes that can be used to specify the alignment of a class.

Aliasing

Another barrier to optimization is **aliasing**. This is where a single piece of data (or a collection of data) is referenced by two or more pointers or references. This is problematic because the order of operations is very important when there are dependencies between the different referenced values. For instance, suppose we called our `saxpy` function with `x` and `y` both pointing to the same block of data. This is technically valid, but it means there is a strong dependency between loads from `x` and writes to `y`. In this case, the compiler is limited and must maintain the order of operations so as not to break functionality. However, if we know that `x` and `y` always point to different blocks of data that do not overlap, the compiler is free to reorganize the instructions to achieve the maximum performance.

The dispatcher function could perform such a check, and instead dispatch to different versions of the saxpy function depending on whether x and y overlap. This can have fairly profound performance impacts. The obvious question then arises: how do we tell the compiler that the x and y spans do not alias? In C99, the pointer arguments can be annotated with the `restrict` keyword to inform the compiler that no other pointer in scope refers to the same data. Unfortunately, this keyword doesn't exist in C++, so we have to turn to the compiler for help. All three of the major compilers have the `__restrict` directive, which functions the same way as the `restrict` declaration from C. Here's how this could be used in our saxpy implementation function:

```
#if defined(__GNUC__) || defined(__clang__) || defined(_MSVC)
#  define CT_RESTRICT __restrict
#else
#  define CT_RESTRICT
#endif

void ct::saxpy_nonaliasing(float a, size_t size,
                           const float* CT_RESTRICT x,
                           float* CT_RESTRICT y) {
    for (size_t i=0; i<size; ++i) {
        y[i] += a*x[i];
    }
}
```

Just to be safe, and to allow for different compiler extensions to be used, we declare the `CT_RESTRICT` macro to abstract away compiler-specific choices. When `__restrict` is available, the macro expands to this; otherwise, it expands to nothing, so the code will always compile. Notice that we can no longer use `std::span` to pass our data arguments, but that's fine because this function should only be called from our dispatcher function, where we can perform the necessary checks to make sure the arguments are appropriately sized.

Branch prediction and speculative execution

Most modern processors include sophisticated branch prediction circuitry. This circuitry attempts to guess the branch (say, the block that follows `if` versus the block following `else`) that will be executed and start performing these calculations in advance. This allows the processor to occupy more of its computational capacity in the pipelining process, which means that before the first result is ready to be committed to memory, several computations may already be in flight, even if these later computations are discarded.

To illustrate the power of this speculative execution, we're going to look at an example of a "clamp loop," which iterates through a span of data and replaces values larger than 255 with 255. A similar example appears in Chandler Carruth's excellent CppCon 2017 talk *Going nowhere fast*, where he gives far more detail about what is happening here (`https://youtu.be/2EWejmkKlxs?si=diXN9-4gO9X0JfUM`). Let's start by writing down some basic code for this clamp loop:

```
inline constexpr uint16_t max = 0xFF;

[[gnu::optimize("no-tree-vectorize")]]
void ct::clamp_min(std::span<uint16_t> x) {
    for (auto& v : x) {
        v = std::min(v, max);
    }
}
```

We've used the attribute to disable auto-vectorization so the generated assembly code does not become too long. Using GCC to generate assembly code for this (with all other optimizations turned on) gives us the following:

```
ct::clamp_min(std::span<unsigned short, 18446744073709551615ul>):
    lea rcx, [rdi+rsi*2]
    cmp rdi, rcx
    je  .L1
.L3:
    movzx   eax, WORD PTR [rdi]
    mov edx, 255
    cmp ax, dx
    cmova   eax, edx
    add rdi, 2
    mov WORD PTR [rdi-2], ax
    cmp rdi, rcx
    jne .L3
.L1:
    ret
```

This implementation uses a conditional move instruction to replace large values with the maximum and then stores the result back into memory. The interesting thing with this implementation is that the `cmova` instruction (the conditional move) cannot complete until the comparison on the line above has finished. With a very small change to the code, we can instead force the compiler to only write to memory if the value is larger. For this, we use the following alternative code:

```
[[gnu::optimize("no-tree-vectorize")]]
void ct::clamp_conditional(std::span<uint16_t> x) {
    for (auto& v : x) {
        if (v > max) {
            v = max;
        }
    }
}
```

The UNLIKELY macro expands to a compiler intrinsic that signals to the compiler that the branch is unlikely to be taken. (Interestingly, that's not actually true in our benchmarks, but we'll come back to that in a moment.) This allows the compiler to structure the assembly code differently making use of the fact that the fact that certain branches won't be taken often. Compiling with the same presets as before yields the following assembly code:

```
ct::clamp_conditional(std::span<unsigned short, 18446744073709551615ul>):
    lea rax, [rdi+rsi*2]
    cmp rdi, rax
    je  .L8
.L11:
    cmp WORD PTR [rdi], 255
    jbe .L10
    mov edx, 255
    mov WORD PTR [rdi], dx
.L10:
    add rdi, 2
    cmp rdi, rax
    jne .L11
.L8:
    ret
```

Here, instead of performing a store every time, we only store if the value is indeed larger than 255, and otherwise skip past the two instructions that implement this store. Unlike the previous code, the processor can speculate past the store operation. The result is faster code. In our benchmark, we fill a vector with 1,000 `uint16_t` values distributed uniformly from `0` to `65535` (the maximum possible value). For the `clamp_min` function, this yields an average execution time of 605 ns, but `clamp_conditional` has an average execution time of 500 ns. That's not a huge improvement, but it is an improvement.

Interestingly, given the distribution of integers that we provided as inputs, we only skip the store step 256/65536 of values. Most of this difference is down to the way the CPU can stack operations in the instruction pipeline. For these situations, it is imperative that you measure accurately before making changes to your code to make sure that you always see an improvement (see the *Profiling your code* section in *Chapter 15*).

There are tools to help understand what is going on here. For instance, Intel's excellent VTune software contains a suite of tools for analyzing the microcode operations that are executed at the hardware level, and can give excellent insight into why these kinds of curious situations occur.

Speculation-based vulnerabilities

Speculative execution provides a huge boost to performance, but it is also the source of some fairly major security vulnerabilities through the **Spectre** family of side-channel attacks discovered in 2017 and 2018. Here, speculative execution is used to bypass the normal guards against reading data from other parts of memory imposed by the operating system. This allows the attacker to read potentially sensitive fragments of memory. This has some major implications for those who have to implement secure computations, for example, in cryptographic applications. More modern processors have been designed to mitigate these vulnerabilities, but they still pose a risk.

In order to protect against these kinds of attacks, one method you can employ is to include speculative execution barriers in your code to prevent the CPU from performing speculation past certain points in your code, thus reducing the risk of exploitation. If you are writing code that works with sensitive information, you should absolutely be aware of these kinds of vulnerabilities and how to guard against them. Microsoft provides a very detailed write-up of some common risks and how to mitigate them at `https://learn.microsoft.com/en-us/cpp/security/developer-guidance-speculative-execution?view=msvc-170`. Since the security best practice area changes rapidly and this is an area of significant nuance, we won't go into any detail here.

We've spent quite a lot of time discussing how the hardware interacts with our programming efforts, but we have missed out one of the most important middle layers: the operating system. This is the topic of the next section.

The operating system

The **operating system** is a piece of software that controls the operation of the whole computer (hence the name). It runs in a special privileged state, commonly called **kernel mode**, that can execute instructions on the CPU that cannot usually be accessed by user-level (unprivileged) applications. The operating system has many roles, such as managing the hardware, scheduling processes on the CPU cores, and managing the mapping between process memory addresses and the physical RAM.

Virtual memory and pages

Common operating systems such as Windows and Linux do not let user code access memory directly. Instead, the addresses that are provided by the operating system and that are used for instructions are addresses in **virtual memory**, which is unique to each process. This is done for a number of reasons, with one being security. Another reason for using virtual memory is that each process can operate as if it had more memory than is physically available. Of course, that doesn't mean it can use all of it. The larger addressing space allows for more flexibility that is not tied to the actual amount of physical RAM installed in the computer.

Virtual memory is divided into a sequence of **pages**, typically around 4 KiB. Addresses are formed by a page number and an offset into the page. The operating system maintains a page table, which translates the virtual pages to corresponding chunks of contiguous physical memory. In this way, large blocks of process data can be distributed across free blocks of physical memory, which means that more of the physical memory can be used. (Otherwise, one must search through for a big enough chunk of contiguous memory, which inevitably leads to fragmented, unusable gaps.)

Every time the CPU looks up data in memory, it must perform a translation from a virtual address to a physical address using information provided by the operating system. Looking an address up in the page table every time would incur a significant and unacceptable performance penalty, so modern processors provide a cache in the form of the **translational look-aside buffer** (**TLB**). This is a small, high-speed mapping from virtual page number to physical address that the processor can query. If the page of a queried address exists in the TLB, then there is essentially no performance penalty. However, if the page cannot be found in the TLB, one goes to the full page table to resolve the reference.

The TLB tends to be rather small, typically between 32 and 1,024 entries, to maintain performance. Like the cache, the processor might keep several layers of TLB, and may also separate data and instruction TLBs. Accessing large blocks of data that are split over manage pages can lead to TLB **thrashing**, where the miss rate of the TLB is abnormally high. To avoid this, one might try to use pages of a larger size, as permitted by the operating system. The operating system might do this automatically, for example, **transparent huge pages** on Linux, or this might need some input from the programmer. Generally, it's advisable to let the operating system do this work where possible rather than attempting to control this yourself.

It is sometimes useful to know what the default page size is when programming, such as for implementing a pool allocator to keep subsequent allocations local to a small number of pages. On Linux and other POSIX-based operating systems, one can obtain this information from the `sysconf` function, and on Windows, it can be obtained from the `GetSystemInfo` function, as follows:

```
#ifdef __linux__
#include <unistd.h>
#elif _WIN32
#define WIN32_LEAN_AND_MEAN
#include <windows.h>
#endif

int main() {
#ifdef __linux__
    std::cout << "page size: " << sysconf(_SC_PAGESIZE) << 'B' <<
std::endl;
#elif __WIN32__
    SYSTEM_INFO info;
    GetSystemInfo(&info);
    std::cout << "page size: " << info.dwPageSize << 'B' << std::endl;
#endif

    return 0;
}
```

Again, if this information is needed for operational purposes, then it is best to cache this somewhere that can be accessed without requiring another system call.

Interacting with the scheduler

The scheduler is the part of the OS that decides what process (or threads within a process) are executed on each core at any particular time. There are generally more processes with work to do than there are CPU cores on which to run them, so it is typical that the OS will occasionally have to pause one process to let another make some progress. During this process, a process might be moved from one CPU core to another, and if the computer has more than one CPU, it might be moved from one CPU to another. This is obviously not ideal if the performance of the application relies on having data in cache. For this and many other reasons, one might want to assert some control over which (logical) CPUs the operating system should assign to your process.

Generally speaking, it is best to interfere with the usual operation of the OS as little as possible since this might have other undesirable implications for the rest of the system. However, if the need arises, most operating systems allow the software to set a preference as to which CPU cores can be used to execute the software. This is called **CPU affinity**. For instance, on Linux, one can set the process scheduler affinity using the `sched_setaffinity` system call, as follows:

```
#include <sched.h>

void set_process_affinity(int core) {
    cpu_set_t cpuset;
    CPU_ZERO(&cpuset);
    CPU_SET(core, &cpuset);

    if (!sched_setaffinity(getpid(), sizeof(cpu_set_t), &cpuset) != 0) {
        throw std::runtime_error("failed to set affinity");
    }
}
```

This is certainly an incomplete example. One should always check what processors are available and make sure the core is valid before locking to the given core. It is much better to make use of higher-level abstractions that take care of all these details, as this is obviously preferable to managing each operating system yourself.

That concludes our brief overview of modern computer hardware and operating systems. Let's look back at what we have seen.

Summary

This chapter contained a very brief introduction to computer hardware, specifically those parts that are crucial to the performance of the system. We also looked at some of the responsibilities of the operating system. Understanding the way that hardware is designed and put together is not essential for being a programmer, but it is for designing code that will perform at the cutting edge. Having an understanding of how your actions as a programmer are realized in the hardware will make you a better programmer.

Two of the most important features of modern processors are the cache memory and vector instructions. Understanding how to make sure the cache is fully utilized and how to maximize the throughput using SIMD instructions will give your code the performance edge that it needs. However, one must also remember that not all processors are designed equally and, as a result, some might not possess all these features. Remember that sometimes it is best to lean on the tooling, especially since the purpose of a high-level programming language is to abstract away the architecture-specific instructions that it is translated into. In the next chapter, we'll take a closer look at data structures and memory layouts, and the impact that these can have on performance.

5

Data Structures

In order to solve problems, we need to work with data. At a basic level, this involves interacting with single values either on the stack or on the heap (and managing their lifetime). The next level is storing and interacting with many values of a given type. For this, the standard library provides several different containers with different characteristics. The basic container type is a vector, which stores values in contiguous (linear) memory and has very good traversal performance. Alternatively, one can use linked lists, which provide some flexibility for insertion and deletion at the cost of traversal performance. At the highest level, we have special-purpose containers such as sets and maps.

The goal of this chapter is to highlight some of the nuances of working with different kinds of data storage and high-level container classes so one can choose the most appropriate container for specific tasks and understand the performance implications of these choices. Along the way, we will look at how using heap allocations and pointer indirection can afford a great deal of flexibility, and how we can use smart pointers to manage the allocation and deallocation of memory. We will survey the different kinds of basic containers (arrays, vectors, lists, etc.) and the abstractions that are built on top of these (stacks and queues, sets, and maps). Most of the time, you should use one of the standard container types, either from the standard library or variants from other libraries such as Boost or Abseil.

The final part of the chapter deals specifically with maps and sets. These are extremely useful as look-up tables in all kinds of applications, including for memoizing results of expensive computation functions. The implementation of these maps has a great impact on performance and the usability of the maps in certain situations: the standard library implementations are based on linked lists and thus are expensive to traverse (iterate over the values). There are alternatives, such as flat (hash) maps. We will look at some of these issues and see how to run benchmarks to expose the performance characteristics of operations such as random access for maps.

In this chapter, we're going to cover the following main topics:

- Computer memory, pointers, and indirection
- Linear memory: vectors, stacks, and queues
- Linked lists
- Maps and sets

Technical requirements

The focus of this chapter is on data structures and the way we store the data that code operates upon. Some familiarity with C++ is assumed, but we try to explain more modern features that you might not have encountered before. This chapter contains several exercises, possible solutions to which can be found in the `Chapter-05` folder of the GitHub repository for this book (`https://github.com/PacktPublishing/The-CPP-Programmers-Mindset`), along with a system of tests so you can test your own solutions. Some snippets of code also have tests in this repository.

Computer memory, pointers, and indirection

All data stored on a computer, however complicated, is at the most basic level a (perhaps not contiguous) sequence of bits (grouped together into bytes). How we interpret these bits is the task of the programmer and, perhaps more so, the compiler. Basic types such as integers and floating-point numbers form the basic building blocks. If this were all we had, we could achieve some things, but our programs would be greatly limited. **Addresses**, or **pointers**, allow us to reference other sequences of memory, thus adding one additional layer of indirection and adding room for dynamic representations. This is extremely powerful: it allows a compact block of memory to hold the representation of a much larger piece of data.

Memory itself is divided into two main parts: the **stack** and the **heap** (or **free store**). The stack is a block of memory that is used to store local variables and temporary values, and is managed by the operating system. The programmer has limited ways to influence the size of the stack through allocating inline arrays (more on this later), local variables, and the signature of the function. (Stack allocations are possible via `alloca`, but not generally encouraged.) Each new function call extends the stack by a small amount, called a **stack frame**. The head of the stack will usually reside in low-level cache (the stack frame might reside entirely in the L1 cache, for example), so there is minimal performance penalty for accessing stack values. Individual stack frames are usually quite small, though sometimes functions with larger stack frames are necessary.

The heap represents the bulk of memory used by a program. It is longer-term storage that must be managed by the programmer, either explicitly or implicitly. Unlike the stack, the heap can hold vast amounts of data and can outlive a single function call. This is essential, or all data could only be defined in the outermost function that interacts with it. This is obviously too restrictive to be of any use. In modern C++, much of the difficulty of managing memory is handled by the **resource acquisition is initialization** (**RAII**) idiom. Here, we use an object to hold the pointer to external memory, and the destructor invokes the necessary code to clean up; the compiler inserts this whenever the object goes out of scope, even if an error occurs. This is almost always preferable to managing freeing memory by hand.

Infinite precision integers

A perfect example of how the addition of a pointer can greatly expand the flexibility of our data types. Fundamental integer types are very useful, but are limited by the number of binary digits they can represent; the maximum number a 32-bit signed integer can represent is 2,147,483,647. Simply increasing the number of bits from 32 to 64, or from 64 to 128, does increase this beyond many practical applications, but some require very large numbers (e.g., cryptography) that cannot be represented in even a 128-bit integer. However, using a single level of indirection, we can create a 128-bit object that can represent an integer that can grow its precision as required. The data part of the class is as follows:

```
class InfinitePrecisionInt {
    uint64_t *limbs_ = nullptr;
    int32_t alloc_ = 0;
    int32_t size_and_sign_ = 0;
    // ... methods
};
```

This is essentially a `std::vector`, except for some minor differences. The `alloc_` member stores how many "limbs" are allocated, the `size_and_sign_` member stores the number of limbs that are actually in use and the sign of the integer: if there are n integers in use and the number is negative, then `size_and_sign_` stores $-n$. The `limbs_` pointer points the start of the `limbs` array. Notice that we're using 4-byte integer for the size and allocation, which should be sufficient for any number we need to represent. (For instance, the prime numbers one needs for RSA cryptography typically max out at 4,096 bits, which is an allocation of sixty-four 64-bit limbs.)

In each calculation, we must first decide how many bits are going to be needed to represent the answer, and re-allocate our `limbs` array as necessary. This process is obviously more involved than the very simple operations for fixed-size integers, but this is the trade-off for the additional flexibility. That being said, this kind of implementation can be made very fast. For instance, see the **GNU Multiple Precision Arithmetic Library** (**GMP**).

Arrays

An **array** is a sequence of values of a single type arranged contiguously (side by side) in memory. However, this is a somewhat overloaded term, so instead of adding to this problem, we shall refer to such a sequence of objects as **linear memory** instead. Linear memory can be **inline** (in that they live on the stack and thus enjoy fast access), but is limited in size, or they can be heap allocated, increasing their utility and maximum size. Arrays, in one form or another, are our main tool for handling bulk data.

The standard library contains the `std::array` template class, which is essentially a wrapper around a C-style array that provides a more C++-idiomatic interface to inline arrays. The size of such an array is static – it can only be defined at compile-time, like C-style arrays – and thus offers less flexibility. These still have their uses as small buffers on which a large number of operations can be performed in rapid succession. (See the tiling that we used in the matrix multiplication example in *Chapter 4*.)

Dynamic arrays come in various forms, but most commonly as a `std::vector`, which is essentially growable linear memory. An alternative is `std::unique_ptr<T[]>`, although the benefits are limited compared to a vector. This introduces the mantra of this chapter: *just use a vector.*

Structured memory

Most of the time, the objects we create are not single integers or floats and are instead an aggregate of these and other objects (possibly indirectly through pointers). The C++ class or struct is the means of defining such aggregations. The programmer has some choices about the design of these aggregates. For instance, if many instances of a struct appear in typical workflows, then making the struct compact might be wise, especially if one does not usually need to interact with any data hidden behind a pointer interaction. This is the case with our preceding infinite precision integers; we only need to interact with the limbs when an operation is performed, and we might well need to interact with many at once. Size is important here, so an array of these structs can fit in the cache.

Compare this to a global configuration object, which contains many settings for different parts of the program. This object needs to be large, to hold all the settings, and will likely only appear on the heap (because it is global). Thus, using fewer pointer indirections here might be preferable. We must create a single pointer indirection to get to the object itself, so more will hurt performance. (These indirections might be necessary, however.) At all times, you should consider the intent of an object and where it is likely to be used, which determines what characteristics to prioritize.

Allocation and allocators

Creating objects or arrays of objects on the heap requires **allocation**, usually by means of `operator new`, and is cleared up with `operator delete`. Of course, in modern C++, it is preferable to make use of smart pointers such as `std::unique_ptr` or `std::shared_ptr` and their corresponding factory functions, `std::make_unique` and `std::make_shared`. More on these later.

Standard library objects that deal with memory, such as `std::vector`, make use of **allocators** to customize their memory interactions. The default allocator simply uses `new` and `delete`, but the programmer can change the allocator via a template argument. In addition to the standard allocator, the standard library also provides polymorphic allocators, which use a composition of `memory_resources` to determine how memory is allocated. The standard library provides a few of these: the standard `new` and `delete`-based resources and memory pool-based resources. (These essentially implement a pool or arena allocator.)

If one is working with vectors of floating-point values and intends to operate on them with SIMD instructions, then one might want to use an aligned allocator. This is essentially the same as the default `std::allocator`, but it makes use of the variant of `operator new` that takes an alignment argument (`std::align_value_t`) and aligns the memory on a specific byte boundary. (We used this variant in *Chapter 4*.) Typically, one would include the alignment as a template argument. Note, however, that `std::vector` with different allocators are different types in C++, so they might not operate the way you intend (e.g., they can't be passed by reference to `std::vector<T>`). A very basic aligned allocator can be implemented as follows:

```
#include <cstddef>
#include <memory>
#include <new>

namespace ct {
template <typename T, std::size_t Alignment=32>
class AlignedAllocator {
```

```
    static constexpr std::align_val_t alignment { Alignment };
public:
    using value_type = T;

    constexpr AlignedAllocator() noexcept = default;

    template <typename U>
    constexpr AlignedAllocator(const AlignedAllocator<U, Alignment>&)
noexcept
    {}

    template <typename U>
    constexpr AlignedAllocator&
    operator=(const AlignedAllocator<U, Alignment>&) noexcept {
        return *this;
    }

    [[nodiscard]]
    T* allocate(std::size_t size);
    void deallocate(T* ptr, std::size_t size) noexcept;

    template <typename U>
    struct rebind {
        using other = AlignedAllocator<U, Alignment>;
    };

    template <typename U, std::size_t OtherAlignment>
    constexpr bool operator==(const AlignedAllocator<U, OtherAlignment>&)
noexcept
    { return Alignment == OtherAlignment; }

    template <typename U, std::size_t OtherAlignment>
    constexpr bool operator!=(const AlignedAllocator<U, OtherAlignment>&)
noexcept
    { return OtherAlignment != Alignment; }
};
```

```
template <typename T, std::size_t Alignment>
T* AlignedAllocator<T, Alignment>::allocate(std::size_t size) {
    auto* ptr = ::operator new[](size*sizeof(T), alignment);
    return static_cast<T*>(ptr);
}
template <typename T, std::size_t Alignment>
void AlignedAllocator<T, Alignment>::deallocate(T* ptr, std::size_t size)
noexcept {
    ::operator delete[](ptr, size, alignment);
}
} // namespace ct
```

This implementation is somewhat minimal. The standard library `allocator_traits` takes care of providing the methods and type definitions that are not provided by the class itself. The key functions here are the `allocate` and `deallocate` methods, which, unsurprisingly, do the work of allocating and freeing memory, respectively. The `rebind` member struct is the mechanism used by standard library containers to quietly change the type being allocated when the `value_type` of the allocator is not quite the same as the internal type needed. (For instance, a linked list might rebind from its element type to the node type.)

The standard library provides two allocators. The first is the default allocator, `std::allocator`, and the second is a polymorphic allocator that has customizable behavior based on a chain of memory resources. By using nothing but the tools provided in the standard library, we can implement a simple pool-based allocator as follows:

```
#include <memory_resource>
// ...
std::pmr::unsynchronized_memory_resource resource {{512, 16}};
std::pmr::polymorphic_allocator pool_allocator(&resource);
// or std::pmr::set_default_resource(&resource);
```

Clearly, this snippet of code is not so usable. A more robust way of handling the memory resource would be to hold it in a static variable inside an `init` function that is called to set the default memory resource for all instances of `std::pmr::polymorphic_allocator`. This is especially powerful if one uses the containers re-exported through the `std::pmr` namespace. These exports swap the default `std::allocator` argument to `std::pmr::polymorphic_allocator` instead.

Smart pointers

Something we haven't spent much time discussing is smart pointers, which are absolutely fundamental to modern C++ memory management. A **smart pointer** is an object that holds a pointer to some other (sometimes polymorphic) object and manages its lifetime. The basic smart pointer is `std::unique_ptr`, which simply deletes the pointed-to object when the `unique_ptr` object goes out of scope. Each unique pointer has unique ownership (hence the name) over the pointer that it manages. An alternative is `std::shared_ptr`, which maintains a reference count alongside the pointed-to object. Each time a shared pointer is copied or destroyed, the reference count is increased or decreased, respectively. Once the reference count reaches `0`, the object is deleted.

The `std::make_unique` and `std::make_shared` factory functions hide the explicit `operator new`; in idiomatic C++, every `new` should be paired with a corresponding `delete`, which is hidden by the use of smart pointers. These factory functions might do more than just allocate and construct, depending on the library vendor. Note that `std::make_shared<T[]>` was introduced in C++20, but the other functions were added in C++14. There are other variants of this function, too.

The implementation of `shared_ptr` from the standard library contains two pointers. The first is to the data and the second is to a control block that contains the reference count, along with a deleter function and a **weak reference** count. A `std::weak_ptr` is a non-owning reference to an object managed by a shared pointer. How this works is that the weak reference carries a pointer to the control block of a shared pointer. The weak reference can tell, by inspecting the main reference count, whether there is a `shared_ptr` that currently references the data or not (whether or not the object is still alive and valid). Weak pointers can be turned into a strong pointer, provided the object is still alive, which makes them useful for caching purposes. Weak pointers allow us to construct data structures that might otherwise lead to reference cycles (which are essentially a memory leak in this scenario). For instance, in a tree data structure, one might use a weak reference to point to the parent node, and strong references for the children, as illustrated with the following struct definition:

```
struct TreeNode {
    std::weak_ptr<TreeNode> parent;
    std::vector<std::shared_ptr<TreeNode>> children;
};
```

Shared pointers are thread-safe and generally the safest way of managing shared memory resources in a multithreaded environment, although the usual arguments hold for making sure that the pointed-to object cannot be mutated in a thread-unsafe way. They do have a downside, however, in that they are twice as large as a basic pointer. This can be problematic in instances where space is at a premium. Effort can also be duplicated if the objects themselves provide some means of managing their reference counts (COM objects in the Windows ecosystem, for instance). In these cases, the Boost smart pointer library provides an alternative: the `intrusive_ptr` smart pointer. This smart pointer uses external functions to define how the reference counts are incremented and decremented, and how the object is deleted. This pointer is also the size of a single pointer.

Now that we understand memory resources and data layouts, we can take a deeper dive into vectors and other objects that have a linear memory layout.

Linear memory: vectors, stacks, and queues

Vectors are just the prototypical example of a data structure that holds a dynamic linear memory. They grow by means of reallocating and moving/copying data when the old buffer runs out of memory. We actually discussed the algorithm for vector growth back in *Chapter 2*. Each time the vector grows, the size of the allocation grows by a multiple of the existing allocation; in practice, this almost always means the size of the allocation doubles each time. This means that most insertions do not require an allocation, and the cost of reallocating is amortized. This means that a vector has very fast push operations (on average) at the back (as in, the end where `push_back` operates). However, inserting elsewhere in the vector is very expensive since this requires moving all the elements from the insertion point forward one position toward the back.

Structure of array versus array of structures

Linear memory is great. It provides fast access times and good cache locality for your data, so it can be operated upon as fast as the processor can handle it. This is fine if the whole structure held in the linear memory is relevant to the computation being performed. This need not be the case all the time. Sometimes, the programmer might want to co-locate several pieces of information together. For example, the following struct defines a player in a game:

```
struct Physics {
    float x, y;
    float delta_x, delta_y;
};

struct Player {
    std::string username,
```

```
    Physics physics;
    // other fields
};
```

One of the operations that we probably want to run as part of the game is to update the physics (position) for each new frame to be generated. This could be accomplished by the following function:

```
void update_physics(std::span<Player> players, float delta_t) {
    for (auto& player : players) {
        player.physics.x += delta_t * player.physics.delta_x;
        player.physics.y += delta_t * player.physics.delta_y;
    }
}
```

The problem here is that there is a large amount of data in the struct that is not touched at all during this calculation. This essentially spaces out the data and degrades the nice cache locality and fast accesses promised by linear memory. This pattern is called an **array of structs**.

This might seem like the most sensible way to store aggregate data about the player (and other entities within the game), but there is an alternative. The **struct of arrays** pattern reverses the aggregation from the player to the components (usernames, physics, etc.). The repackaged version might look like this:

```
class Players {
    std::vector<std::string> usernames;
    std::vector<Physics> all_physics;
public:

    void update_physics(float delta_t) {
        for (auto& physics : all_physics) {
            physics.x += delta_t * physics.delta_x;
            physics.y += delta_t * physics.delta_y;
        }
    }
};
```

But why stop there? Why not collect together all the components from all the different entities within the game (not just the players) into a single struct of arrays, and we can update them all at once as necessary? The physics component update is always the same regardless of what entity it belongs to, as is the update.

This is the makings of an **entity component system** that is the basis of most modern game engines. (Such a system has to be accompanied by a sophisticated indexing system to keep track of which entities are still active and which component belongs to which entity, but this is beyond the scope of this book.)

Stacks and queues

A **queue** is a data structure that supports two operations: **push** and **pop**. There are two kinds of queue: **first in first out** (**FIFO**) queues and **last in first out** (**LIFO**) queues. A LIFO queue is sometimes called a **stack**. (Not to be confused with *the stack*, the temporary memory that provides the environment for function executions.) The stack is a LIFO queue containing stack frames and operates in exactly the same way. When a new function is called, a new stack frame is pushed onto the stack. When the function returns, the stack frame is popped from the top of the stack. This is what gives LIFO queues the name: the push and pop operate on the same end of the data, at the back.

Conversely, in a FIFO queue, the first element pushed to the queue is the first to be removed; the push and pop operate at opposite ends of the data: pop at the front and push at the back. A stack can be efficiently implemented as a vector, because push and pop at the end of the vector are cheap, but a FIFO queue would be ill-suited to a vector. A `pop_front` operation on a vector is inefficient because it would induce a move/copy of every other element in the vector. The C++ standard library provides a data structure that supports fast push and pop operations on the front and back, called a **double-ended queue** (**deque**). This structure is vector-like in that it grows as the allocated space becomes exhausted, but the strategy for growth is somewhat different. Unlike vectors, the elements are not stored contiguously as a whole; typically, small blocks of elements are stored in linear memory along with some metadata.

The C++ library also provides some adapter classes that abstract the implementation details of an underlying container class so that the interface presented only contains the methods required for the specific kind of queue: `std::queue` for FIFO queues, `std::stack` for LIFO queues, and `std::priority_queue` for priority queues. In a **priority queue**, the next element to be obtained from a `pop` operation is the element with the largest (or smallest) priority according to some comparison operation. Each of these adapters takes two (or more) template arguments, the first is the value type and the second is the container type (the default for `std::stack` and `std::queue` is `std::deque`).

More on vectors

Vectors are our main concern in this section. We've discussed how a vector allocates its memory and how to add elements, but we haven't discussed the important parts: access to the elements. Like all containers, the C++ standard sets out an **iterator**-based interface that provides access to the elements in a sequential manner. For a vector, these iterators are essentially pointers (they may even be pointers, depending on the implementation of the standard library). Accessing all elements in the vector sequentially obviously has linear complexity (in the number of elements). However, unlike other containers we will see in this chapter, these accesses are very cheap and predictable for the compiler and CPU. This means that using a vector might have a profound impact on the runtime performance of your code, even if it doesn't change the underlying computational complexity of the algorithm (and sometimes even if it does). This is especially true in cases where the data structure will be relatively small or if one needs to traverse the data structure often. One of the problems with vectors is the iterator invalidation that occurs when the buffer is reallocated. There is no way around this without compromising the performance of the whole container. For this reason, we might describe a vector as a **non-stable container**. (Linked lists are stable containers, as we shall see later.) This is usually not a concern. Most algorithms don't modify the size of the source container, and we can enforce this by passing the arguments as iterators (ranges) or, in the case of a vector or other linear memory containers, `std::span`. In cases where this is unavoidable, keeping iterators around is an easy place for bugs to creep into code. Indexes are a more stable alternative to iterators if the reference must live longer than a scope where the vector is guaranteed not to be resized. This approach is common in game engines in conjunction with an entity component system, which we described earlier.

Static vectors

A **static vector** is a variant of a vector, but where the capacity of the vector is fixed at compile time. One can still add and remove elements, but the vector cannot grow if there is no more space. These kinds of vectors are very useful if the maximum size of the vector is known (and is not too large) or in situations where a heap is not implemented (e.g., embedded applications). These vectors are not implemented in the standard library, but there is an implementation in the Boost.Container library. If the Boost library is not suited to your application, a static vector is easy enough to implement by hand.

Since static vectors never resize, iterators are never invalidated (though what they point to might change after insertion or deletion operations), and there is virtually no cost to insertion and deletion from the end of the vector (there is no need for complicated resize logic).

However, there are some special considerations. First, one must deal with the fact that insertions could fail. A basic implementation might simply throw an exception, but this itself requires a heap allocation, which is what we were trying to avoid with a static vector. Instead, insert operations could (additionally) indicate whether they were successful. This can be achieved by returning `std::optional` or a `std::outcome` (or one of the equivalents from Boost or Abseil, or another library), or simply returning a `bool`.

Implementing a static vector can be rather tricky. The complication comes from the fact that the template type, `T`, might not be default constructible (or not constructible at all from the container's point of view), so we cannot simply make use of simple storage such as `std::array`. In the following code, we give the skeleton of a static vector. We won't implement the full class, but we will show the `emplace_back` implementation to show how one would operate on such a structure. The code is as follows:

```
template <typename T, size_t Size>
class StaticVector {
    alignas(T) char storage_[Size * sizeof(T)] { 0 };
    size_t current_size_ = 0;
public:
    // constructors and other methods.

    [[nodiscard]] T* data() noexcept
    { return std::launder(reinterpret_cast<T*>(storage_)); }

    [[nodiscard]] const T* data() const noexcept
    { return std::launder(reinterpret_cast<const T*>(storage_); }

    [[nodiscard]] // the programmer must handle failure
    bool emplace_back(T&& value) {
        if (current_size_ < Size) {
            ::new (data() + current_size_) T(std::move(value));
            ++current_size_;
            return true;
        }
        return false;
    }
    // more methods
};
```

You might have noticed our rather curious choice of storage here. Why didn't we just use `T[Size]`? In this case, it is about communicating intent (there may well be other reasons). Here, the buffer is uninitialized memory to begin with. We don't want the compiler to try and construct values in this space; as we mentioned before, this might not be possible. We should only ever access the buffer via the `data` methods, eliminating the need to invoke pointer conversions elsewhere. The inclusion of `std::launder` here is not strictly necessary, but advisable. This is a barrier for the compiler to "forget" the previous type metadata of the pointer (as a `char`) and consider it only as a pointer to `T`. C++23 adds the perhaps more appropriate `begin_lifetime_as` function that is explicitly for this purpose. (Unfortunately, not all current compilers have support for C++23 features.)

Insertion operations need to be performed with the placement `new` operator, as shown in the `emplace_back` method. In this instance, we move the data from the r-value reference provided, but this could be a copy construction or construction from arguments. This method, along with all of the methods involved, should ideally be marked `noexcept` with the appropriate condition; this is omitted to keep the code readable.

Small vectors

A hybrid between a static vector and a normal vector is a small vector or, more precisely, a vector with a small-size optimization. As a **small vector** contains a small buffer of static storage space, customizable by template parameter, within which no heap allocation is required. If the vector grows beyond this statically allocated space, the vector grows as normal. This provides a very fast storage solution for vectors that are more likely to remain relatively small, but still have the flexibility to grow beyond their statically allocated capacity. Unfortunately, the standard library does not contain a general-purpose implementation of a small vector (except for `std::string`), but several other frameworks do: Abseil and Boost.Container are notable providers of a small vector implementation. A small vector implementation is slated for inclusion in the C++26 standard.

Small vectors are very effective in situations where the expected number of entries is relatively small. This is certainly the case for strings; most are very small (a handful of characters). The standard library `string` has an internal buffer for `char` – it is a small vector specifically for characters – so creating a string with a single character or a small number of characters incurs no cost at all. (However, `std::string`, like any small vector, are fairly large objects because of the internal buffer, which can occasionally be problematic.) More generally, small vectors can be used anywhere you would use `std::vector` with minimal changes to your code, but remember that they can't be passed by reference to a function expecting `std::vector` or some other kind of vector (including a small vector with a different internal buffer size, since this will be a different type).

Views and spans

Most of the time when operating on linear memory, one does not need to know how the data is actually managed. The only thing that matters is where the data is located (a pointer to the beginning of the block in question) and the size of the block. The C++ standard library contains `string_view` (C++17) and `span` (C++20), which are management-agnostic views into a block of linear data. They are, essentially, a pair of a pointer and a size and can be used anywhere linear memory is expected (and does not need to change size), regardless of the structure used to manage the allocation. Typically, this will be in function parameters. These objects should always be passed by value so the compiler is free to optimize the function call. Unlike `span`, a `string_view` only provides non-mutable access to the buffer. This is necessary because a `UTF-8` character modification might change the number of bytes required, necessitating a reallocation.

Spans come in two flavors. One has a template size that does not change (in which case, `std::span` behaves very much like `std::array`). The second form has a dynamic size, which is indicated by passing a `std::dynamic_extent` constant in the template argument for size. This second use is the default usage and generally more flexible (most linear memory does not have a size known at compile time).

There is a disadvantage to using `std::span` and `std::string_view`. These are both relatively recent additions to the standard library and have not propagated throughout the interfaces contained therein. Notably, the Regex library does not use a string view and, as a result of making many copies of data internally, suffers performance penalties. This may change in future revisions of the C++ standard. There are other limitations too, for instance, a map whose key type is `std::string` cannot be queried with a string view. That is, the following code will not compile:

```
std::unordered_map<std::string, double> map;
map["test"] = 1.0;
std::string_view sv_key ("test");
auto& val = map[sv_key];
```

Pitfalls like this make it rather difficult to completely embrace `std::string_view`. There are other issues, too. In *Chapter 4*, we saw that it is sometimes important to annotate pointer parameters to functions with `__restrict` (or equivalent) to indicate that the pointed-to range is not aliased by any other pointer in the scope of the function (provided, of course, that this is true!). This is not possible if the argument is provided in `std::span`. However, these obstacles are rather niche and should not discourage using `std::span` and `std::string_view`.

This concludes our discussion of vectors and other linear memory containers for now. The next category of data structures we discuss is linked lists.

Linked lists

A **linked list** is another fundamental data structure in computing, generally coming in two flavors: singly linked and doubly linked. A linked list is a collection of nodes, each containing some data and a pointer to the next node in the list, as illustrated in *Figure 5.1*. Each node in a doubly linked list also contains a pointer to the previous entry in the list. This offers a great deal of flexibility. The data in each node is independent of its position in the list; new insertions only require modification to the pointers in the node and not the data itself. Insertions at a known point in the list (such as at the beginning or end) are also very cheap, as they only involve modifying the pointers in the surrounding nodes (if there are any).

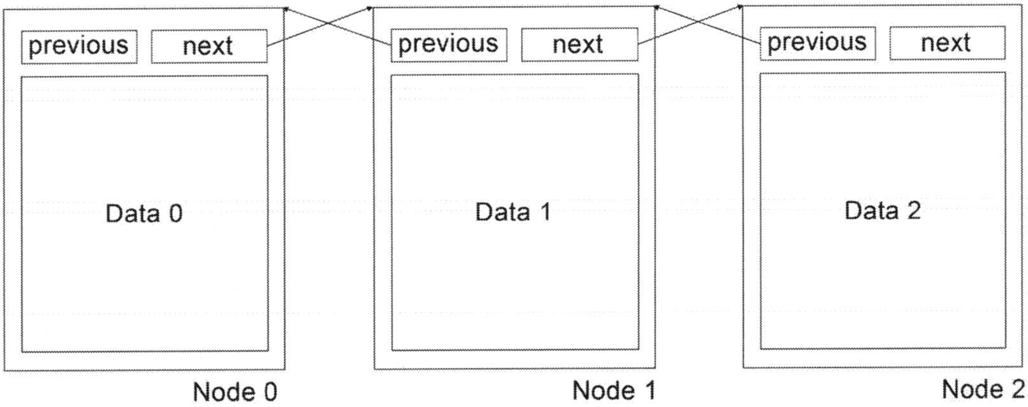

Figure 5.1: A linked list with three nodes. Each node contains pointers to the previous and next node in the list, which could be null if no such node exists, indicated here by missing arrows. Each node also contains user data

Linked lists are more stable and cheaper to insert into than vectors, but this comes at a cost. Traversing a linked list is very expensive, compared to traversing a vector. This is because moving from one node to the next involves following a pointer indirection, which makes predicting which page in memory to find rather tricky for the processor and disrupts the operation of the cache. This is not to say that linked lists aren't useful. We've already described a use of these in *Chapter 4* in the free list of memory pages. This is a linked list where the nodes are unallocated memory pages. Moreover, many standard library data structures, such as maps, are implemented on top of linked lists.

Linked lists are most effective when the size of the data is fairly large, or where insertion and deletion are frequent, and in other situations where it is essential that operations on the data structure as a whole do not invalidate references to data within the list. However, if the application requires repeated traversals, then a different data structure (i.e., a vector) might be more appropriate.

Stable vectors

A **stable vector** is a hybrid between a vector and a linked list. It can grow like a vector and has (mostly) contiguous data, but instead of moving data upon growth, it allocates a new block of linear memory as a new node in a linked list. This eliminates the need to copy elements when the vector grows, which has the additional property that a growth operation does not invalidate references to the data, hence the name. This has most of the desirable properties of both linked lists and vectors, although it incurs a slight penalty in traversal because of the need to follow a pointer at the end of each block of linear memory. The standard implementation of `deque` follows a pattern similar to this.

Boost.Container provides a stable vector implementation, should this be necessary, but we've already discussed some ways that pointer invalidation can be mitigated through the careful use of indexing. Stable vectors, being partly based on linked lists, do suffer from performance penalties when traversing the structure or obtaining a specific element. In many cases, it might be more appropriate to make use of `std::unique_ptr` to ensure value-pointer stability (if not iterator stability) in a `std::vector`. Of course, there is a performance penalty for this, too.

One of the main uses for linked lists in the standard library is to implement maps and sets, which are the topic of the next section.

Maps and sets

A **set** is a container in which all the contained objects must compare not equal. Thus, adding a new object that is a duplicate of (or is equal to) an element that already exists in the set does not insert a new element. This is useful if one needs to keep track of all of the elements seen thus far. Determining whether an element is contained in a set should be a fairly fast operation (logarithmic in the size of the container for `std::map`), depending on the backing storage layout, as should adding new members. The standard library set stores the elements in order and uses a binary search to find elements. Maps and sets are often implemented as binary trees, such as a red-black tree, the structure of which is illustrated in *Figure 5.2*.

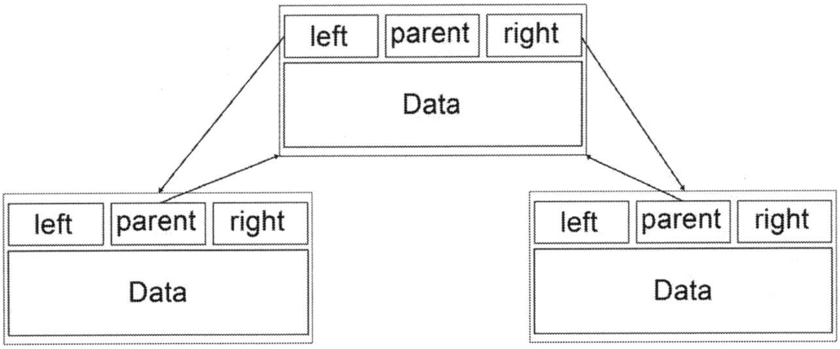

Figure 5.2: A simple tree with three nodes, one root node with two child nodes. Each node contains pointers to the left and right child nodes and a pointer to the parent node. Any of these can be null if there is no further node. Each node contains data, which may include a marker such as a red/black color in the case of red-black trees

Maps are closely related to sets, but instead of simply recording the elements that appear, a relationship is formed between a key type and a value type. (They are sets where part of the key does not contribute to determining equality of keys.) The standard library map again uses an ordering on the keys to achieve the desired property.

Maps are extremely useful in almost any situation, for example, for memoizing the results of expensive calculations. Accessing the element associated with a key in a map has logarithmic complexity, due to the binary search. However, it is worth remembering that, because these structures are backed by linked lists, the performance of these data structures is somewhat limited. Depending on the application, one might want to use a flat variant of maps instead.

Flat maps and flat sets

A **flat set** is a set that is implemented in a vector. This has the benefit of far greater performance over the standard implementation. As we have already seen, linear memory has a distinct advantage in performance over linked lists. This boost in performance only works for accesses to data; insertion and deletion from a flat set is far more expensive (because it is backed by a vector). The same holds true for **flat maps**. As before, here, the items are pairs of keys and values.

From C++23, the standard library provides `flat_set` and `flat_map` adapters that provide a flexible means of constructing such sets. The `flat_map` adapter is essentially a `flat_set` of keys combined with a vector (or some other container) of values. The Boost.Container library provides a different implementation of a flat map, where both keys and values are stored together in `std::pair` inside a single vector.

This is a less flexible approach, but it likely has better performance characteristics because one does not need to look in a separate block of memory to get the keys, which are possibly located a long way from the key block. Regardless of implementation, flat maps have similar algorithmic properties to `std::map` based on linked lists.

Hash functions

Order-based maps only work for types that have a well-defined ordering, which certainly doesn't include all types. Aside from this, the order-based operation has logarithmic lookups, which is fine when there are relatively few elements, but will eventually become problematic. An alternative strategy for implementing a map is to use a **hash** to quickly distinguish between different keys. A hash is a function that turns an object into an unsigned integer (`size_t`) that satisfies various properties. Most importantly, the function should produce the same value for any objects that compare equal: if `obj1 == obj2`, then `h(obj1) == h(obj2)` (within a single run of the program). A good hash function should evenly distribute its values over the entire range, and non-equal objects should produce hashes that are somewhat far apart. One property that is missing from the list is speed. For a hash function to be useful, it needs to operate relatively quickly.

The standard library provides `std::hash`, a function object template that implements a hashing algorithm that is sufficient for container use. However, this implementation is a little limited. The problem is implementing `std::hash` for your own types. Moreover, even fairly standard types such as `std::pair` do not have an implementation of `std::hash`, which is a major pitfall. Consider the following very simple object:

```
struct KeyObject {
    std::string name;
    int index;
};
```

One might wish to implement `std::hash` for this `KeyObject` by computing the hash of each element and combining them in some way:

```
namespace std {
template <> struct hash<KeyObject> {
    size_t operator()(const KeyObject& obj) noexcept {
        auto h1 = std::hash<std::string>{}(obj.name);
        auto h2 = std::hash<int>{}(obj.index);
        return h1 + h2; // what goes here?
        }
    }
}
```

The standard library does not provide a specific means of combining hash values, and for good reason. A general-purpose `combine` function would disrupt the carefully crafted properties of the underlying hash algorithm. There are some reasonable solutions, such as the `hash_combine` function provided in the Boost.Container hash library. The Abseil library provides a somewhat better solution. Using this framework, one implements a `friend` function as follows:

```
struct KeyObject {
    std::string name;
    int index;

    template <typename H>
    friend H AbslHashValue(H hasher, const KeyObject& obj) noexcept {
        return H::combine(std::move(hasher), obj.name, obj.index);
    }
};
```

Here, the internal state of the hash algorithm is exposed to the implementing function. This is a far more flexible system than provided by the standard library and eliminates the need for an externally defined combination function. Once this function is defined, `absl::Hash<KeyObject>` should work as a drop-in replacement for `std::hash<KeyObject>`.

Hash sets and hash maps

Hash sets and **hash maps** store their data in buckets, using a hash function to determine which data goes in which bucket. This creates a fast means of accessing a particular entry by first computing the (relatively cheap) hash value, and then locating and retrieving the corresponding bucket. Unfortunately, the hash function is not guaranteed to be perfect, and **collisions** in hashes can occur. This is where two values are given the same hash value by the function, causing them to be placed in the same bucket. This is not catastrophic, but it does need to be handled in some way. There are several strategies for handling collisions, each with its own strengths and weaknesses (we won't get into those here).

The **load factor** of a hash set is the ratio of the number of entries to the number of buckets (the average number of entries per bucket). As the size of the hash set grows, the load factor increases and the performance degrades. Thus, insertions that cause the load factor to become too large trigger a **rehash** (resize) of the array of buckets available to the set. This should be a relatively infrequent operation. For instance, in an open addressing implementation of a hash table, we might set the maximum load factor at around `0.7`. Other implementations might have different ranges for the maximum load factor.

Retrieving a specific key from a hash map has constant complexity ($O(1)$), but the constant is usually quite large (computing the hash and performing collision resolution). Insertions have amortized constant complexity, with linear worst-case complexity (a rehash must touch each entry in the set). Computing hashes can be expensive, particularly if the objects are large. The standard library hash is not the fastest hash implementation: on GCC, for integers, `std::hash`, `abls::Hash`, and `boost::hash` are broadly comparable, but for doubles and strings, `std::hash` is notably slower than the others (benchmark code is given in the code folder for this chapter).

The C++ standard library provides hash sets and hash maps as `std::unordered_set` and `std::unordered_map`, respectively. The name comes from the fact that the elements in the buckets are not kept in any particular order. Other implementations of hash sets do preserve (insertion) order or have other properties (Python's `dict` structure is a hash map that maintains insertion order since Python 3.6). C++ containers are based on linked lists, which, as we have discussed, are good if there are frequent insertions or deletions but incur some performance penalties for accesses and traversals.

As with most standard library containers, the hash function, equality function, and allocator can be customized by template parameters. Using `boost::hash` or `absl::hash` instead of `std::hash` will allow you to use `std:pair` (or `std::tuple`) as keys in a map or set without any additional code.

Flat hash maps and sets

An alternative implementation of a hash set stores values in linear memory instead of a linked list, reducing the performance overhead for accesses and traversals, but increasing the complexity of insertions and deletions. These are not implemented in the standard library, but both Boost (unordered library) and Abseil provide implementations of flat hash maps and sets. (A large collection of benchmarks is provided in the Boost unordered documentation.) Care is needed with these types, though, since they aren't quite drop-in replacements for `std::unordered_set`/`std::unordered_map`. Obviously, the methods on these containers have different complexity, since they're backed by linear memory instead of a linked list, but they also have different properties. For instance, the elements must be move-constructible, and rehashing will invalidate pointers and references to the values stored within.

Map benchmarks

To understand the performance characteristics of different kinds of maps, we can benchmark them. To demonstrate how this works, we've constructed a relatively simple benchmark for accessing a single element from various kinds of maps. For this particular benchmark, we're going to choose the key to look up uniformly randomly. This should disrupt some of the cache locality effects that would not give us meaningful numbers if a constant key value were used. (Typically, one does not repeatedly look up the same key every time in a map.) This will add a small overhead to each benchmark, but crucially, it will be exactly the same for all of them. In the remainder of this section, we will show how we construct the benchmark code.

The first thing to do is import the relevant libraries. For this, we'll use the Google benchmark framework, which makes writing these kinds of benchmarks extremely easy. We need to import this and headers for all the different maps we're going to benchmark; these include standard maps, the map types from Abseil, and the maps from Boost.Container and unordered. We don't show all of these (there are a lot of them), but here is a snippet:

```
#include <random> // to generate random keys
#include <map>
#include <unordered_map>

#include <benchmark/benchmark.h> // Google benchmark

// abseil maps
#include <absl/container/flat_hash_map.h>
#include <absl/container/node_hash_map.h>

#include <boost/container/flat_map.hpp>
// more boost maps
```

We're going to use templates to generate the benchmarks so they all use precisely the same code (to make the test fair). The first thing we will need to do is generate an instance of a map that contains values for a known set of values. To keep things simple, our key types and value types are going to be (signed) 64-bit integers. The function that constructs and fills the maps is as follows:

```
template<template <typename, typename> class Map>
Map<int64_t, int64_t> make_map(int64_t size) {
    Map<int64_t, int64_t> m;
    for (int64_t i = 0; i < size; ++i) {
        m[i] = i;
```

```
    }
    return m;
}
```

Now, we can set up the benchmark code. The outline is very simple. First, we set up a new map using the function. Then, we set up our random number generator. Next, we run the benchmark loop, where, on each iteration, we generate a random key and get the reference to the corresponding element. Now, we need to make sure the optimizer doesn't simply delete the accesses because the value is unused, so we use the `benchmark::DoNotOptimize` function to force the compiler to retain the instructions necessary to perform the lookup. This is the code that implements this procedure:

```
template<template <typename, typename> class Map>
void bench_map_random_access(benchmark::State &state) {
    auto m = make_map<Map>(state.range(0));

    std::mt19937_64 rng(std::random_device{}());
    std::uniform_int_distribution<int64_t> dist(0, m.size() - 1);

    for (auto _: state) {
        int64_t i = dist(rng);
        auto &value = m[i];
        benchmark::DoNotOptimize(value);
    }
}
```

The final step is to instantiate and register these benchmarks with the Google benchmark runtime, using the `BENCHMARK_TEMPLATE` macro. Now, we also want to run the benchmark with two different sizes to explore the effect of lookups on differently sized containers. This argument will be passed to the benchmark via the `state` object and is passed to the `make_map` function on line 3 of the previous code block. The first two register statements are as follows (the rest are the same, but with the second argument replaced by the remaining map templates):

```
BENCHMARK_TEMPLATE(bench_map_random_access, std::map)
->Arg(256)->Arg(1024);
BENCHMARK_TEMPLATE(bench_map_random_access, std::unordered_map)
->Arg(256)->Arg(1024);

// register the rest of the templates

BENCHMARK_MAIN(); // add the standard `main` function.
```

The results of these benchmarks are shown in the following table.

Map class	Arg	CPU time (ns)	Iterations
`std::map`	256	23.3	29,718,334
`std::map`	1024	34.9	20,013,830
`std::unordered_map`	256	3.56	196,713,903
`std::unordered_map`	1024	3.81	183,563,793
`absl::btree_map`	256	19.5	35,186,272
`absl::btree_map`	1024	24.1	29,140,587
`absl::flat_hash_map`	256	3.81	183,544,058
`absl::flat_hash_map`	1024	3.89	181,007,764
`absl::node_hash_map`	256	3.95	177,309,001
`absl::node_hash_map`	1024	4.29	163,764,827
`boost::container::flat_map`	256	25.9	27,124,320
`boost::container::flat_map`	1024	31.4	22,278,930
`boost::unordered_map`	256	3.68	189,779,848
`boost::unordered_map`	1024	3.66	189,826,896
`boost::unordered_flat_map`	256	3.93	178,792,524
`boost::unordered_flat_map`	1024	4.03	173,829,279

Table 5.1: Results of benchmarking random access to elements in various maps

There are two important features to pull out here. The first is that hash maps are universally faster than ordered maps, roughly 10 times faster. The second is that the unordered maps have (more or less) constant access time regardless of size, whereas the ordered maps do not. This is precisely the behavior we expected, since the complexity of a binary search is $O(\log N)$ but the hash map has lookup complexity $O(1)$. Surprisingly there doesn't seem to be any difference between the flat variants and the node variants. This is probably because the number of elements is small enough to fit into higher levels of cache. (These numbers were generated on an AMD Ryzen 7900x; your results may vary.)

This concludes the main content for the chapter. Let's take a look at what we have seen.

Summary

This chapter covered the various options for storing and representing data in C++ code. At a basic level, data in C++ is either fundamental (integers, floats, pointers, etc.) or instances of classes. These can live on the stack or on the heap, where most of the time, one will want to manage the memory using a smart pointer. The main content of this chapter concerns the various kinds of containers that we can use. These generally fall into two categories: linear memory containers (vectors and arrays) and linked lists (essentially, everything else). Generally speaking, linear memory has better performance for traversal and direct memory access, but is less performant when inserting or deleting elements, especially when these operations occur at the beginning of the data. For almost every data storage problem that doesn't require some additional structure, a vector is almost certainly the right tool for the job: *just use a vector*.

The second half of the chapter covered maps and sets. These are containers that store only values that it does not already contain and, in the case of maps, for an association between a key object and a value object that allows for very fast key-value lookup. Some of these types utilize an ordering on the keys and binary search to find the value of the key. The other kind of set/map uses a hash function to place keys in buckets, plus some logic to disambiguate between keys that end up in the same bucket. Hash maps have very fast (constant time) lookup. We also looked at some alternatives from other libraries that fill in some gaps that are left in the standard library.

In the next chapter, we will look at how to structure your code and use features of modern C++ to make your code modular and reusable.

6

Reusing Your Code and Modularity

The code you write to solve problems is only useful if you, or others, can use it. This means you have to think quite carefully about how others (including yourself, who might have forgotten how things work) interface and otherwise interact with your solution. This starts with the interface to your solution, which should be simple and stable, but allow for flexibility where it exists. The next challenge is packaging the solution into a library that can be used elsewhere in applications (or other libraries). This is the main topic of this chapter.

In the first part of the chapter, we will discuss some of the considerations of building libraries in C++, particularly some of the challenges associated with building shared libraries. Designing interfaces is something we discussed in previous chapters and appears again here. This time the focus is on stability which is critical, especially for shared libraries, for making your code usable. We also look at C++ modules as a potential replacement for traditional header files as the description of the interface that is used by the compiler. We will see how to build a basic module-based interface that can be consumed (more efficiently) by the compiler instead of header files. The final section deals with some practical concerns for working with large projects, specifically around breaking up very large and complicated projects into smaller pieces. The main ingredient of this process is understanding dependencies.

In this chapter, we're going to cover the following main topics:

- Libraries: static and shared
- Designing stable interfaces
- Using C++ modules
- Separating components in the build system

Technical requirements

The focus of this chapter is on building modular, reusable, and portable code that can be built and used in multiple configurations. This includes some example code and the associated CMake files that are necessary to make this possible. These are all contained in the `Chapter-06` folder of the GitHub repository for this book, at `https://github.com/PacktPublishing/The-CPP-Programmers-Mindset`, along with a system of tests so you can test your own solutions.

Libraries: static and shared

Libraries are the containers into which code is collected so that it can be reused. These (usually) come in two forms: static libraries and shared libraries. **Static libraries** contain raw compile code plus some metadata that allows the linker to find and incorporate specific functions and classes. These are relatively simple archives of functions and data (including classes) that are pulled in to each application that links them during **linking**. **Shared libraries** are somewhat more complicated. Like static libraries, these contain code and metadata, but the code is not pulled into the application binary during linking. Instead, this process happens during **loading** when the application is first loaded into memory. This work is carried out by the dynamic loader (`ld` on Linux). The dynamic loader uses an offset table inside the dynamic library to locate each of the needed symbols and make them available to the application.

Static libraries have a slight advantage in speed since the code necessary is incorporated into the application binary file, and no indirection is needed to load or use these functions. (Modern dynamic loaders and the supporting CPU functions make the performance advantage of using static libraries over shared libraries somewhat negligible.) However, incorporating the additional code leads to larger binary sizes. In some rare cases, linking the same static library in multiple components of an application can lead to problems with memory allocation or global initialization tasks. Shared libraries, on the other hand, are, as the name suggests, shared between many applications and can be efficiently loaded by the operating system to facilitate this.

On Linux, all C/C++ applications link to the main system runtime library, `libc`, which contains parts of the C standard library that interact with the operating system, such as `malloc` and `free`. macOS and Windows have similar mechanisms for exposing basic system calls to end user applications. There are generally a number of support libraries that go alongside it, such as the math library (`libm` on Linux) and other operating system-specific libraries.

In C++, libraries that consist only of template code don't require a compiled component and thus can be distributed purely as a set of header files. These are commonly referred to as **header-only libraries**. Much of the C++ standard library is header-only, as are many of the Boost libraries. Templates are instantiated at compile time directly into the application binary, making them more like static libraries in behavior. Templates can be extremely flexible and, since it is essentially source code, can be compiled anywhere there is a compliant compiler available. However, templates too carry a cost, which is the increased compilation time. Instantiating templates is expensive for the compiler, particularly if these templates are recursively defined.

Public and private components

Library code is often divided into two parts: the external-facing functionality and the internal implementation details that are not intended to be accessible or used externally. These form the public and private components of the library (respectively). The header public header files determine what is accessible for consumers of the library, although these may also contain some implementation details – especially for libraries that make use of templates. These details can be obscured using namespaces that signal to the end user that these details are not intended for external use. (Internal namespaces called `detail`, or `dtl` for short, and `internal` are common for this purpose.) One can also note in comments and documentation that certain functions are for internal use. This is important because internal functions might not have the same guarantees or perform the same kind of checking as those intended for external use. Shared libraries have additional controls on symbol exports since these are deployed to end users, unlike static or header-only libraries.

The distinction between public and private is not so much about detail and guarantees but instead about stability. One of the most important factors in the longevity of a software library is the stability of the interface, both the programming interface (**API**) and the binary interface (**ABI**). Public interfaces should be stable and dependable, at least within well-defined timeframes, but private interfaces need no such guarantee. If the public interface does need to change, symbol versioning can be used (possibly through the use of **inline namespaces**), and symbols that need to be removed should first go through a deprecation cycle. For instance, one can use short vx_x style namespaces, as shown here:

```
namespace ct {
    inline namespace v1_0 {

        int versioned_function(int a, int b);

    } // inline namespace v1_0
} // namespace ct;
```

Inline namespaces essentially re-export the symbols declared within into the surrounding scope. (Unnamed namespaces do the same thing.) This way, one can refer to the `ct::versioned_function` symbol even though its actual fully qualified name is `ct::v1_0::versioned_function`. This allows one to create a new version of a symbol without removing the old one by changing the namespace to be non-inline and adding a new-inline namespace.

Modules introduced in C++20 provide a far more fine-grained means of controlling references to symbols, though these are not a replacement for namespaces. (See the *Using C++ modules* section later in this chapter.) This is an effective means of indicating that parts contain private implementation details, but it does not address the versioning.

Dynamic libraries

Dynamic libraries offer some advantages when it comes to deploying code to users. The main advantage is size: shared libraries, as the name suggests, can be shared among several applications, needing only a single copy for multiple applications. Shared libraries can also be upgraded – providing the interface they provide has not changed – without needing to recompile the main binary. This allows for bug fixes and performance improvements to be distributed without interrupting user applications. This is important for operating systems and distributors of frameworks that must not break applications that rely on them.

Most of the time, shared libraries are linked statically just like static libraries. At link time, the linker inserts the code and data necessary to locate and load the symbols that should be provided by a dynamic library. However, the address of symbols cannot be fully resolved until run/load time. As mentioned before, this dynamic linker is responsible for performing this final address resolution. If you want to read more about this process, the book *Linkers & Loaders* [1] is an excellent place to look.

On Linux and macOS, linking to a shared library only requires the library itself and the associated header files. On Windows, linking is done against a stub file (usually adorned with the `.lib` extension, which is confusingly similar to the static library). The shared library object must then be packaged along with the application binary (or otherwise made available on the end user's computer). This can actually be rather complicated because the main executable needs to be able to find all the dynamic libraries that are required. Linux and macOS binaries can be provided with a list of paths (the `RPATH` attribute or equivalent) that is used by the dynamic linker to find the correct shared libraries at runtime (especially those that are not distributed as part of a package manager). Windows binaries do not have this facility, which makes finding DLLs rather frustrating at times. (Especially during testing, which is commonly done within the build tree rather than in the final install locations.)

Occasionally, one might want to load a dynamic library by hand and locate specific functions contained therein. This is a useful mechanism for loading extensions that are not essential to the running of the main application but augment the functionality or performance in some way. This is achieved using the `dlopen` and `dlsym` functions on Linux and their equivalents.

As a library developer, it is important to keep the different ways that your library can be consumed in mind. From a programming point of view, you don't need to worry about the means of loading a shared library, or the exact details of linking. But you do need to understand how to provide the correct type of library for the task. You may even wish to provide a choice between a shared library and a static library to link against.

Building and distributing a shared library correctly can be rather tricky. Using CMake makes this process easier by taking care of some of the platform-specific problems, but there is more to it than one might think. The main concern is deciding what functions and classes should be exposed in the interface, which should be as stable as possible. Setting up library versioning and other metadata (such as the `RPATH` attribute for finding dependent libraries) helps to ensure compatibility and a smooth loading experience, but we won't cover these here.

Exporting symbols

Shared libraries do not make all of the functions they contain findable to the dynamic linker. The default behavior in GCC and Clang is that all symbols are exported. In MSVC, symbols that are exported must be explicitly marked as `dllexport`, and similarly, functions that are to be imported from a DLL must be marked `dllimport`. In this case, it is far better to explicitly choose the functions and classes that should be exported as part of the shared interface. This is easily accomplished with the assistance of CMake. The following CMake code defines a shared library target and takes care of setting the appropriate visibility flags:

```
# set the defaults for the whole cmake project
set(CMAKE_VISIBILITY_PRESET hidden)
set(CMAKE_VISIBILITY_INLINES_HIDDEN ON)

add_library(MySharedLibrary SHARED)

# or set for an individual library with properties
set_target_property(MySharedLibrary PROPERTIES
    VISIBILITY_PRESET hidden
    VISIBILITY_INLINES_HIDDEN ON
)

# define sources for library etc.
```

Now, regardless of the compiler and platform, no symbols will be exported unless we have explicitly marked them as exported. The usual practice for marking symbols as exported (or imported, when consuming the library) is by using a preprocessor macro. We actually don't need to construct these macros ourselves; we can just let CMake do this for us:

```
include(GenerateExportHeader)

generate_export_header(MySharedLibrary)

# Make the generated header findable by the .cpp/.h files
target_include_directories(MySharedLibrary PRIVATE
    ${CMAKE_CURRENT_BINARY_DIR})
```

This will generate a header file called `mysharedlibrary_exports.h` in `CMAKE_CURRENT_BINARY_DIR` containing a number of macro definitions, but most importantly, the `MYSHAREDLIBARY_EXPORT` macro. You will need to make sure this file is installed along with other header files if that's part of your deployment workflow. When building the library, this macro will expand to the compiler-specific instruction to export the symbol (e.g., `__declspec(dllexport)`) and otherwise to the instruction to import the symbol (`__declspec(dllimport)` on Windows, and blank otherwise). The following code is an example of how this can be used in a library header file to mark functions and classes as exported:

```
#include "mysharedlibrary_export.h"

namespace ct {

class MYSHAREDLIBRARY_EXPORT MyExportedClass {
public:
    void exported_method();
};

MYSHAREDLIBRARY_EXPORT int exported_function(int arg);

namespace dtl {

class UnexportedInternalClass;

} // namespace dtl
} // namespace ct
```

The names of these macros (and the header itself) are derived from the name of the CMake target, but, like most things in CMake, these are customizable. This same construction does work if the target library is not a shared library, but in that case, the macros expand to nothing.

One of the most important features of libraries that are distributed to end users is a stable interface. How to design such interfaces is the topic of the next section.

Designing stable interfaces

Public interfaces need to be stable. Intermediate users (which may include yourself) will build applications and other libraries that consume your interface and use it. Asking those users to recompile their software every time you ship a new shared library is unreasonable (and in many cases impossible). Static libraries don't have the same problem since the code is baked into those applications, but stability is important there too. Having an interface that doesn't change in ways that break existing functionality is important. There are many things to consider here, such as how to add new functionality, how to change behavior, and how to deprecate and eventually remove old functionality.

Before we get to some of the ways to safely change interfaces, we can give some general tips for how to build good interfaces that are flexible from the start, and thus are less problematic to change later. Here are a few general tips:

- **Layer your interface**: Separate core functionality from the convenience and user-facing functions and classes. Templates and inline functions can be used on top of these core routines to implement more simplified interfaces that can be used. The core routines are then free to present a more complex interface that covers a wider array of use cases. This serves two purposes: to provide flexibility and as a prototype for users to develop their own interface around your core routines.
- **Keep the interface minimal**: The larger the interface, the more work to maintain it. Ensure the number of functions and classes that are provided by the shared interface is relatively small. You can expand these using the layered approach, employing templates and inline functions (that are more amenable to changes) to fill out the details.
- **Encapsulate implementation data**: Changing data members in a class is a sure way to break binary compatibility and force end users to recompile. To avoid this, you can encapsulate implementation-specific data behind opaque objects (using a pimpl idiom), giving you room to change these internal details if the need arises. Many design patterns (e.g., from the Gang of Four book [2]) make use of this kind of abstraction.

With these points in mind, we can look at some more specific concerns that can lead to problems.

Handling memory across boundaries

One of the easiest ways to cause errors with (heap) allocated memory is to use a different allocator to free the data than the one used to allocate it. In modern C++, this should not be a problem; smart pointers and the allocator framework provided by the standard library should all but eliminate this problem. However, many libraries provide a C interface that you might have to propagate. In this case, C++ smart pointers will not immediately help to manage the data correctly.

Consider the C standard file IO system as an example. A `FILE` pointer created with `fopen` must be closed using the `fclose` function when you're finished. Passing a `FILE*` over an interface boundary is problematic because your client (the downstream application that uses your library) now does not know how to safely close the file and release the resources. (Of course, this is a very simple example.) Worse still, if the client application has a different version of `fclose`, then using their version of `fclose` might result in undefined behavior. A very simple way to handle this problem is to wrap the `FILE` in a `std::unique_ptr` with a custom deleter function. Here is how to achieve this:

```
#include <memory>
#include <cstdio>

struct FileDeleter {
    void operator()(FILE* f) noexcept {
        fclose(f);
    }
};

using FilePointer = std::unique_ptr<FILE, FileDeleter>;
```

Of course, the `FileDeleter` call operator should be defined in the corresponding `.cpp` file rather than inlined (to avoid the dual copy situation mentioned before). A similar effect can be accomplished with `std::shared_ptr`, which stores a type-erased deleter function in its control block allocated on the heap.

A similar technique can be used to handle deleting opaque types when encapsulating data if these appear outside a class. For instance, consider the following class definition:

```
class MyClass {
    // opaque data
    struct ImplementationData;

    std::unique_ptr<ImplementationData> data_;
```

```
    // methods etc...
};
```

At the moment, this will fail to compile outside of a scope where the definition of `MyClass::ImplementationData` appears. A simple fix for this is to declare a destructor in the class that is implemented (by `= default`) in the `.cpp` file. If this isn't possible, or if an opaque object doesn't appear in such a class definition, then the same technique as previously can be used to make sure the `std::unique_ptr` wrapper knows how to properly destroy the `ImplementationData` struct. (Defining the destructor is certainly easier, and much less intrusive, and is preferable in almost all cases.)

With a stable interface defined, we need to expose this to our downstream users (which may just be yourself). Traditionally, this is done using header files, but C++20 introduces an alternative mechanism for sharing symbols and definitions (and several other things) in modules, which are the topic of the next section.

Using C++ modules

Modules were introduced in C++20 as an alternative means of sharing declarations/definitions across multiple translation units; essentially, they are a partial replacement for header files. These are similar to how other programming languages, such as Rust, organize their code; entities are organized into modules (derived primarily from the file structure). Modules do not replace namespaces; you should continue to use these in addition to modules. An **interface module** is declared using an `export module` statement. In the following code snippet, we declare a new module named `computational_thinking` (in `module_example.cpp`). Entities that should be exported in the module must be prefixed with the `export` keyword; we include some examples here:

```
export module computational_thinking;

export namespace ct {
    // defined elsewhere
    void exported_fn(int a);
}

// Not exported
int non_exported_fn();

// defined elsewhere
export int another_exported_fn(int b);
```

```
// exported inline function
export inline int inline_fn(int c) {
    return non_exported_fn() * c;
}

// defined elsewhere
export struct MyStruct;

export template <typename T>
T template_fn(T e) { return e; }

export template <typename T>
class TemplateClass {
    T f;
public:
    T get_f() { return f; }
};
```

Note that the functions in the module that are not explicitly exported are still usable by the module, even in code external to the module. The difference, though, is that external code cannot reference these symbols by name. For instance, our inline function makes reference to the non-exported `non_exported_fn` function, but a consumer of this module would not be able to refer to `non_exported_fn` by name. We can implement the functions and classes that are declared in the export header in a separate **implementation module unit**, such as in `function_impls.cpp` here:

```
module;

// Include should appear in the global module fragment
#include <iostream>

// extend the module definition
module module_example;

// preferably, use this instead of include
// import <iostream>

void ct::exported_fn(int a) {
    std::cout << a << std::endl;
}
```

```
int another_exported_fn(int b) {
    std::cout << b << std::endl;
    return b;
}

struct MyStruct {
    int d;
};
```

Notice that the `include` directive appears above the declaration of the `module_example` module and after a bare `module;` declaration. This part of the file is called the **global module fragment**. The general guidance is that, if includes are necessary, they should appear within the global module fragment and not after the module declaration. We've included a standard header here as an example, although we could have imported this as a module directly using the `import <iostreams>;` statement (currently commented out). Currently, GCC (v14.2 at the time of writing) does not provide precompiled modules for the standard library, and these must be explicitly compiled before such an import statement can be used.

Also note that the C++ module semantics are also separate from the shared library import/export mechanics, and these will still be required in the module interface unit. It isn't exactly clear yet in the documentation how this should be achieved; on Windows, the requirement of using both `dllexport` and `dllimport` depending on context might present a problem here. In MSVC, it seems that one needs only to specify `dllexport`, and the compiler will take care of `dllimport` when consuming a module (see `https://stackoverflow.com/a/38078341/9225581`).

Once created, using modules is very easy. The module needs to be imported by name, just like for a header file, and then all the exported symbols will become available. Note that the module name is only used for the import and does not modify the names of the imported functions; namespaces are the mechanism for scoping symbols. Brief example code for using the module we just defined is shown here:

```
import computational_thinking;

int main() {
    MyStruct s { 2 }; // exported, but defined elsewhere
    auto r = another_exported_fn(s.d) // exported in the global namespace
    ct::exported_fn(r); // exported in a namespace
}
```

There is a lot more to C++ modules than we have covered here. These include **module fragments**, which are a mechanism for breaking up the definition of a module into smaller parts. These fragments can then be declared with `export import` in the main module export unit. This not only brings all the symbols exported from the fragment into the current module but also re-exports these symbols.

C++ modules are a great addition to the language, but writing this chapter made me feel that, at the moment at least, there are too many problems for them to be widely adopted. As of early 2025, compiler support is spotty at best, and that doesn't account for the many of us who are stuck using compilers where C++20 is not an option. There are still many difficulties with modules, such as the problem of shared library exports that are just not sufficiently explored yet. Until these kinds of issues are resolved, using modules is not going to be a portable and stable experience.

This concludes our discussion of C++ modules. In the next section, we'll see some practical tips on how to decompose a large project into smaller, more manageable parts to ease the burden of maintaining large projects and facilitate testing.

Separating components in the build system

Once a project reaches a certain size, it becomes rather difficult to manage as a single large project. One strategy for dealing with this is to separate the large project into small components, at least within the build system. However, this carries some risks, and it can be rather difficult to get right, particularly if the output of the large project is a shared library. One instance where these issues appear is in testing. Testing the internals of a shared library can be rather problematic, since these details might not be externally visible (exported). Sometimes these internals don't need to be tested in isolation, but if you do, pulling these into a small static library that is linked into the larger library and tested independently is one strategy. Understanding when and how one can separate parts into their own component and how to integrate them into the larger whole is crucial to getting this right.

The key to modularizing your projects is to understand dependencies. Ideally, modules should be standalone, without requiring other modules from the same larger project and certainly not from the shared library itself. If this is not possible, the concepts cannot, and should not, be separated. This is best illustrated by means of an example.

Suppose you're writing a library for solving differential equations numerically. (Don't worry, the mathematics here is not important.) There are numerous different numerical methods that can be employed for this, including Euler's method and the Runge-Kutta family of solvers. At a higher level, the user-facing interface needs a means of selecting the solver to use, but nothing more, defined in a shared library. The interface we use might look something like this:

```
#include <functional>
#include <span>
#include <vector>

namespace ct::ode {

enum class SolveMethod {
    Euler,
    RK4
    // other methods
};

class OdeSolution {
    std::vector<double> solution;
    std::vector<double> step_params;

// methods omitted
};


using ODEFunction = std::function<
    void(std::span<double>, double, std::span<const double>)>;

OdeSolution ode_solve(
    SolveMethod method,
    ODEFunction func,
    std::span<const double> initial_condition,
    double initial_param,
    double final_param,
    double step_size
);

} // namespace ct::ode
```

In this setup, the `ODEFunction` function evaluates on the second argument and places the return value in the first. This is called (at least) once for each step of the solving process. Inside the implementation of `ode_solve`, we set up the solution class (details omitted here) and then pass to another function, selected by the enumerator, to actually perform the solving process.

The signature of each of these functions must be the same (and not involve any of the definitions from the main library). Fortunately, this is quite reasonable since we can just pass the two vectors by reference that can be populated by the solver, which might look like this:

```
void solver_method(
    std::vector<double>& soluton,
    std::vector<double>& step_params,
    const ODEFunction& func,
    std::span<const double> initial_condition,
    double initial_param,
    double final_param,
    double step_size
);
```

This is the *internal* interface that is implemented for the different methods, such as Euler and RK4, mentioned in the enumeration in the source sample. None of the other details for how this works matter for the shared library that uses this, but as programmers, we need access to this in order to perform testing. To make this work, we can compile each solution method in a separate static library that has no external dependencies. The question now becomes how to achieve this. Let's start with the directory structure:

```
ctode
  | euler
    | CMakeLists.txt
    | euler.h
    | euler.cpp
    | test_euler.cpp
  | rk4
    | CMakeLists.txt
    | rk4.h
    | rk4.cpp
    | test_rk4.cpp
  | CMakeLists.txt
  | ctode.h
  | ctode.cpp
  | test_ctode.cpp
```

The two solver methods are segregated into their own directory with implementation, a set of tests, and their own `CMakeLists.txt`. The Euler solver component will contain the following:

```
add_library(ctode_euler STATIC euler.h euler.cpp)

set_target_properties(ctode_euler PROPERTIES
    POSITION_INDEPENDENT_CODE ON
)

if (ENABLE_TESTS)
    add_executable(test_ctode_euler test_euler.cpp)
    target_link_libraries(test_ctode_euler PRIVATE
        ctode_euler
        GTest::gtest_main
    )
endif()
```

The only odd line here is setting the properties on the `ctode_euler` target to build position-independent code. This sets `-fPIC` or equivalent during compilation, which is required if the code will eventually be linked into a shared library, as is the case with `ctode_euler` (see *Chapters 2* and *9* of [1]). Note that none of the functions declared in `euler.h` will be exported from the `ctode` library, which is declared in the higher-level `CMakeLists.txt`, which contains the following code:

```
if (ENABLE_TESTS)
    enable_testing()
    find_package(GTest CONFIG REQUIRED)
endif()
include(GenerateExportHeader)

# Import the two solver's that we've implemented
add_subdirectory(euler)
add_subdirectory(rk4)

add_library(ctode SHARED ctode.h ctode.cpp)
target_link_libraries(ctode PRIVATE ctode_euler ctode_rk4)

generate_export_header(ctode)
target_include_directories(ctode PRIVATE
    ${CMAKE_CURRENT_BINARY_DIR}
)
```

```
if (ENABLE_TESTS)
    add_executable(test_ctode test_ctode.cpp)
    target_link_libraries(test_ctode PRIVATE
        ctode GTest::gtest_main)
endif()
```

With this structure, the solver method functions are available internally (in `ctode.cpp`) for use when requested by the external user via the `ode_solve` function. This hides all of the implementation details from the user, but these are available for internal testing (in, for example, `test_ctode_euler.cpp`). This situation is very simple, and the separation of concerns is somewhat obvious. (Does this sound familiar? It should! Separating concerns is one of the four components of computational thinking.)

Sorting code like this is generally advisable even if the code is all part of a single target. One can use the `target_sources` CMake function to extend the list of source files associated with a target, even if these cannot be logically separated into a new target. This helps anyone reading your code (including *future you*) to find all the files associated with a particular piece of functionality more easily, reducing the cognitive overhead. It also allows for easier reuse of code.

Unfortunately, most situations are not as simple as this one. Let's consider a slightly different scenario where the solver methods are provided in the form of an abstract interface with a common base class. Now we have a common dependency between the implementation libraries that needs to be dealt with carefully. Sometimes it's possible to collect together these common dependencies in another target on which all the libraries can depend; the linker should take care of removing duplicates during the final linking step. For instance, in our example, we could declare a new `ctode_common` target containing the necessary base class, and link this target into all of the solver targets and the main `ctode` shared library target.

Summary

This chapter covered several challenges of modularizing code and making your code available to others (or possibly just yourself) to reuse in the future. In the first section, we talked about static and shared libraries, and some of the things that should be considered when building these, especially shared libraries. Next, we talked about C++ modules, which are conceptually a more efficient replacement for header files. However, compiler support is a little lacking, and there are many technical problems with these that don't have compelling answers right now. In the final section, we reviewed how to divide a large project into smaller parts using CMake to reduce the cognitive burden of understanding the library and make it easier to test the internal mechanics of your libraries.

The main point of this chapter is that designing and maintaining (re)usable code is its own challenge that needs to be thought through carefully. At a basic level, this involves designing interfaces that are flexible enough that they don't need to be changed frequently, yet simple enough that they can be used easily. At an intermediate level, it's about how one packages their code into libraries and the complications that may arise there. Finally, it's about how to divide your code into manageable chunks that are semi-independent of one another, and yet come together to make a cohesive whole. This chapter concludes the first part of the book, where we covered the theory and background for how to solve problems using C++. In the next chapter, we outline a larger project that will allow us to put our new skills to the test.

References

1. Levine, J.R. 2000. *Linkers and Loaders*. San Francisco: Morgan Kaufmann.
2. Gamma, E., Helm, R., Johnson, R., and Vlissides, J. 1994. *Design Patterns: Elements of Reusable Object-Oriented Software*. Boston: Addison-Wesley.

7

Outlining the Challenge

In this chapter, we introduce a large, central challenge that we will discuss over the next few chapters. The first part of this chapter outlines the challenge in the form of a brief from a hypothetical client and a discussion of the data they have provided. The remainder of the chapter is the first stage of solving this particular challenge, which at this stage involves identifying several smaller problems that make up the whole. The larger of these problems here makes up the content of *Chapters 8* through *12*.

In this chapter, you will see one approach to breaking down large challenges and identifying concerns that one might want to address within the process of solving. Some of these issues only make sense from a high-level perspective, and need to be considered up-front rather than after solving the intermediate problems; for instance, whether and how to incorporate multithreading support into the solution. It is always important to maintain an overview of the whole project to make sure the intermediate pieces fit together properly.

In this chapter, we're going to cover the following main topics:

- The challenge
- The major challenges
- Some smaller challenges
- Putting everything together
- Setting up the repository

Technical requirements

This chapter outlines the central challenge, which will be the focus of the next few chapters. There is not much code associated with this chapter, but we do include the Python scripts used to generate the data we use for this challenge. These are all contained in the `Chapter-07` folder of the GitHub repository for this book (`https://github.com/PacktPublishing/The-CPP-Programmers-Mindset`), along with a system of tests so you can test your own solutions.

The challenge

The challenge is presented here in the form of a brief, as if this were a problem provided by a client. The first part is a description of the problem and its context, followed by a description of the data.

The brief: The curious cases of the rubber duckies

All over the world, there are reports of mysterious rubber ducks appearing in odd places. These duckies appear quite harmless, politely floating along waterways and sitting atop public landmarks. By many accounts, they sit and politely listen to problems, which onlookers describe as somehow calming and even helpful. We want a tool that can identify the hot spots.

The data we have gathered comes from various sources. Some are emails to our information address, and some have been gathered using a web form that provides a little more structure. The rest of the data is gathered from an app and is downloaded in JSON format from the public API. You will have to find a way to combine all of these sources in your analysis.

What we need is a command-line tool that takes a set files (`.txt`, `.csv`, or `.json`) and produces a set of approximate coordinates (printed back to the terminal) for the locations where the rubber ducks are congregating around the world.

The data

The client sent a number of sample data files along with the brief. It's always a good idea, when it is possible, to look at the data and figure out what you're working with. The client already mentioned that the data comes in three different formats (plain text, comma-separated values, and JavaScript object notation), and it's good to know what the differences are between the formats. In the brief, the client makes it sound like the majority of the information was reported using a mobile app, and the responses are/have been gathered from an API endpoint in JSON format. These results probably have the most structure – it also sounds like the other methods are fillers while they commission the app. The email data sounds like it has the least structure, so it might be the most problematic for us. Let's have a look at the first JSON entry.

```
{
    "latitude": 51.5074,
    "longitude": -0.1278,
    "date": "2024-09-10",
    "description": "A curious rubber ducky sighted in London."
}
```

There are three crucial pieces of information here. The longitude and latitude are the most important, since these tell us where on the globe the sighting took place. The date is also important, though not directly. Trends can change over time, and having a date allows one to localize these trends to specific periods. The client didn't ask about this, but that doesn't mean they're not interested. The description field is largely redundant, and might well be empty on many of these JSON reports. (App users will often only fill out the required fields, particularly if they make a lot of reports.) Next, let's have a look at the CSV data.

```
2024-09-10, 51.5074, -0.1278, A mysterious rubber ducky was seen floating
in London.
```

The key components are the same here: date, latitude, longitude, and description. Notice that they have not provided the column headings. This might be a problem, but we can infer the order because we know the coordinates of London. Given the similarity between the JSON record and the CSV record, we might wonder whether these two reports are of the same rubber duck. At the moment, we don't know how widespread these sightings are. We might want to account for the fact that there might be multiple records of the same sighting. Finally, let's look at the unstructured email reports.

```
June 10 2024: This morning I saw a bright yellow rubber duck was spotted
cruising leisurely on the Thames River in London (51 30' 26''N, 7' 39''W).
It had a tiny blue scarf around its neck.
```

As expected, these responses have much less structure, but the vital information is obviously still here. (They even include the coordinates in degrees, minutes, and seconds.) We shouldn't assume that all the records are as complete as this. Some might omit the data, or give a relative date (e.g., yesterday, last Tuesday), and some might not include the location. In the latter case, there really isn't anything we can do except perhaps log that we can't find a date.

This kind of initial exploration of the data can really help you to devise a plan for how to deal with the problem as a whole. Now that we're done with this, we can start to formulate a plan, starting with identifying the major challenges.

The major challenges

This problem has three obvious substantial challenges.

- How do we read in the numerous forms of data?
- How do we construct, from the data that we have read, a coherent dataset to work with?
- How do we find the various epicenters of rubber duck activity that the client asked for?

There is also a final problem: how this data is returned to the user. The client said this should be printed back to the terminal, but in what form? They didn't specify exactly how this should happen. Given that they asked for a command-line utility, it is quite reasonable to follow the Unix philosophy and expect that our output is to be consumed by some other tool. Ideally, we could ask the client for clarity. Sometimes the problem is more than just the initial briefing, and sometimes (perhaps frustratingly) the brief will change over time.

Out of the three major problems, there is a common thread among all of these: how do we represent the data internally? We actually need to make this decision quite early, because this will change the way we read the files and how we pass data from one stage to the next. Since we've only been asked about the physical locations, a simple `struct` containing the longitude and latitude in decimal format might be sufficient, such as here.

```
struct Coordinates {
    float latitude;
    float longitude;
};
```

Given our earlier discussion about trends evolving over time, we might want to include date information too. This presents a new problem of how to present the date. Common formats use seconds from a common epoch (e.g., Unix time), or perhaps some other timescale. However, given that our task is to process the spatial data only, we should prioritize the performance of this task alone. (This might be another thing to take back to the client for clarity.) We also need to think about the kind of algorithm that we're going to use to locate the hot spots of duck activity, since this, too, might place requirements on the way we store data. For instance, it might be better to follow the *struct of arrays* philosophy and store the longitude and latitude coordinates separately.

```
struct CoordinateArray {
    std::vector<float> latitudes;
    std::vector<float> longitudes;
};
```

Given that we're using floats (more on that in a moment), and the two coordinates are likely to be used together (to compute distances between points, for instance), we probably don't need to separate these into different arrays; indeed, this might be bad for performance. However, if we had decided to include other metadata, this might not be the case. (In fact, we will do this so as not to throw away the additional metadata in the preprocessing step.) Our common data structure is thus going to be something like this.

```
struct RubberDuckyData {
    std::vector<Coordinates> coordinates;
    std::vector<std::chrono::year_month_day> dates;
    std::vector<std::string> descriptions;
};
```

We also need to talk about our decision to use `float` to represent our data. Here, the question is about accuracy. The data that we have is very coarse; we have approximate locations at a city level. Nothing that we can produce from this will result in greater accuracy than that afforded by the data. The advantage of using `float` rather than `double` is the effective doubling of throughput (a `float` is half the size of a `double`). This means we can process the data faster and thus produce results faster for our client. This has some implications, though. Internal calculations of distances will be less accurate, and this could cause problems in the convergence of our clustering. However, given the scale of the differences we expect between cities of the world, this is less likely to be something to worry about. For the purposes of this book, we're going to assume that `float` has sufficient accuracy, but you will need to check that this is really the case in your own work.

Reading the data

Reading the data is our entry point problem. We can't do anything until we have ingested all of the data from the various files. The main challenge here comes from the fact that the data comes in different formats, and we will need a set of file readers with the same interface, combined with a simple method for dispatching to the correct reader for the given file type. The client already told us the different file extensions that are used for each type of data: plain text responses are in `.txt` files, tabulated responses in CSV format have the `.csv` extension, and JSON-formatted data has the `.json` file extension.

From a technical point of view, reading CSV and JSON data is well-trodden ground, and there are many libraries out there for dealing with these kinds of data (for instance, `https://rapidjson.org/` and `https://simdjson.org/` for JSON, and `https://github.com/p-ranav/csv2` or `https://github.com/d99kris/rapidcsv` for CSV). Ideally, whenever the opportunity arises, one should use well-tested library code rather than writing your own solutions. The problem with this is that libraries mean dependencies. C++ header-only libraries are ideal since they don't require any linking.

You might wonder, if CSV and JSON are so well understood, what is the challenge here? The answer is the *interface*. The objective is to read all the data from the different formats into a common data structure. This means that, for each file, one must dispatch to some kind of handler to read the relevant data and perform the conversion into our agreed data format. We will dive into the details of designing and constructing these interfaces in *Chapter 9*.

The free-text responses certainly pose the greatest challenge, since we will have to parse these ourselves, undoubtedly making use of regular expressions or similar to extract the relevant parts of the text to construct the data. This is a more difficult challenge, so we will tackle this separately in *Chapter 10*. This way, we will have already solved all the interface design problems and can focus on the task at hand.

Clustering the data

The central challenge in this whole exercise is to reduce the (presumably) large set of coordinates down to a relatively small number of "hot spots," where the observations are clustered. The keyword here is **clustered**, which narrows the kind of algorithm we're looking for to clustering algorithms. We're going to use a ***k*-means clustering** algorithm (see [1]) for this task. It won't always be this obvious what the best choice of algorithm is, or even what the major problem is.

In some cases, the major problem will involve one or more "standard" problems (such as a clustering of data) that you must sew together into a coherent pipeline. There will be instances where you, as the problem solver, will need to devise new algorithms to meet the requirements of the problem. It's difficult to anticipate the nuances that determine exactly what algorithm should be used until one explores the problem more deeply. However, it is always best to start with standard, well-known algorithms, especially those that have existing high-quality library implementations, before moving into bespoke technology. In this book, we will create our own implementation of a standard algorithm, which can be found in *Chapter 11*.

Besides the big challenges outlined here, there are several smaller challenges that are involved. These are outlined in the next section.

Some smaller challenges

We've already identified one small problem that we will have to solve before we can write our file readers: extracting the location data from the free-form text sightings. This might not always be possible – for instance, the coordinates might not be present in the text at all.

Formatting the results

One problem that needs a good discussion is how we format the results to be returned to the client. The only instruction given here is that it should print the results to the terminal, and, as we've already mentioned, we can infer that they might want to take this as input to another program. Thus, a sensible strategy here is to return a simple table of latitude and longitude, illustrated here.

```
51.5074    -0.1278
19.432608  -99.133209
19.076090  72.877426
```

(The first coordinate here is London, which we have already seen. The latter are Mexico City and Mumbai, which are surprisingly close in latitude!) There are some other options here. We could return the data in JSON format or some other object notation. We could include other metadata alongside, such as the number of observations that are grouped into each cluster, or map the coordinates to cities and present these alongside.

Allowing for expandability

Before we commit to a particular path and start to write code, we should consider the possibility that we might have to change our approach based on new information from the client, or because something doesn't work as intended. One example of this is keeping the additional metadata (date and description) instead of ignoring this at the data ingestion stage. We could also build out a little infrastructure within the remaining sections that allows us to make use of this data in the analysis or simply aggregate it alongside the results. We've already looked at the data, and noted that there is not a lot of additional data to be found.

One option here is to provide a base (shared) library that contains all the logic, and a small, lightweight frontend that exercises the relevant functionality within the shared library. (This is a model employed by cURL, for instance.) This allows other developers to add new functionality without modifying the base library by implementing new interfaces (abstract classes in this instance) that can then be used in the larger workflows. This is somewhat overkill for a simple project like this.

Multithreading and computation environment

The clustering task in this project will be computationally intensive. As such, it might be wise at this stage to think about introducing multithreading to ease the computation bottleneck and speed up the process. When using multithreading, it is wise to provide some mechanisms for controlling the number of threads used. The default for threading packages is to use all CPU cores, which is quite reasonable on a laptop or desktop where there are no other jobs running, but is probably not optimal for use on a server with hundreds of CPU cores. (Using too many cores might even hurt performance because of the cost of starting so many threads.)

Most threading packages provide such a mechanism, at least internally. For instance, the number of OpenMP threads can be controlled with the `OMP_NUM_THREADS` environment variable, although this requires the end user to be aware that this is the threading model that is employed and that this is an option. It is wise to provide a different option, such as a command-line flag (`-j` is common on Unix). At the very least, the options should be made obvious via the command-line interface – don't count on users reading the long-form documentation.

Error handling

We will need a mechanism for handling errors gracefully without terminating the program early because we couldn't find coordinates inside a free-form text response. The C++ exception framework is good for libraries, but the default behavior is to do exactly this, printing debug information to the terminal. This is not ideal behavior for a command-line application. Instead, we will need to make sure we catch any exceptions and either deal with them or log error messages and gracefully terminate the program, setting the error code to something non-zero. We need to give some high-level consideration to what our strategy will be for handling errors throughout the application.

Caching preprocessed data

Reading and preprocessing data into a usable form can be an expensive operation. If this utility is to be run more than once, it might be sensible to cache data that has already been preprocessed in some kind of binary form that we can load quickly instead of repeating the processing step. This can be rather tricky to get right. A robust means of handling this data will inevitably involve hashing and an efficient binary format; flat buffers are a good option: `https://flatbuffers.dev/`

In more complex problems, one might also cache intermediate values. This has several functions. One is to speed up re-computation with the same values. Another is to introduce some redundancy so that, if the process crashes or is terminated for some reason, restarting does not force the program to start again from scratch. Finally, the same mechanism can be used to distribute work to a number of nodes if it is too large to be performed on a single machine.

This challenge is not so complex that this is a concern, and the client did not indicate that they intend to run this many times with the same inputs.

This concludes the discussion of some of the minor challenges associated with this problem. Next, we will see how each of these challenges can be put together to construct a single cohesive solution to the client's brief.

Putting everything together

It is important to keep one eye on the bigger picture when solving problems. It can be easy to get stuck into the details and forget that the pieces must fit together. We will go back over each of the components and construct the final solution in *Chapter 12* and reflect on the whole process. (Reflecting on the problems that you have solved is an important part of the learning process.) The general flow of the corresponding internal components that we need to develop over the next few chapters is shown in *Figure 7.1*. Understanding the flow of the final program allows us to structure our efforts and how we might want to group the work into manageable packets.

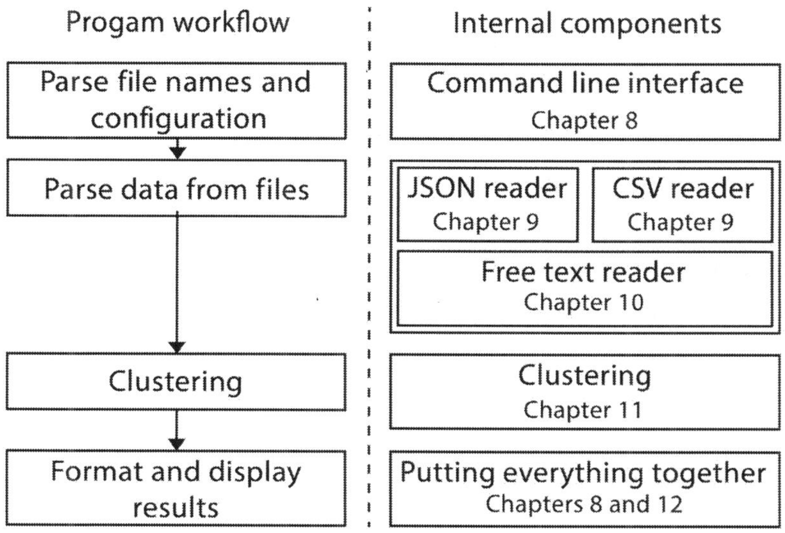

Figure 7.1: The program workflow and the corresponding components that must be developed to solve the client's brief

One thing we need to think about before we start is what the rough process of the application will be. A good way to do this is to think about what the `main` function will look like. For instance, the `main` function might have the following parts.

```
int main(int argc, char** argv) {

    // get all the arguments and configure the execution
    auto files = parse_args_and_environment(argc, argv);

    // Read the files into usable format
    auto data = parse_data_files(files);

    auto clusters = do_clustering(data);

    present_results(clusters, data);

    return 0;
}
```

Filling in these functions will be the topic of the following chapters. In *Chapter 8*, we discuss parsing arguments, setting up the computation environment, and presenting the results. In *Chapter 9* and *Chapter 10*, we deal with reading and preprocessing the data. In *Chapter 11*, we write the clustering step. Finally, we put everything together and reflect on our work in *Chapter 12*.

Setting up the repository

All that remains is to set up the repository for this particular project. We'll follow some of the points we followed in the previous chapter about modularizing the project. We might consider splitting out the file reading infrastructure into a separate library so it can be extended with optional shared libraries. However, given that the client has not mentioned any other file types, this is not really necessary. (On the contrary, it looks as if they have run through the natural progression of formats and there is not likely to be another.) However, we should still separate out the components so we can test them independently of one another. The final structure of the repository will thus look something like this.

```
rubber_duckies
  | clustering
    | CMakeLists.txt
    | clustering.h
```

```
      | clustering.cpp
      | test_clustering.cpp
    | readers
      | CMakeLists.txt
      | file_reader.h
      | file_reader.cpp
      | test_file_reader.cpp
    | CMakeLists.txt
    | main.cpp
```

Over the next few chapters, we will populate this repository until it contains a complete implementation of our solution. With all this done, let's summarize what we have discussed here.

Summary

This chapter introduced the main challenge that we will work on over the following five chapters. The challenge is to produce a command-line application that reads data from files of various formats and performs a clustering operation, and then prints the results to the terminal. We have identified three big challenges: reading the data from the different file formats, homogenizing the data, and performing the clustering. We also identified several smaller challenges, including formatting the results and setting up the computation environment.

This chapter serves as the first pass of decomposing the overall challenge into a number of smaller challenges and, in at least one case, breaking these smaller challenges down further. This is a great start for solving the problem. Of course, each of these sub-challenges is a fair challenge in its own right. Indeed, we have chosen these challenges carefully to address specific aspects of the computational thinking framework. In the next chapter, we build out the command-line interface for our eventual solution and discuss the configuration options that we might want to add to control the execution.

References

1. James, G., Witten, D., Hastie, T., and Tibshirani, R. 2013. *An Introduction to Statistical Learning: with Applications in R*. New York: Springer.

Subscribe to Deep Engineering

8

Building a Simple Command-Line Interface

Our first task is to set up a command-line interface for the application that provides our solution to the challenge set out in *Chapter 7*. This will be the main way the user interacts with the application and contains most of the feedback mechanisms that they can use to understand what our program is doing, such as logging. A good interface is expressive but minimal and well defined; the interface should give good feedback if the user provides a bad argument and provide ample usage information. This chapter shows how we set up the interface, including the command-line parser, and some ancillary functionality, such as logging and error handling, at a high level. This is a very minimal interface, but leaves open the possibility for easy expansion later.

At the very least, this interface needs to parse the command-line arguments to obtain the list of files that should be processed. However, there are a few other things we want to control too. The threading environment, logging, error handling, and signal handling are all other things we need to set up ready for later challenges. Quick-reference usage information (usually provided by passing the `-h` or `--help` option) is essential for users, including you as the author, to remember what options are available and what arguments are expected. Setting up options for all of these is relatively simple if one uses a framework such as the Boost program options library.

In this chapter, we will cover the following basic topics:

- Setting up program options
- Setting up logging
- Controlling the threading environment
- Error handling and signals
- Formatting for the terminal

Technical requirements

This chapter shows the first stage of developing our rubber duckies application and involves some additional libraries. In particular, you will need to install the Boost program options and `spdlog` libraries. These can be obtained from a package repository on Linux (`apt`, `yum`, etc.), Homebrew on macOS, or via a package manager such as `vcpkg` on any system. (You will need to follow the instructions at `https://vcpkg.io` on setting the CMake toolchain file and installing the libraries in the latter case.) We do provide a `vcpkg` manifest file for those who want to use this mechanism for installing dependencies.

The code for this chapter can be found in the `Chapter-08` folder in the repository for this book on GitHub: `https://github.com/PacktPublishing/The-CPP-Programmers-Mindset`.

Setting up program options

The first task we need to address is setting up the command-line interface for the program. At the very least, this must be able to parse the names of one or more files to process to pass to the inner workings of the program that we will write later. However, there are several other things we want to add here, such as turning on verbose logging, controlling the threading environment, and controlling the format of the output. We also want our command-line interface to produce usage information when the arguments are malformed or when the standard `-h` or `--help` option is passed.

There are a few libraries that we could use to create such an interface quickly and easily, including Abseil's program options library, but we're going to use Boost program options because it is very standard and easy to use. The library can be installed in many different ways and, depending on your operating system, you might opt for a different option. We're just going to assume that it is installed on the developer's system somewhere that can be found by CMake. With this in mind, we can write our first pass of `CMakeLists.txt` containing the following:

```
project(curious_rubber_duckies)

find_package(OpenMP REQUIRED COMPONENTS CXX)
find_package(Boost CONFIG REQUIRED COMPONENTS program_options)
find_package(spdlog CONFIG REQUIRED)

add_executable(duckies main.cpp)

target_link_libraries(rubber_duckies PRIVATE
    Boost::program_options
```

```
    OpenMP::OpenMP_CXX
    spdlog::spdlog
)
```

This adds one executable target, called `duckies`, that will be our main executable. In the next few chapters, we will expand this basic CMake file with additional targets that implement the various components of the larger application, but this is our starting point. As discussed, we've used the `find_package` function in CMake to find the Boost program options library, but we've also found the OpenMP runtime, which we will need in order to set up the threading environment. The other package we import here is `spdlog`, which is a lightweight logging library. The `duckies` executable has one source file, called `main.cpp`, which will contain our `main` function and the other functions needed for parsing arguments; we will populate this as we proceed through the chapter.

In *Chapter 7*, we gave an example of what our main function might look like. This had four function calls. The first parses the arguments and environment and returns a container of files to parse. The next parses the data from each of the files and returns an array of data. Next comes the clustering, returning an array of cluster points, and finally a function that presents the results to the user. This describes quite well the functional part of the application, but it ignores some of the other task setup steps that we want to perform before we start the analysis. Moreover, it doesn't allow us to use command-line arguments to customize the output format. For this reason, we're going to change our main function slightly.

Our revised `main` function itself will be very simple, delegating all of the actual work to several helper functions. This will help us keep the different parts of the setup, execution, reporting, and cleanup phases of the running time separate for easy maintenance. Having simple separation of concerns like this makes a big difference when you come to add functionality or change the way certain options are parsed. For the time being, we will have four stages in the execution. The first is reading in the arguments, environment variables, and configuration files into a single set of values to be passed to other components. The second is setting up the logging and reporting. The third component sets up the computation (threading) environment that will be used in the remainder of the program. The final component runs the function that we will write in later chapters to obtain and print the results. With this in mind, our basic skeleton application looks like this:

```
#include <filesystem>
#include <string>
#include <vector>

#include <boost/program_options.hpp>
#include <spdlog/spdlog.h>
```

```
#include <spdlog/sinks/stdout_sinks.h>
#include <omp.h>

// headers for our logic
#include "clustering/clustering.h"
#include "readers/file_reader.h"

// This is a huge time saver
namespace po = boost::program_options;
using namespace duckies;

static void setup_signals();
static po::variables_map parse_config(int argc, const char *const *argv);
static void setup_logging(const po::variables_map& args);
static void setup_threading(const po::variables_map& args);
static void run_and_report(const po::variables_map& args);

int main(int argc, char * argv[]) {
    setup_signals();

    const auto args = parse_config(argc, argv);

    setup_logging(args);
    setup_threading(args);

    run_and_report(args);

    return EXIT_SUCCESS;
}
```

In the remainder of this section and the next, we focus mostly on the `parse_config` function. Our first task is to write the command-line parser. To make this part easier, we create some static variables that hold the strings that will be printed when the version is requested and the help or usage information. Omitting the longer strings, these are defined as follows:

```
static const char version_string[] = "duckies Version 1.0.0\n";
static const char program_synopsis_string[] =
    "duckies [options] file1 file2 ... \n";
static const char program_usage_string[] = /* omitted */;
```

The first step of setting up a command-line parser using the Boost program options library is to define an `options` description object. Then we have to add the individual options that the parser should look for in the array of program arguments passed via `argv` to the main function. We have four options that we want to define. First, we want to define the standard `-h` or `--help` and `--version` options, which print information about the executable itself. The next option is a flag to change the verbosity level, which is usually given the short `-v` flag and the long `--verbose` flag. The final option sets the maximum number of threads that can be used in the computation. Following the `make` program, we will use `-j` and `--jobs` for this option. In addition to the four options, we also want to accept any number of filenames as positional arguments. To accomplish this, we need to add the following lines to the body of the `parse_config` function:

```
using PathVec = std::vector<std::filesystem::path>;

po::options_description options { "Options" };
options.add_options()
    ("help,h", po::bool_switch(), "produce_help_message")
    ("version", po::bool_switch(), "print the version and exit")
    ("verbose,v", po::bool_switch(),
     "print logging information to the terminal")
    ("jobs,j", po::value<int>(),
     "set the maximum number of threads to use")
    ("paths", po::value<PathVec>(), "paths to process");

po::positional_options_description positional;
positional.add("paths", unlimited_arguments);
```

This groups all the options together and, perhaps unsatisfactorily, all of the options are presented together, including the positional `paths` argument. We could break this into separate groups to fix this, but this would add significant complication to the code. Now the job is to take the options description and then actually do the work of parsing the options and positional arguments into a `map` object that can be used elsewhere. The code, as follows, is placed next in the `parse_config` function:

```
po::variables_map cli_args;
try {
    // parse the command line arguments
    po::command_line_parser parser(argc, argv);
    parser.options(options);
```

```
    parser.positional(positional);
    po::store(parser.run(), cli_args);

    // parse environment variables
    po::store(po::parse_environment(options, "DUCKIES_"), cli_args);

    po::notify(cli_args);
} catch (const std::exception &exc) {
    std::cerr << exc.what() << "\n\n"
              << program_synopsis_string << options << '\n';
    std::exit(EXIT_FAILURE);
}
```

The command-line parser object is provided the descriptions of the options and positional arguments before storing the results of running the parser in the `cli_args` variable map. The `parser.run()` method call can throw exceptions if the parser encounters a problem, such as an unrecognized option, so we need to wrap at least this function inside a `try-catch` block. On failure, we just print out the error message for the exception and then the short usage of the program and exit.

The Boost program options library can also inspect environment variables to fill out the expected options. We've added this to show how easy reading the environment can be. The second argument to this function sets a prefix for the environment variables to avoid conflicts with other applications. Here, Boost will check for variables such as `DUCKIES_VERBOSE` in the environment and use these to set the options, if these are not already set at the command line. We could have coded this ourselves using the `std::getenv` function, but it is certainly more convenient to allow the program options library to do this work for us. (Don't reinvent the wheel!)

Once parsing arguments is complete, we move on to other aspects of the program. However, two of the options should cause the program to exit early. The `--help` (or `-h` for short) option should print the (extended) usage information and exit, and the `--version` option should print the version string and then exit. In addition to these successful invocations, we can also check whether the user has provided any files to process, and exit early if none have been provided. This is achieved with the following chain of conditionals:

```
if (cli_args["version"].as<bool>()) {
    std::cerr << version_string;
    std::exit(EXIT_SUCCESS);
}
```

```
if (cli_args["help"].as<bool>()) {
    std::cerr << program_synopsis_string
              << program_usage_string
              << options
              << '\n';
    std::exit(EXIT_SUCCESS);
}

if (cli_args["paths"].empty()) {
    std::cerr << program_synopsis_string << options << '\n';
    std::exit(EXIT_FAILURE);
}
```

The only remaining task for the `parse_config` function is to simply return the `cli_args` variables map for use in the remaining components of the application. (We won't show the code for this here.) The next task is to set up the logging functionality, which is done in the next section.

Setting up logging

Logging is important for us to see what a program is doing during execution. There are several options for when, how, and where to log the information about what your program is doing, but generally, one either logs directly to the console (as we will do here) or logs to a file. Some operating systems, such as Linux, also provide a system logging facility, but since this is not universal, we won't use that here. Most logging frameworks provide filters based on severity to decide which messages actually make it to the log. High-severity messages such as errors and warnings are generally allowed through to the log in all but the most conservative settings, while general information, debug information, and very fine-grained trace information are usually filtered out.

As shown in the `CMakeLists.txt` file and in the includes listed in the previous section, we're using the `spdlog` library to implement logging in the `duckies` program. This is a header-only library that is very easy to use, which makes it perfect for our purposes. There are two steps to setting up the logging. The first is creating the logger sink object, which in our case simply writes to `stderr`, and then setting the filter level. Our default level will only print out warnings and errors, but setting the verbose flag will relax this condition to also allow general information. Setting up the logger is fairly straightforward with the following code inserted into the `setup_logging` function:

```
auto console_logger = spdlog::stderr_color_mt("console");
console_logger->set_pattern("[%Y-%m-%d %T] [%L] %v");
spdlog::set_default_logger(console_logger);
```

Here we construct a `std::shared_ptr` to a `stderr` logger object, and we immediately set the pattern for the actual log items. This format string prints the date (in ISO 8601 YYYY-MM-DD format) and the time, followed by the short one-letter indication of the logging level (`D` for debug, `I` for info, `W` for warning, etc.), followed by the actual message. Finally, we set this to be the default logger for `spdlog`. Next, we need to set the logging level to use in the remainder of the program. The `args` argument passed in contains the `verbose` setting we took from the command line or environment. If this is true, we want to set the logging level to `info`, as described previously, and otherwise set the logging level to the default `warn` level. This is achieved as follows:

```
console_logger->set_level(spdlog::level::warn);
if (args["verbose"].as<bool>()) {
    console_logger->set_level(spdlog::level::info);
}

spdlog::info("Fininshed setting up logger");
```

We've added a line that logs at the info level that setting up the logger is complete. This line will be printed to the console (via the logger) if the verbose option is set, but otherwise will not be shown. The real purpose of this line is it show how we can use the logger to emit information about what our program is doing. `spdlog` provides several convenience functions for writing to the default logger at various severity levels. We can also use the `spdlog::warn` function to emit a warning when something isn't quite right, such as if we provide a file in an unexpected format or if the file doesn't exist, or `spdlog::error` if something is very wrong. More on this later.

With the logger set up, the next job is to set up the threading environment, which is done in the next section.

Controlling the threading environment

Since we're using OpenMP for our multithreading support, setting up the threading environment is very easy. All we need to do is take the number of threads specified by command-line arguments or from environment variables and call `omp_set_num_threads` to set the number of threads to use in subsequent parallel blocks. If you're using other threading libraries, such as **Intel Thread Building Blocks** (**TBB**) or **Apple Grand Central Dispatch**, or some bespoke implementation, this might involve setting up the thread pool and configuring the settings just like here. In our case, the only code that is needed is as follows, which is the body of the `setup_threading` function:

```
auto num_threads = omp_get_max_threads();

if (args.count("jobs")) {
```

```
        auto requested_threads = args["jobs"].as<int>();
        num_threads = std::min(num_threads, requested_threads);
    } else {
        // set a very conservative default
        num_threads = 2;
    }

    omp_set_num_threads(num_threads);

    spdlog::info("We will use {} threads", num_threads);
```

This is not a large part of this example, but it is important. Leaving the number of threads uncontrolled might lead to the application starting too many threads, resulting in other resource contention or contention with other processes, particularly if one is running the application on a large-scale compute machine with many hundreds of cores. (Top-of-the-line server processors can have more than 200 cores, and with 2 sockets per server, this might lead to OpenMP trying to use more than 400 threads by default.)

By default, OpenMP will use a number of environment variables to initialize its internal variables, such as the number of threads to use in parallel blocks. The variable that sets the number of threads is `OMP_NUM_THREADS`. This number will essentially be ignored here because we set our own default. Generally, we shouldn't rely on these kinds of mechanisms to control the internal parameters of the program. There are two reasons for this. The first is that one might have to change the mechanism that powers the multithreading, and second, environment variables are not as explicit (and therefore somehow less reliably used) than command-line arguments.

In the next section, we discuss our strategy for handling errors in the deeper parts of the code and how to handle external input via signals.

Error handling and signals

There are two kinds of errors we need to deal with. The first kind are expected errors, such as files not being found or of an unrecognized format, and unexpected errors, where some operation lower down catastrophically fails for some unknown reason. We might also call these recoverable and unrecoverable errors, respectively. In both cases, we will use the logging framework to first report the error and, if necessary, terminate the application using `std::exit` as we did before. Ideally, we will report recoverable errors that happen lower down also using the `spdlog` functions, and only use the exception mechanism for unrecoverable errors.

When we're writing the code for the other parts of this challenge, we can be careful to catch errors that are thrown in any library functions, where it is appropriate to do so. (Remember, we want errors that are unrecoverable to propagate outward and only be caught at the last level.) However, this still leaves us with the challenge of how to handle errors at the outermost level. Clearly, we need to wrap our actual computation in a `try-catch` block. This is very standard, but here, there is a nice technique we can employ to make this a little cleaner. This starts by defining a template function that takes a function-like object by universal reference and executes this within a `try-catch` block. The `catch` block can then handle the error and gracefully exit. The definition is as follows:

```
template <typename F>
void handle_errors(F&& func) noexcept {
    try {
        func();
    } catch (const std::exception& exc) {
        spdlog::critical(exc.what());
        std::exit(EXIT_FAILURE);
    }
}
```

Note that we've marked this function as `noexcept`. This is an indication to the reader that this function completely handles the exception state, and the exception itself does not escape. This can be easily adapted to handle multiple different types of errors in different ways (either by additional `catch` branches or by a map keyed by runtime type information). It is important, though, that the handler code does not throw itself, as is required by the C++ standard. We can use this function in several different ways. The most obvious way is to use it to wrap a lambda function that captures its environment by reference:

```
handle_errors([&] {
    auto data = read_files(args);
    // ...
});
```

This approach makes it very easy to use and means we don't have to repeat lots of boilerplate error-handling code wherever necessary. Moreover, this can be used with any function (that doesn't accept arguments, although this is easily fixed) and not just lambda functions. Using lambda functions is very convenient because of their effortless ability to capture the environment.

Signals

Signals are a means for the operating system, or some other process, to interrupt or otherwise communicate with an application while running. These are not uniformly supported across different platforms; Unix-based operating systems have far greater signal support than Windows. There are a number of signals that are prescribed by the C/C++ standard, including abort (`SIGABT`), terminate (`SIGTERM`), segmentation fault (`SIGSEGV`), floating-point exceptions (`SIGFPE`), and interrupt (`SIGINT`). One should not ordinarily interfere with these signals. Since this book aims to be as portable as possible, and since other signals are not available elsewhere, we will implement a very basic signal handler. Note that this really isn't necessary to make a perfectly functional program, but it is a nice quality-of-life feature for eventual users.

The C/C++ standard provides the `signal` function (in `<csignal>`), which can be used to set a handler function for a specific signal number. This handler function is a function pointer with the `void (*)(int)` signature that is called whenever the application receives the signal specified, with this signal number passed as the argument to the handler. Obviously, there are some severe restrictions on what can be done inside a signal handler. Most library functions are not safe to use, except functions such as `std::exit`, and nothing that requires allocations is signal-safe. More generally, a signal might be sent multiple times (envisage a panicked user spamming *Ctrl + C* to send `SIGINT` to an application started with the wrong arguments). Signal handler writers should be mindful of this.

A common use that one might see in long-running applications such as web servers is the ability to interrupt with graceful shutdowns. This is where the first instance of `SIGINT` tells the program to exit, but doesn't force it to do so. This allows the program to finish processing pending requests and perform its usual cleanup operations before exiting. If the user wishes to exit immediately, they can send a second `SIGINT` to kill the application. This can be accomplished using something like the following:

```
static std::atomic_int signal_count = 0;

extern "C"
void sigint_handler(int signum) {
    auto current = signal_count.fetch_add(1);
    if (current > 0) {
        std::exit(1);
    }
}
```

```
bool check_interrupts() noexcept {
    auto interrupt = signal_count.load() > 0;
    if (interrupt) {
        std::cerr << "Received Ctrl-C event, terminating gracefully\n"
                  << "Press Ctrl-C again to exit immediately"
                  << std::endl;
    }
    return interrupt;
}
```

Notice that the signal handler itself is very simple. The temptation might be to put the print to `std::cerr` inside the signal handler itself, but this is unsafe because `operator<<` is not reentrant. Moreover, printing to the terminal is a fairly expensive operation that is best kept out of the signal handler itself.

To use this code, one can insert the `check_interrupts` in the body or condition of the main loop to break early (perhaps even at multiple places in the loop) so that if a break happens, one can leave the remaining processing (if it can be safely ignored) and proceed to clean up the application state before exiting. For instance, here is a basic demonstration of how it can be used in general:

```
int main() {
    std::signal(SIGINT, &sigint_handler);

    // main loop
    while (!check_interrupts()) {
        // first bit of processing
        if (check_interrupts()) { break; }
        // more processing ...
    }
    // cleanup
}
```

In our case, we will sprinkle the use of `check_interrupts` throughout our `run_and_report` function to exit early. Note that we won't be able to use this inside our computation routines themselves because of the way we have structured our application, but our application won't be so long-running and this won't be much of a hindrance. All that remains is to populate the `setup_signals` function, which will register the signal handler at the start of the application. This function just calls `std::signal`, as follows:

```
void setup_signals() {
    std::signal(SIGINT, &sigint_handler);
}
```

Unix provides a more sophisticated signal-handling system to better match the greater variety of signals available and the greater flexibility of the signal system exposed there. A good resource to get started is the signal man page, `signal(7)`, and the pages linked therein.

Now that we have set up error handling and signals, we can start to think about how we want to format the results after the computation is finished. This is the content of the next, and final, section.

Formatting results for the terminal

Formatting results is a tricky topic, and there are many different ways to approach it. One thing we want to be particularly sensitive to is the Unix philosophy of assuming that the output of our application will be immediately consumed by another (such as `grep` or `sort` or similar), and as such, we should be sure that our output is predictable and machine-readable. On the other hand, we also want our output to be human-readable if it is just printed to the terminal or written to a file. We may even want to change the behavior slightly depending on whether the output is actually a terminal or a file or another program (but we won't do this here). In all of this, we want to keep the actual code relatively simple.

The most flexible approach, which would be necessary if we wanted to support a variety of output formats, would be to provide an abstract interface for printing results. This would allow us to provide several implementations that we could choose from based on our configuration. However, this pattern is more or less the reverse of the mechanism we will discuss at length in the next chapter, so we won't do that here. To keep things very simple, we will simply print the cluster information, one result per line, directly to `stdout`. The manner in which we do that, though, is what we need to discuss.

Our results are global coordinates, represented as a pair of floats, that give the latitude and longitude of our clusters. In *Chapter 7*, we gave an example of what the printed output of a small set of clusters should approximately be. This consists of two aligned columns, providing the coordinates of the cluster mean. These numbers are between -90 and 90 in latitude and -180 and 180 in longitude. (ISO 6709 specifies that latitude should be given first. We will follow this convention in our interface.) Ideally, we want to arrange the latitude and longitude values into neat columns, which helps human readers differentiate between the two values; computers can easily ignore padding spaces.

To accomplish neat columns, we need to dive into the standard library format functions until we arrive at something that produces the output that we want. First, the numbers themselves are floating points, with two or three digits (at most) preceding the decimal point, and we need a reasonable number of decimal points to follow. The numbers can be positive, for latitudes in the northern hemisphere or east of the meridian, or negative. We should add space for this regardless of whether the numbers need a negative sign or not. The number of decimal places needed is an interesting problem. One degree of longitude at the equator corresponds to approximately 111 km resolution, so one decimal place gives 11 km resolution and two decimal places give 1 km resolution. (Further north or south, the resolution gets better.) A resolution greater than a few hundred meters is probably sufficient for the kind of output we have, which means at least three decimal places. We'll stick to the minimum of three decimal places.

It remains to write the code to produce each line of output. Obviously, we need to loop over the results obtained from the clustering function that we have yet to implement. For now, we will create an empty vector of `Coordinate` structures that will eventually be filled with results so we can also write the output loop. We can update this later as we fill in the other parts of the `run_and_report` function. The implementation body that we will add now looks like this:

```
std::vector<Coordinate> results;

// fill this vector

for (const auto &coordinate : results) {
    std::cout << std::format("{: 7.3f} {: 8.3f}\n",
                             coordinate.latitude,
                             coordinate.longitude);
}
```

Let's quickly review the format string here. The colon indicates the start of the formatting. The initial space means that an additional space is left that will be replaced with a - character if the value is negative. (We could also have used + to add + for positive numbers and - for negative numbers, but people are generally not used to seeing + before a positive number.) The number that follows (7 and 8 in the two terms, respectively) is the width of the field in total, and `.3f` sets the precision mode to a fixed three decimal points. Using this code to print out some sample coordinates, we produce the following output:

```
 51.507   -0.128
 19.433  -99.133
 19.076   72.877
 19.899 -155.666
-19.015   29.155
```

This is perfect. We have two neat columns, leaving space for a - character if negative, with at least one space between the two numbers in each line, and all the numbers are given to the desired number of decimal places.

This covers all the issues that we need to discuss for building the command-line interface. In the next chapter, we'll look at parsing the list of files provided from the command-line arguments into raw data that we can process later.

Summary

In this chapter, we discussed various issues that one might encounter when building a command-line interface for an application. The most important part is parsing options and positional arguments provided by the user, implemented here using the Boost program options library. This library parses the `argv` array passed to the application, the environment variables, and configuration files (although we don't use this functionality here). We also covered setting up logging (using the `spdlog` library), error handling, signal handling, and formatting the results to be printed to the terminal, or otherwise.

There are many ways to design a command-line interface, and there is a lot that can be done using such an interface. It is important that you have a sensible, predictable, and functional interface even if you are the only one who will use it. The addition of help and usage information will be invaluable and save vast amounts of time if you forget what options are needed. The ability to simply check the help options at the command line is a great time saver with basically no upfront cost.

In the next chapter, we will start to build the file reader infrastructure that will allow us to ingest data from CSV and JSON files.

9

Reading Data from Different Formats

The next challenge that we face is reading each of the file formats provided by our client containing the data of the observations of the rubber ducks from around the world. We already know that some of these files will be in structured formats, namely **comma-separated values** (**CSV**) and **JavaScript Object Notation** (**JSON**). To read these structured files, we will need to make use of external libraries to quickly process the data contained within and turn this into the data structures that we can process later. There are many choices of libraries, each with different strengths, but very few have consistent interfaces. Thus, we must define our own interface that is consistent and allows us to hide the details of how each file format is parsed and turned into data.

In this chapter, we will choose the libraries that we are going to use and see how to use them. Then we will define the data structures (continuing our discussion from *Chapter 7*) and construct the single interface that we will use at the top level to process our files. We will look at what options we have for selecting the appropriate reader type to use for each file, and write some basic tests for our newly constructed reader interfaces.

In this chapter, we will cover the following basic topics:

- Reading CSV and JSON
- Designing an interface
- Dispatching according to file type
- Writing some simple tests

Technical requirements

This chapter shows the second stage of developing our rubber duckies application and involves some additional libraries. In particular, you will need to install the RapidJSON and csv2 libraries. These might be available from a package repository on Linux (apt, yum, etc.), Homebrew on macOS, or via a package manager such as vcpkg on any system. (You will need to follow the instructions at `https://vcpkg.io` on setting the CMake toolchain file and installing the libraries in the latter case.) We have provided a vcpkg manifest file for those who want to use this mechanism for installing dependencies.

The code for this chapter can be found in the `Chapter-09` folder in the repository for this book on GitHub: `https://github.com/PacktPublishing/The-CPP-Programmers-Mindset`.

Reading CSV and JSON

Our first task is to decide how best to parse the two different formats that the bulk of our data is stored within: CSV format and JSON format. For parsing, we're going to use two different libraries, of which there are several choices. For JSON, two very good options are simdjson (`simdjson.org`) and RapidJSON (`rapidjson.org`). We're going to use RapidJSON because the interface is slightly simpler. Similarly, there are many choices of CSV parsers, including csv2 (`https://github.com/p-ranav/csv2`) and lazycsv (`https://github.com/ashtum/lazycsv`). We're going to use csv2 here because it is cross-platform, whereas lazycsv does not seem to be. Having decided on the tools that we're going to use (in the form of libraries), we need to work out how to parse the files that we have been provided as samples (which are hopefully indicative of what the rest of the data looks like) and turn each entry into a piece of data that we can use later.

In terms of what data is needed, we obviously need to extract the latitude and longitude, recorded as decimal degrees and stored in floats, for each record. These are the most important records to extract for our basic analysis. We will also extract the date, stored as a `std::chrono::year_month_day` struct, which might be important for follow-up analysis. Finally, we will extract any text description provided and store this in a `std::string` alongside. Eventually, we will have to figure out how to store this in a data structure that allows us to access this, but we won't do this until we understand what is needed from each of the interfaces and come to design in the next section. In the remainder of this section, we'll work on understanding the libraries and building the guts of the parser.

Parsing CSV files

Parsing CSV files is a little challenging because of the limitations of the format itself and the library that we're using. The first major challenge is to determine which columns correspond to which quantities or strings. The sample we gave in *Chapter 7* was a single row with the fields (ordered as date, latitude, longitude, and description), as shown here:

```
2024-09-10, 51.5074, -0.1278, A mysterious rubber ducky was seen floating
in London.
```

What we can't see from this sample is whether the files themselves include a header row or not. We might assume that this is not the case since we don't see such a header in the example. We could, in theory, write code that determines whether the file has a header or not, but this would involve adding one more case to the beginning of the processing loop. Equally, we could assume that the headers are not given and that all the data appears in the same order as shown in the preceding code. However, this hides some interesting details about how to parse and use the header information. So, we will implement the reader assuming that headers are given but the headers do not necessarily match the order of the preceding code. (In reality, this is something we could ask our client.)

To get started, we need to use the `csv2::CSVReader` template class. The template options on this class customize the delimiter, the quotation character, whether the first row is a header or not, and whether to trim excess whitespace. The settings we use are actually the defaults, but we include them anyway to be explicit. Once we've created an instance of the class, we must load in the target file by calling the `mmap` method with the file path. This function returns `true` if the load was successful and `false` otherwise. We're not going to insert the wrapping functions until later when we have properly designed the interface. The first part of the code is as follows:

```
#include <csv2/reader.hpp>
//...
using Reader = csv2::Reader<csv2::delimiter<','>, csv2::quote_character<'"'>,
    csv2::first_row_is_header<true>, csv2::trim_policy::trim_whitespace>;
using Row = typename Reader::Row;

// inside the function
Reader csv;

if (!csv.mmap(path)) {
    return;
}
```

Now the task is to figure out which columns correspond to the values that we want. There are four columns that we're interested in being present, and if not, this file is malformed and should be ignored. These columns might be presented in any order. The only interface provided by the reader is forward iterator-based. This means we need to devise a system for isolating each value as we iterate through the cells in each row. There are two things to think about here. The first is the selection of columns that we're interested in, and the second is the mapping from these sub-selected column indices to the four values we need to decode. We're going to manage this using an index array and an array of `string_view` to hold the values to be located. The following function populates the index array by searching through the header for the four items we want:

```
static constexpr std::array<std::string_view, 4> col_headings = {
    std::string_view("date"),
    std::string_view("latitude"),
    std::string_view("longitude"),
    std::string_view("description")
};

static std::array<int, 4> parse_headers(const Row& header)
{
    const auto begin = col_headings.begin();
    const auto end = col_headings.end();

    std::array<int, 4> interests = {-1, -1, -1, -1};

    int col = 0;
    for (auto cell : header) {
        auto cell_view = cell.read_view()
        auto it = std::find(begin, end, cell_view);

        if (it != end) {
            auto value_index = static_cast<int>(it - begin);
            interests[value_index] = col;
        }
        ++col;
    }

    for (const auto& check : interests) {
        if (check == -1) {
          throw std::invalid_argument("not all required headings are provided");
```

```
        }
    }

    return interests;
}
```

The array contains the indices in the list of all columns of those that we want. As we iterate through the columns, we will check whether our current index matches one that we want, and if so, store a string view of the cell into our temporary array, as shown in the following code:

```
const auto ind_begin = interests.begin();
const auto ind_end = interests.end();
for (auto row : csv) {
    std::array<std::string_view, 4> values;

    int col = 0;
    for (auto cell : row) {
        auto pos = std::find(ind_begin, ind_end, col);
        if (pos != ind_end) {
            auto index = static_cast<int>(pos - ind_begin);
            values[index] = cell.read_view();
        }
        ++col;
    }

    // parse string values to actual values
}
```

After this inner loop, we have an array containing views of the text in the four columns that we're interested in. Obviously, we will need to parse the first view into a `std::chrono::year_month_day` object, and the second and third values need to be converted to floats. The final value just needs to be converted to a string. The easiest way to convert the date is to use an `istringstream` and the `from_stream` function to parse the `string_view` to the `date` object. This is achieved using the following code:

```
std::string tmp(values[0]);
std::istringstream ss(tmp));
std::chrono::year_month_day date;
std::chrono::from_stream(ss, "%F", date);
```

We could use the stream operators to obtain the latitude and longitude values, but the stream interface is a little cumbersome and better alternatives exist in the form of `std::stof`, so we're going to use these instead. We are going to reuse the `tmp` string as storage since all these functions take a `const std::string&` argument and not a `std::string_view`. (The addition of `std::string_view` to the standard library was great, but the rest of the library has not followed suit.) The remaining value parsing code looks like this:

```
tmp = values[1];
auto latitude = std::stof(tmp);

tmp = values[2];
auto longitude = std::stof(tmp);

tmp = values[3];
```

All that remains is to insert this into the data structure that will be passed to the next part of the analysis pipeline. However, we haven't decided what this will look like yet. Before we design the interface, we need to figure out how to parse the JSON files.

Parsing JSON files

Reading JSON is a little easier than the CSV. We're going to parse the JSON file via a C++ `istream`. For the real application, this will be an `ifstream`, but this gives us some flexibility for testing to pass in a string stream containing test data. We won't worry about the function signature just yet, and instead focus on the code that will eventually become the body of the `read_stream` function. To start with, we need to consult the documentation to see how to read in a JSON file from a C++ string. It turns out that we need to make use of a wrapper, `rapidjson::IStreamWrapper`, from the `rapidjson/istreamwrapper.h` header. We construct this and use the `ParseStream` method on the `Document` class to read the data from the stream into the document. This is achieved with the following lines of code:

```
#include <rapidjson/document.h>
#include <rapidjson/istreamwrapper.h>

//...

// inside the function
rapidjson::IStreamWrapper json_stream(stream);
rapidjson::Document doc;
doc.ParseStream(json_stream);
```

The doc document holds the root element of the JSON file, which in our case should be a JSON array. The size of this array is the number of elements that we need to process (this will be relevant later). We can check that the root element is indeed an array by calling the IsArray method on doc and obtaining the size using the Size method. The bulk of the work we need to do now is to parse each of the entries contained within this root array, which should all be objects of the following form:

```
{
  "latitude": 51.5074,
  "longitude": -0.1278,
  "date": "2024-09-10",
  "description": "A curious rubber ducky sighted in London."
}
```

For our purposes, we really only need the coordinate data. The date and description are optional, but at least the date will always be there. Any entry that doesn't contain a latitude, longitude, and date member (or is not itself an object) will be considered malformed and ignored. We'll add the code for checking whether the description is given. In terms of getting at the entries, we can use a range-based for loop that iterates over the array obtained using the GetArray method. Parsing the date string into year_month_day uses the same sequence as before, using the from_stream function. The finished loop looks like this:

```
for (const auto& entry : doc.GetArray()) {
    // checks for well-formedness
    if (!entry.IsObject() || !entry.HasMember("longitude")
        || !entry.HasMember("latitude") || !entry.HasMember("date")) {
        continue;
    }

    // parse coordinate
    float latitude = entry["latitude"].GetDouble();
    float longitude = entry["longitude"].GetDouble();

    // parse date
    std::chrono::year_month_day date;
    std::istringstream stream(entry["date"].GetString());
    std::chrono::from_stream(stream, "%F", date);
```

```
        // optionally get description
        std::string descr;
        if (entry.HasMember("description")) {
            descr = entry["description"].GetString();
        }

        // insert data into container
    }
```

The only thing that remains is to insert the additional function calls necessary to add each entry to the data array. We can't add this until we decide on the interface that we have yet to design. The design of this interface will be the topic of the next section.

Designing an interface

Having spent some time with the two implementations, we are now able to start designing the interface. Skipping ahead to this stage might be problematic since we don't know what kind of constraints we need to place on the interface, what parameters need to be passed, and what structures are needed to facilitate the loading. We've learned already that the JSON library supports an abstract stream interface but the CSV library does not; thus, passing the file as an `ifstream` or other file descriptor will not be sufficient. We will have to pass a valid filesystem path. If we don't want implementation details to leak, we're also limited in what supporting functions can be added to the class itself. This isn't really a concern here because the file readers library is so small, but in larger libraries, this might be important.

To add the interfaces to the project, we're going to add an additional directory to the project called `common`, which will contain our basic types that we use elsewhere in the project. This will be accompanied by a very basic `CMakeLists.txt` that declares an interface library with a single header file, as follows:

```
add_library(duckies_common INTERFACE duckies_types.h)

target_include_directories(duckies_common INTERFACE
    ${CMAKE_CURRENT_LIST_DIR}
    )
```

We've added a single header file to this interface target called `duckies_types.h` that will contain the `Coordinate` and `RubberDuckData` classes that we're about to define. This `CMakeLists.txt` is included in the main project using `add_subdirectory(common)` at the bottom of the main `CMakeLists.txt` (in the top-level directory of the project).

We already discussed this briefly in *Chapter 7*, where we described several strategies for storing the four values associated with an entry: date, latitude and longitude, and description. The question there was whether the data should be stored together in a single vector or instead be a class containing several vectors. Since we only really need the coordinates, we decided that these should be stored together, and the date and descriptions are free to be kept in separate vectors, leading to a class that looks like this:

```
#include <chrono>
#include <string>
#include <vector>

namespace duckies {
struct Coordinate {
    float latitude = 0.0f;
    float longitude = 0.0f;
};

class RubberDuckData {
    std::vector<Coordinate> coordinates_;
    std::vector<std::chrono::year_month_day> dates_;
    std::vector<std::string> descriptions_;

public:
    // accessor methods
};

} // namespace duckies
```

Aside from storage, we also need a means of inserting the data into the three arrays. We don't want to force the user to insert into the three constituent vectors individually; this would be error-prone. We need to maintain the invariant that all of these vectors have the same size. Thus, the best approach is to provide an `insert` method defined as follows. (This function is defined in the body of the class itself, so it is implicitly inline.)

```
void insert(float latitude, float longitude,
    std::chrono::year_month_day date, std::string descr)
{
    coordinates_.push_back({ latitude, longitude });
```

```
        dates_.emplace_back(date);
        descriptions_.emplace_back(std::move(descr));
    }
```

This makes sure that we always insert the four pieces of information in the correct places. (Notice that it is easy to accidentally swap the `latitude` and `longitude` values in the `coordinate` struct, so having separate named parameters here allows us to make sure they are inserted correctly.) Now, inserting into a vector like this is fine, but it works best if we don't have to allocate each time, so we should also add a reserve function to pre-allocate enough space to contain the entries. This won't be perfect since the data is coming from a large collection of different sources, all of which have different sizes, but it will at least alleviate some of the pressure. The tiny added complication is to reserve space for an additional number of elements, rather than an absolute number of elements. This function is given here:

```
void reserve_additional(size_t new_elements)
{
    auto current_size = coordinates_.size();
    auto new_size = current_size + new_elements;

    coordinates_.reserve(new_size);
    dates_.reserve(new_size);
    descriptions_.reserve(new_size);
}
```

We have also added several accessor methods to get (non-mutable) access to the data later. We could add some other debugging functions to query the size (and so on), but these are not strictly necessary for what we need. Since the data members are private, we are free to change these, which will have a knock-on effect for users of the accessor methods, but not for the file readers that only access the data through the `insert` and `reserve_additional` methods. With this container class in mind, we can turn our attention to the file reader interface.

The file reader base class

Each of the different file formats will have a different implementation of a file reader abstract interface. Our task now is to define this interface. We already added the stub file for the main `readers/file_reader.h` interface. We will have to add more files. We need to set up our CMake target for the interface and the various implementations.

The readers/CMakeLists.txt contains the following code, and is included in the top-level CMakeLists.txt using the add_subdirectory(readers) command, just below the inclusion of the common folder:

```
find_package(RapidJSON CONFIG REQUIRED)
find_package(csv2 CONFIG REQUIRED)

add_library(ducky_readers STATIC
    file_reader.cpp
    file_reader.h
    json_reader.cpp
    json_reader.h
    csv_reader.cpp
    csv_reader.h
)

target_link_libraries(ducky_readers
    PRIVATE
    csv2::csv2
    spdlog::spdlog
    PUBLIC
    duckies_common
)

target_include_directories(ducky_readers PRIVATE
    ${RAPIDJSON_INCLUDE_DIRS}
)
```

The first two lines find the two dependencies that we need for this component of the project (and only this component). Next, we add a static library for the readers interface and link all the dependencies. (Note that RapidJSON does define a CMake config file, but not an imported target, so we have to use the variable to add the include directories manually.) We also link to the duckies_common target that we defined before, which just makes the duckies_types.h header available for use. This inclusion needs to be public because it is used in the public parts of this target (i.e., the file_readers.h header file). We've added all six of the files that we will construct in the remainder of this chapter.

In terms of functionality, we need to have two functions. One of these will take a reference to the data container we just defined and a file path, and read the contents of the file into the container. The other function is to provide the file extension that will be used to dispatch to the correct handler at runtime (see the next section). The base class is defined as follows, added to the `file_readers.h` header file:

```
#include <filesystem>
#include <string_view>

#include "duckies_types.h" // contains RubberDuckData

namespace duckies {
class FileReader {
public:
    using Data = RubberDuckData;
    using FSPath = std::filesystem::path;

    virtual ~FileReader();

    /**
     * @brief Read the data from file into data
     */
    virtual void read_file(Data& data, const FSPath& path) const = 0;

    /**
     * @brief Get the file extension that this reader can parse.
     */
    virtual std::string_view supported_file_extension() const noexcept = 0;
};
} // namespace duckies
```

To keep the function signatures short, we've added the two member types: `Data`, as an alias for `RubberDuckData`, and `FSPath`, as an alias of `std::filesystem::path`. Other than that, this class is exactly as prescribed. We've moved the definition of the virtual destructor to the corresponding CPP file (`file_reader.cpp`), but it is just the default destructor. With this base class set up, we can start to write the two implementations using the code we've already written in the previous section.

Writing the CSV reader class

Our task now is to take the code to read CSV files we wrote earlier in this chapter and transplant this into the framework of the `FileReader` interface. For this, we add a new `.h`/`.cpp` file pair called `csv_reader`, and derive a new implementation of the `FileReader` class that implements our two methods. We're also going to add a function that reads from a `string_view` (which can be used instead of a memory-mapped file for testing). The contents of the header file are as follows:

```
#include "file_reader.h" // FileReader class

namespace duckies {
class CSVReader : public FileReader {
public:
    using typename FileReader::Data;
    using typename FileReader::FSPath;

    void read_view(Data& data, std::string_view view) const;
    void read_file(Data& data, const FSPath& path) const override;
    std::string_view supported_file_extension() const noexcept override;
};
} // namespace duckies
```

There are no mentions of the csv2 library here since we want to keep those implementation details private. These will only appear in the corresponding `.cpp` file. Note that we haven't stored any settings or preferences on the class itself, which we could use to give some limited customization options for the parser, such as the delimiter character. (Note that we can't easily use these because they are template parameters on the `csv2::Reader` class.) We don't need this customization here, but it is good to keep a mental note of the customization points that exist.

Now comes the slightly trickier task of moving the code from the previous section into the constraints of the two functions required by the interface. We're going to break up the function a little into smaller helper functions to make this easier to read and maintain later. To start with, let's separate the code that parses the header into an array of indices into a helper function called `parse_headers`.

We can separate the remaining parsing code into a new function that takes the data container and the populated `csv2::Reader` object and populates the data. The only addition is to reserve some additional space in the `data` object ready to receive the incoming entries.

This is defined as follows. (In the repository, we've also added some error checking and logging to this code.)

```
static void read_csv(typename FileReader::Data& data, const Reader& csv) {
    auto interests = parse_headers(csv.header());   data.reserve_
additional(csv.rows());

    const auto ind_begin = interests.begin();
    const auto ind_end = interests.end();

    for (auto row : csv) {
        std::array<std::string_view, 4> values;
        // finding relevant comments loop defined earlier
        // ...

        // parse string values to actual values as before
        // ...

        // insert into data container
        data.insert(latitude, longitude, date, std::move(tmp));
    }
}
```

Now, the implementation of the main reader function is trivial since we only need to open (memory map) the file at the path provided and pass this to the function we just defined. The remaining functions are shown here:

```
void CSVReader::read_view(Data& data, std::string_view view) const {
    Reader csv;
    if (!csv.parse_view(view)) {
        spdlog::warn("failed to parse csv from string");
        return;
    }

    try {
        read_csv(data, csv);
    } catch (std::invalid_argument &e) {
        spdlog::warn(e.what());
    }
}
```

```
void CSVReader::read_file(Data& data, const FSPath& path) const {
    Reader csv;
    if (!csv.mmap(path)) {
        spdlog::warn("failed to parse csv from file \"{}\"", path.c_
str());
        return;
    }

    try {
        read_csv(data, csv);
    } catch (std::invalid_argument &e) {
        spdlog::warn(e.what());
    }
}

std::string_view CSVReader::supported_file_extension() const noexcept {
    return "csv";
}
```

With these final additions, the reader class for CSV files is complete. The usage should be fairly clear by now. At the top level, we will use the file extension to select a particular `FileReader` instance, and use the `read_file` member to read the data and populate the data structure. With this already constructed, let's see how the JSON reader works.

Writing the JSON reader class

The JSON reader follows exactly the same pattern but is a little simpler. Here, we don't need as many helper functions because the JSON document format is a little more structured than CSV and requires less heavy lifting. The library also helps significantly by providing conversion functions for elements of the document. The top-level class looks very similar. As we mentioned before, we've added a function that parses a `std::istream` that will be used to implement the main interface function, `read_file`. We add another `.cpp`/`.h` file pair called `json_reader` and add the following code to the header file:

```
namespace duckies {
class JSONReader : public FileReader {
public:
    using FileReader::Data;
    using FileReader::FSPath;
```

```
    void read_stream(Data& data, std::istream& stream) const;
    void read_file(Data& data, const FSPath& path) const override;

    std::string_view supported_file_extension() const noexcept override;
};
} // namespace duckies
```

Now we just have to populate the functions as necessary. We start with the `read_stream` method, which will be the bulk of the work. Again, we've added a little code to reserve space in the `data` object for entries we're about to add and some additional error handling. The only other change is the addition of some logging when a member is malformed. The full definition is as follows, placed in the CPP file:

```
void JSONReader::read_stream(Data& data, std::istream& stream) const
{
    rapidjson::IStreamWrapper json_stream(stream);
    rapidjson::Document doc;
    doc.ParseStream(json_stream);

    // Extra error handling added
    if (!doc.IsArray()) {
        spdlog::warn("could not parse as JSON"
                     ", top level object is not an array");
        return;
    }

    // Add the reserve and logging
    auto num_records = doc.Size();
    spdlog::info("file contains {} entries", num_records);
    data.reserve_additional(num_records);

    size_t index = 0;
    for (const auto& entry : doc.GetArray()) {
        // checks for well-formedness, added logging
        if (!entry.IsObject() || !entry.HasMember("longitude")
            || !entry.HasMember("latitude") || !entry.HasMember("date")) {
            spdlog::warn("entry {} is malformed", index);
            continue;
        }
```

```
        // get the values from the columns as before
        // ...

        data.insert(latitude, longitude, date, std::move(descr));
        ++index;
    }
}
```

This function does all the work of loading the data from a JSON file, so now we just need to write the wrapper that actually translates the path as provided in the `FileReader` interface. The two remaining functions are defined as follows:

```
void JSONReader::read_file(Data& data, const FSPath& path) const {
    std::ifstream input_file(path);
    read_stream(data, input_file);
}

std::string_view JSONReader::supported_file_extension() const noexcept {
    return "json";
}
```

This concludes the implementation of the two file readers. In the next section, we will see how to dispatch files to the appropriate reader.

Dispatching according to file type

There are several ways to dispatch from the list of paths to process to the correct file handler. The first, and most crude, method is to simply try each file reader on a given path until one works. This would require some changes to the interface and the implementations, so we're not going to use that. As you might have guessed from the design of the interface, we're going to check the extension of a file against the supported extension of the reader. The best way to do this, especially if the number of readers is large, is to use an associative map such as `std::unordered_map`, whose keys are the file extensions and the values are (smart) pointers to the corresponding file readers. A basic version of this map can be constructed as follows:

```
std::unordered_map<std::string, std::unique_ptr<FileReader>> get_readers()
{
    std::unordered_map<std::string, std::unique_ptr<FileReader>> readers;

    auto csv_reader = std::make_unique<CSVReader>();
```

```
    std::string csv_ext(csv_reader->supported_file_extension());
    readers[csv_ext] = std::move(csv_reader);

    auto json_reader = std::make_unique<JSONReader>();
    std::string json_ext(json_reader->supported_file_extension());
    readers[json_ext] = std::move(json_reader);

    return readers;
}
```

(This is not really an optimal use of all the resources, but it doesn't need to be. This function will be run exactly once.) The next job is to find the appropriate reader for a path. Using the `std::filesystem::path` class provided by the standard library, we can extract the path extension (and convert this to a string), which we can then use to query the map to obtain the appropriate file reader. The snippet of code to achieve this is given next, assuming the path we are querying is called `path`:

```
const auto readers = get_readers();
// ...

auto ext = path.extension().string();
auto reader_it = readers.find(ext.substr(1));
if (reader_it != readers.end()) {
    spdlog::warn("no reader for path: {}", path.string());
    // handle error
}
auto& reader = *reader_it->second;
// use the reader
```

The relevant parts of this code can be inserted into the `run_and_report` function we declared in *Chapter 8*, but we will save this particular task for later once we have finished writing the remaining code. Our only remaining task is to write some basic tests to make sure our readers operate as expected. This is tackled in the next section.

Writing some simple tests

Our first task is to set up CMake for adding tests. This includes finding the Google Test library and the CMake support functions by adding the following lines to the root `CMakeLists.txt`:

```
find_package(GTest CONFIG REQUIRED)
include(GoogleTest)
```

Now we can link the `GTest::gtest_main` library to our test executables and the `gtest_discover_tests` function to register the tests contained therein to the CTest harness. (This makes actually running all the tests in a project very easy.) The next task is to create a new executable target in the `readers/CMakeLists.txt` file and register the tests. The code is as follows:

```
add_executable(test_ducky_readers
    test_csv_reader.cpp
    test_json_reader.cpp
    )

target_link_libraries(test_ducky_readers PRIVATE
  ducky_readers
  spdlog::spdlog
  GTest::gtest_main
  )

gtest_discover_tests(test_ducky_readers)
```

We've already added the two test source files, though we have yet to create them. As the names suggest, these files will contain tests for the `CSVReader` and `JSONReader` classes, respectively. For now, we will just add a test based on the samples given in *Chapter 7* (and repeated earlier in this chapter). The test for `CSVReader` is as follows. Note that we have to insert the header line into the sample since we assume it will be there:

```
#include <gtest/gtest.h>

#include "csv_reader.h"

using namespace duckies;
using namespace std::chrono_literals;

TEST(CSV, TestReadSample){
    CSVReader reader;
    std::string_view csv_sample(
        "date, latitude, longitude, description\n"
        "2024-09-10, 51.5074, -0.1278, A mysterious rubber "
        "ducky was seen floating in London.\n");
    RubberDuckData data;
    reader.read_view(data, csv_sample);
```

```
    auto& coordinates = data.coordinates();
    ASSERT_EQ(coordinates.size(), 1);
    auto& coord = coordinates[0];
    EXPECT_NEAR(coord.latitude, 51.5074, 1e-8);
    EXPECT_NEAR(coord.longitude, -0.1278, 1e-8);

    auto& dates = data.dates();
    ASSERT_EQ(dates.size(), 1);
    std::chrono::year_month_day expected_date {
        2024y, std::chrono::September, 10d };
    EXPECT_EQ(dates[0], expected_date);
}
```

The tests for the coordinates have to be split up into two parts because we have not defined an `operator==` for coordinates. However, we do need to use `EXPECT_NEAR` here because the coordinates we provided in the text might not be exactly representable as floating-point numbers. Notice also the use of `ASSERT_EQ` to test that the containers have the correct size, but `EXPECT_` macros for the other tests. This is because we want the test to continue if one of the coordinates is off, to see what else has failed to parse correctly. On the other hand, if the container does not contain an element, we cannot perform these tests, so we must exit early.

Also in this file, we add a test for the same sample but where the order of columns has been permuted. This is to test that the parsing we designed is robust to changes in the header in the way we intended. For instance, we've added the `TestReadSamplePermutedCols` test, which replaces the `csv_sample` string with the following:

```
std::string_view csv_sample("latitude, longitude, date, description\n"
                "51.5074, -0.1278, 2024-09-10, A mysterious rubber "
                "ducky was seen floating in London.\n");
```

This test actually exposes a problem in our code. The trailing line break character causes an empty line to be parsed, which in turn provides a cryptic `std::stof` exception to be raised. We can fix this by checking whether the row has any data by adding the following line to the beginning of the loop that processes each row:

```
if (row.length() == 0) { continue; }
```

We should also write tests to make sure the read fails gracefully if the expected columns are missing or if the header is missing, but we leave these as exercises for the reader. Writing the tests for the JSONReader class proceeds in the same way. Here, we'll have to use the read_stream function we added to the class and pass a stringstream instead of passing the string directly (as a string_view). Apart from the sample and the objects passed to the reader, the body of the test is exactly the same. The code is as follows:

```
#include <sstream>
// ...

TEST(JSON, TestReadSample) {
    JSONReader reader;
    std::string json_sample(
    "[{\"latitude\": 51.5074,\"longitude\": -0.1278,"
    "\"date\": \"2024-09-10\","
    "\"description\": \"A curious rubber ducky sighted in London.\"}]");
  std::stringstream ss(json_sample);
    RubberDuckData data;
    reader.read_stream(data, ss);

    // rest of test ...
}
```

The permuted entries test that we added before doesn't really make sense here because the RapidJSON library will handle this internally (according to the JSON specification). We can add a test where the description field is omitted; we made this conditional in the reader code. We should also add graceful failure tests here for when other fields are omitted or malformed. Again, we leave these as additional tests for you to carry out.

With these tests complete, we have finished the design and implementation of two of the three file readers that we will need to complete the task.

Summary

In this chapter, we saw how to examine two libraries that are responsible for parsing two different file formats. We used what we learned to inform the design of the interface that homogenizes the use of them that we will use in the main executable of the project. This pattern allows us to encapsulate the specific details of how each file format is handled and hide these details from the top level. This will make changing details internally easier and also allow for more sensible unit testing. We also discussed our strategy of choosing a reader for each file type by examining the extension of the paths provided via the command-line interface that we constructed in *Chapter 8*.

The addition of these two file readers means that we can now process two of the three file formats that are required by the client for this challenge. We still have to learn how to process the raw text-based responses and implement an additional file reader interface to handle this particular case. This will be handled in the next chapter.

10

Finding Information in Text

The next challenge is to read the free-form text responses that are held in `.txt` files, ready to be processed. This means we need to define a new implementation of the `FileReader` interface defined in the previous chapter, and find some way to extract the date and coordinate data from these unstructured texts. Finding strings matching a particular pattern means using regular expressions. This means we have to think quite carefully about the patterns that we might encounter, such as common date patterns and coordinate patterns. As with all regular expressions, this needs to be a methodical process with ample testing.

In this chapter, we will construct the regular expressions needed to extract dates and coordinates from unstructured text and devise a mechanism for separating the text for the individual entries held within a single file. Both of these different aspects will come together to define a new `FileReader` class, which will finish our file ingestion pipeline for the project.

In this chapter, we will cover the following basic topics:

- Searching text with regular expressions
- Designing the parser
- Extracting individual entries from the whole file
- Writing tests

Technical requirements

This chapter shows the second stage of developing our rubber duckies application and involves some additional libraries. In particular, you will need to install the **compile-time regular expressions** (**ctre**) library (`https://github.com/hanickadot/compile-time-regular-expressions`) either directly from source (into a place where CMake can find the file) or using a package manager such as vcpkg on any system. (You will need to follow the instructions at `https://vcpkg.io` on setting the CMake toolchain file and installing the libraries in the latter case.) We have provided a vcpkg manifest file for those who want to use this mechanism for installing dependencies.

The code for this chapter can be found in the `Chapter-10` folder in the repository for this book on GitHub: `https://github.com/PacktPublishing/The-CPP-Programmers-Mindset`.

Searching text with regular expressions

At the heart of this challenge lies a text pattern-matching procedure. For such tasks, one would usually reach for **regular expressions** (also known as **regex**) to perform this search quickly and efficiently; our case is no different. The tricky part of the task is recognizing the different patterns that we need to find and building the infrastructure around these patterns so we can extract the relevant bits of data that we need. Some of the patterns will be very simple, while others will be more complex. The tricky part is that there are many patterns for each of the different pieces of data we need to find (date and coordinates). We're going to tackle these separately rather than using a single pattern for everything. This will carry a small penalty because each string will be checked several times, but this isn't too bad because the strings involved are relatively short.

The standard library does provide regular expressions, but the performance of this part of the library leaves much to be desired. The are several regular expression libraries out there (such as PCRE and RE2), but we're instead going to make use of the ctre library (`https://compile-time.re`), which uses templates and compile-time programming to implement a basically complete regular expression library similar to PCRE in capability. Naturally, this is a header-only library, which makes it easier to work with as a dependency. Once installed, using your preferred method, you can use the following CMake commands to add this library to the project so it is ready for use:

```
find_package(ctre CONFIG REQUIRED)
# ...

target_link_libraries(ducky_readers
    PRIVATE
    # other libraries
```

```
    ctre::ctre
    PUBLIC
    duckies_common
)
```

Also, at this point, we're going to add a new .cpp/.h file pair named free_reader for the new free-text reader class that we will define later in this chapter. The code we write in this section will form parts of the .cpp file, but we have some choices to make about how to structure it. Before we get started with writing patterns, it makes sense to examine the example string we gave in *Chapter 7*:

```
June 10 2024: This morning I saw a bright yellow rubber duck was spotted
cruising leisurely on the Thames River in London (51 30' 26''N, 7' 39''W).
It had a tiny blue scarf around its neck.
```

This initial look highlights the variety of things we need to search for in the rest of the free-text entries. First is the date. Here, the date is presented in month-day-year format, with the month in its full-text form rather than a numeric representation. This is one of several ways that one might expect a date to be presented in text. Other formats include YYYY-MM-DD ISO format, as we have seen before, or the day-month-year format. We also see that there are potential challenges in finding coordinates. In the example text, the degrees of longitude are not given (because London is at approximately 0 degrees longitude). Our regular expression needs to be robust to small differences such as this.

Regular expressions can be rather problematic. For this reason, we're going to place all the patterns in the header file (free_reader.h) in preprocessor macros (we'll discuss this choice later). This will allow us to use the patterns in independent tests to make sure each part of them does what we need it to. For now, we need to write the patterns for finding dates in the text.

Searching for dates

Dates are the easier of the challenges that we face in this chapter, so we'll deal with this first. We can start with the ISO format, which only consists of numbers in a very specific order. The regular expression that matches the ISO format date is easy to construct (if we ignore the constraints on individual digits for a moment). We have three groups of digits, containing 4, 2, and 2 digits, respectively, possibly including 0. These groups are separated by either a dash (as we've seen already) or possibly a forward slash. A simple pattern that will match these kinds of dates is as follows:

```
(\d{4})(?:-|\/)(\d{2})(?:-|\/)(\d{2})
```

We've added capture groups around the various components of the date, so these can be easily extracted and converted to the components of the date in C++. (In fact, we started out using named capture groups, but this led to problems with repeated names, causing us to alter our approach.) The first group matches exactly four digits, followed by either a dash or a forward slash (uncaptured). The next capture group matches exactly two digits, followed again by an uncaptured dash or forward slash, and the final group matches another two digits. The other date formats that might appear (at least those that we will cover here) all require an additional element, which is the month written out as a word. Moreover, there are shortened versions of these months, such as "Jan" and "Feb" rather than January and February. We can handle both by writing a single regex that matches exactly one of these branches. The other components of the text dates can be reused from the ISO pattern. The first part of the pattern for the months written out in English is as follows:

```
(Jan(?:uary)?|Feb(?:ruary)?)
```

The remaining months are omitted for space, but the pattern is clear. Each branch of this regex contains a single month name, starting with the required three-letter abbreviation followed by the remaining optional letters (surrounded in a non-capture group). Unfortunately, since we're doing everything at compile time using the ctre library, we have to keep these as string literals, so we can't store these in separate variables and use string concatenation functions. The easiest way to do this is to use preprocessor macros that expand to string literals, since adjacent string literals separated only by whitespace will be automatically concatenated by the preprocessor. For instance, if we construct macros named `RE_YEAR`, `RE_MONTH`, `RE_DAY`, and `RE_DATE_SEP` for the digit representations of the year, month, and day, and the separate tokens that appear between these in ISO format, we can write the ISO regex as follows:

```
#define RE_ISO RE_YEAR RE_DATE_SEP RE_MONTH RE_DATE_SEP RE_DAY
```

We've added a named group surrounding the whole pattern, but this will only be used to determine which of the three date patterns have matched. This is ugly and not really idiomatic C++, but it does mean we don't have to write out the full string many times. (In the full date regex, the English months will appear twice, and day and year will appear three times.) Replicating this using compile-time C++ mechanisms would greatly increase the amount of work required and the complexity of the program. (It can be done, but it is certainly not easy.)

Putting the whole string together, with some appropriately defined macros such as RE_MONTHS to be the month names, as indicated before, we can construct the following regular expression for all the date strings we want to find:

```
#define RE_DMY RE_DAY RE_WS RE_MONTHS RE_WS RE_YEAR
#define RE_MDY RE_MONTHS RE_WS RE_DAY RE_WS RE_YEAR

#define RE_DATE RE_ISO RE_OR RE_DMY RE_OR RE_MDY
```

RE_OR expands to "|" and RE_WS expands to "\\s" for the or operator and whitespace characters, respectively. All of these macros will be expanded to their string literal meaning, which will be concatenated by the preprocessor into a single string literal with the correct meaning. The one remaining task is to set up some compile-time constants that enumerate the various groups that appear in the date pattern. This helps us write the code to extract the various parts later, and also allows for our code to be more maintainable, since the meaning of constants will be obvious to the reader. These are placed in the header file (within the duckies namespace) and are defined as follows:

```
inline constexpr int iso_date_year_group = 1;
inline constexpr int iso_date_month_group = 2;
inline constexpr int iso_date_day_group = 3;
inline constexpr int dmy_date_day_group = 4;
inline constexpr int dmy_date_month_group = 5;
inline constexpr int dmy_date_year_group = 6;
inline constexpr int mdy_date_month_group = 7;
inline constexpr int mdy_date_day_group = 8;
inline constexpr int mdy_date_year_group = 9;
```

These names are a little verbose, but as long as they are updated whenever the pattern is updated, they will make writing later code much easier and prevent the appearance of magic numbers with no explanation. With this pattern in good shape, now it's time to tackle the coordinate pattern.

Searching for coordinates

Coordinates pose a much greater challenge than the dates because there is more variety in the presentation. First, we could receive coordinates in the degree-minute-second format that we saw in the sample text, or we could find decimal degrees as seen in the CSV and JSON samples from the previous chapter. These could be provided with or without surrounding brackets, and with or without separating commas, and using either negative or cardinal direction markers ("N/S" or "E/W") to indicate direction. Since our sample starts with the degree-minute-second format, let's start there.

In the degree-minute-second format, we provide two strings of the form `DDD° MM' SS" C'` where `D`, `M`, and `S` denote digits and `C` denotes a cardinal direction. Sometimes, the degree symbol might be omitted, as might groups of digits that are 0. Notice too that longitude degrees range from 0 to 180 (or -180 to 180 if you use decimal degrees and negative direction indications), while latitude varies from 0 to 90 (or -90 to 90), so the patterns for longitude and latitude are subtly different. These small variations soon add up to a large number of possibilities that we must accommodate in our pattern. Once again, we can use some macros to simplify the construction of our full pattern.

The regex patterns we need for the degree-minute-second will again be constructed from a number of macros that expand to string literals containing the various parts of the pattern. The latitude and longitude in the DMS format each have four components: the digits of the degree, minutes, and seconds along with the cardinal direction (as discussed before). Thus, our DMS patterns have four components too. This time, we've named each component so we can extract it from the match later and made some of the terms optional. This is mostly to demonstrate the alternative approach. The patterns for the latitude are as follows:

```
#define RE_LAT_DEG "(?:(?<lat_deg>\\d{1,2})(?:\u00b0)?\\s*)?"
#define RE_LAT_MIN "(?:(?<lat_min>\\d{1,2})'\\s*)"
#define RE_LAT_SEC "(?<lat_sec>\\d{1,2}(?:\\.\\d+)?)(?:\"|'')\\s*"
#define RE_LAT_NS "(?<lat_card>[NS])"

#define RE_DMS_LAT RE_LAT_DEG RE_LAT_MIN RE_LAT_SEC RE_LAT_NS
```

The Unicode `\u00b0` character is a degree symbol, °, which is optional in our pattern. (This is enclosed in a non-capture group to avoid some bugs we discovered in testing.) Each of the numbers here is at most two digits, since degrees can range from 0 to 90 in latitude, and the seconds have optional decimals, although it's unlikely that these will ever actually be used.

Minutes are followed by a single quotation and seconds are followed by either a single double quotation or two single quotation marks. All of the numbers (and cardinal direction) are wrapped in named capture groups, and the degrees and minutes are also wrapped in a non-capture group, so they can be marked as optional. The whole pattern consists of all four components in sequence. Notice that the whitespace is included within each component (and is optional). The longitude patterns are exactly the same except for a change to the names, and the degrees term can have three digits instead of two, as shown here:

```
#define RE_LON_DEG "(?:(?<lon_deg>\\d{1,3})(?:\u00b0)?\\s*)?"
// .. etc
#define RE_DMS_LON RE_LON_DEG RE_LON_MIN RE_LON_SEC RE_LON_EW
```

Now that we have patterns for the degree-minute-second format of coordinates, we need to do the same for the decimal degree format. This is much simpler as each group only contains a single number (though this time with a decimal point and following digits). We also have an optional sign ahead of each number to capture, but this is easy. As before, we name the groups uniquely so we can extract them from the pattern later. The patterns are defined as follows:

```
#define RE_DD_LAT "(?<dd_lat>[+\\-]?\\d{1,2}\\.\\d+)(?:\u00b0)?"
#define RE_DD_LON "(?<dd_lon>[+\\-]?\\d{1,3}\\.\\d+)(?:\u00b0)?"
```

Now we have to pull these together. In both cases, a full coordinate is a pair of latitude and longitude, separated by a comma or whitespace (or both). The whole pattern is an optional between the two aggregated pattern, so as before, we have to group each in a non-capture group surrounding the | operator using our `RE_OR` macro from before. The result is the following final pattern:

```
#define RE_CO_SEP "(?:,|\\s)\\s*"
#define RE_DMS RE_DMS_LAT RE_CO_SEP RE_DMS_LON
#define RE_DD RE_DD_LAT RE_CO_SEP RE_DD_LON
#define RE_COORD RE_DMS RE_OR RE_DD
```

Now that we have all the patterns we need, we need to start putting these together into a system for extracting them from the string inputs.

Designing the parser

We need to pause here before we dive into matching regular expressions against text. We need to think about what our strategy will be for searching. We really have two options:

- We could combine the regular expressions into a single pattern and perform an iterative search through each string to find all the matches, and then disentangle the results after the fact
- We could parse the string several times, with each pass looking for a different pattern, keeping the results separate

The first strategy has the advantage of speed, especially if the strings are long. The second strategy has better separation of concerns, which allows us to focus on each component at a time. At the start of the section, we said we would use the second strategy. The main reason for this is that we can write the code much more quickly since it dramatically simplifies the process of unpicking the various groups into the numbers we need.

To facilitate the process, we're going to define two functions that operate as a kind of filter. (A true filter design would consume the input stream and modify it in some way to be passed on to the next stream. We're just extracting data from the stream here.) Each of these functions will take a (Unicode) view of the text and return a `std::optional` wrapping the corresponding struct (`Coordinate` or `std::year_month_day`). This will allow us to see whether the parse has been successful, so we can early exit and report a failure. This logic will be handled a little higher up.

At this stage, we need to look closely at our chosen regular expression library, ctre. This is a Perl-compatible regular expression library that uses compile-time strings as patterns (in `ctll::fixed_string` objects). The library provides several of the standard regular expression functions, such as `match` and `search`; we'll be using the latter here. Since our patterns contain Unicode characters, we need to make sure we include the additional headers that pull in the Unicode support, in the form of `ctre-unicode.hpp`. We also have to use `std::u8string` and `std::u8string_view`, added in C++20, which inform the functions from the library that they should match Unicode. Let's get started with the date match function:

```
static std::optional<chrono::year_month_day> parse_date(std::u8string_view
text)
{
    // Pattern as fixed_string
    constexpr ctll::fixed_string date_re { RE_DATE };
```

```
    std::optional<chrono::year_month_day> result;
    auto match = ctre::search<date_re>(text);
    if (!match) {
        spdlog::warn("no date string match found");
        return result;
    }

    auto year = get_year(match);
    auto month = get_month(match);
    auto day = get_day(match);
    if (!year || !month || !day) {
        spdlog::warn("missing year, month, or day");
        return result;
    }

    result = chrono::year_month_day { *year, *month, *day };
    if (!result->ok()) {
        spdlog::warn("parsed an invalid date");
        result = std::nullopt;
    }

    return result;
}
```

This function delegates the decoding of the various parts of the date to three helper functions, which we also need to define. These return a `std::optional` containing the relevant object that we can test to see whether the conversion was successful, which it should almost always be, unless the component is missing from the string. Note that these functions don't check the validity of the date in question; they just parse the numbers from the segments of the string. Validity checking is handled right at the end with the `results->ok()` call. The get_year and get_day functions are very similar, since these are always numerical values. The get_year function is defined as follows:

```
template <typename Match>
static std::optional<chrono::year> get_year(const Match& match)
{
    std::optional<chrono::year> result;

    std::u8string_view view;
```

```
    if (auto group = match.template get<iso_date_year_group>()) {
        view = group.to_view();
    } else if (auto group = match.template get<dmy_date_year_group>()) {
        view = group.to_view();
    } else if (auto group = match.template get<mdy_date_year_group>()) {
        view = group.to_view();
    } else {
        spdlog::warn("no matching day pattern");
        return result;
    }

    int num = 0;
    if (str_to_num(view, num)) {
        result = chrono::year { num };
    }
    return result;
}
```

We've made these template functions to avoid having to deduce the type of the regex match group. The strategy here is to test each of the groups that contain a day value (i.e., a number with 1 or 2 digits). Since all three have the same textual presentation, we can simply select the present group and collect the view before processing further. The `str_to_num` function used here is a thin wrapper around the `std::from_char` function that returns `true` on a successful parse and `false` otherwise based on a string view. (Please note, the `std::from_char` function from the standard library might not be supported on all compilers yet.) The `get_day` function is defined similarly:

```
template <typename Match>
static std::optional<chrono::day> get_day(const Match& match)
{
    std::optional<chrono::day> result;

    std::u8string_view view;
    if (auto iso = match.template get<iso_date_day_group>()) {
        view = iso.to_view();
    } else if (auto dmy = match.template get<dmy_date_day_group>()) {
        view = dmy.to_view();
    } else if (auto mdy = match.template get<mdy_date_day_group>()) {
        view = mdy.to_view();
```

```
    } else {
        spdlog::warn("no matching day pattern");
        return result;
    }

    unsigned num = 0;
    if (str_to_num(view, num)) {
        result = chrono::day { num };
    }
    return result;
}
```

The final function, get_month, is a little more complicated. Here, we have to deal with two different cases. In the ISO year-month-day format, the month is given as a number, whereas in the other two, the month is given by its name. Thus, we have to split the implementation, checking first for a match on the ISO month group, and performing a numerical conversion in this case, or testing the other two groups and converting from name to a numerical value. To convert the month names to a numeric value, we only need to look at the first three letters of the name, which is enough to distinguish them. Most months can be distinguished by their first letter. The exceptions are those that begin with "J" (January, June, and July) and "A" (April and August). For the "A" months, we can just look at the second letter to disambiguate. For the "J" months, we need to check the second and possibly the third letters. We package all this into a long switch statement that sets the value accordingly. The body of the function is as follows, though we've omitted all but the "J" case of the switch to save space:

```
template <typename Match>
static std::optional<chrono::month> get_month(const Match& match)
{
    std::optional<chrono::month> result;
    if (auto month = match.template get<iso_date_month_group>()) {
        unsigned month_num = 0;
        if (str_to_num(month.to_view(), month_num)) {
            result = chrono::month { month_num };
        }
    } else {
        std::u8string_view view;
        if (auto dmy = match.template get<dmy_date_month_group>()) {
```

```
            view = dmy.to_view();
        } else if (auto mdy = match.template get<mdy_date_month_group>())
{
            view = mdy.to_view();
        } else {
            spdlog::error("no matching month");
            return result;
        }

        switch (view[0]) {
        case 'J':
            if (view[1] == 'a') {
                result = chrono::January;
            } else if (view[2] == 'n') {
                result = chrono::June;
            } else {
                result = chrono::July;
            }
            break;
        // ...
        }
    }

    return result;
}
```

Parsing the coordinates presents a greater challenge. We have two possible branches in the regular expression: one for decimal degrees and one for degree-minute-second. The decimal degrees branch is much simpler since there are no optional groups and only two numerical values to parse. The degree-minute-second branch is trickier. Here, there are optional groups, and the conversion from the matched strings and their associated numerical values is more complicated than a simple conversion (that's not to say that the computation is difficult; it's just more complicated). With all that in mind, we'll separate out the conversion of the DMS format coordinates into a separate function, get_dms, which is defined as follows:

```
template <typename Match>
static std::optional<Coordinates> get_dms(const Match& match) {
    constexpr ctll::fixed_string lat_d_name { "lat_deg" };
```

```
// ... other group names omitted

std::optional<Coordinates> result;

auto lat_d = match.template get<lat_d_name>();
auto lat_m = match.template get<lat_m_name>();
auto lat_s = match.template get<lat_s_name>();
auto lat_cd = match.template get<lat_cd_name>();

auto lon_d = match.template get<lon_d_name>();
auto lon_m = match.template get<lon_m_name>();
auto lon_s = match.template get<lon_s_name>();
auto lon_cd = match.template get<lon_cd_name>();

float longitude = 0.0f, latitude=0.0f, tmp=0.0f;
if (lat_d && str_to_num(lat_d.to_view(), tmp)) {
    latitude += tmp;
}
if (lat_m && str_to_num(lat_m.to_view(), tmp)) {
    latitude += tmp / 60;
}
if (str_to_num(lat_s.to_view(), tmp)) {
    latitude += tmp / 3600;
}
if (lat_cd.to_view()[0] == 'S') {
    latitude = -latitude;
}

if (lon_d && str_to_num(lon_d.to_view(), tmp)) {
    longitude += tmp;
}
if (lon_m && str_to_num(lon_m.to_view(), tmp)) {
    longitude += tmp / 60;
}
if (str_to_num(lon_s.to_view(), tmp)) {
    longitude += tmp / 3600;
}
```

```
    if (lon_cd.to_view()[0] == 'W') {
        longitude = -longitude;
    }

    if (-90.0f <= latitude && latitude <= 90.0f
            && -180.0f < longitude && longitude <= 180.0f) {
        result = Coordinates { latitude, longitude };
    } else {
        spdlog::warn("parsed invalid coordinates {}, {}",
                     latitude, longitude);
    }

    return result;
}
```

For the optional parts of the pattern (degrees and minutes for both longitude and latitude), we must check whether the `match` object (`lat_d`, `lon_d`, etc.) holds a value before we convert it to a numeric value. Minutes should be divided by 60 before being incorporated into the result, and seconds should be divided by 3,600. (There are 60 minutes per degree, and 60 seconds per minute.) To save time, we parse each of these directly into floats. The final step in the function is to check whether the parsed coordinates are valid and set the result if this is true. With this work out of the way, we can write the wrapping function to search for coordinates in the text:

```
static std::optional<Coordinate> parse_coord(std::u8string_view text)
{
    constexpr ctll::fixed_string coord_re { RE_COORD };

    std::optional<Coordinate> result;
    auto match = ctre::search<coord_re>(text);

    if (!match) {
        spdlog::warn("no coordinates found in text");
        return result;
    }

    constexpr ctll::fixed_string dd_lat_name { "dd_lat" };
    constexpr ctll::fixed_string dd_lon_name { "dd_lon" };

    if (auto dd_lat = match.get<dd_lat_name>()) {
```

```
        auto dd_lon = match.get<dd_lon_name>();
        float lat, lon;
        if (str_to_num(dd_lat.to_view(), lat)
            && str_to_num(dd_lon.to_view(), lon)) {
            if (-90.0f <= lat && lat <= 90.0f && -180.0f < lon
                && lon <= 180.0f) {
                result = Coordinates { lat, lon };
            } else {
                spdlog::warn("parsed invalid coordinates {}, {}", lat, lon);
            }

        } else {
            spdlog::warn("unable to parse decimal degree lat or long");
        }
    } else {
        result = get_dms(match);
    }

    return result;
}
```

These two functions will form the bulk of processing free-form text into usable data for these free-text entries. To keep the wrapping code clean, we can wrap these two functions in one additional function that turns a single text entry into a single record (if this can be done successfully). This is defined as follows:

```
static void parse_entry(typename FileReader::Data& data,
                        std::u8string_view text) {

    auto date = parse_date(text);
    auto coords = parse_coords(text);

    if (date && coords) {
        data.insert(coords->latitude, coords->longitude, *date,
                        std::string(text.begin(), text.end()));
    }

}
```

Now we have a complete pipeline for converting a single text entry into a set of usable data. The remaining challenge is to extract the text for each of the entries from the containing file. This is the challenge for the next section.

Extracting individual entries from the whole file

The final challenge is to find individual entries within the text file. On the surface, one might assume that the entries are stored in the file with one line per entry, but this might not be the case. Indeed, each entry might consist of multiple lines, in which case we would need some additional structure in the file to separate the entries. In this case, the individual entries will be separated by blank lines. We will need to write the code to read consecutive lines of text into a buffer from where it can be processed using our `parse_entry` function. The trick here will be to detect when we have a blank line. For the purposes of this section, we will assume that newlines are denoted using only a `\n` character (no CRLF endings) as this will make the code dramatically simpler.

We have to write a function to read a single entry. We need to be a little careful here to make sure we properly handle the case where we encounter an error or reach the end of the file. Both of these cases will need careful thought. Splitting the whole process into a `get_entry` function, analogous to `std::getline`, and using this in the condition allows us fairly fine-grained control over the execution. Before we write this, we need to understand the different cases that might happen:

- The most common case is where we reach the end of the entry without incident. In this case, we process the text in the buffer and repeat the loop once again.
- We reach the end of the file while reading. Here, we want to process the data that was read into the buffer before the end of the file, but then terminate the loop. (We have finished at this point.)
- An error occurs during reading. We need to log what has happened and gracefully exit the parse. We don't want to completely abandon the computation if we fail to read a single file, but we do want the user to know that it has happened. (We will set the stream to not emit exceptions and instead handle errors via the flags.)

As we've already discussed, the `peek` function allows us to inspect the next character in the stream without consuming it. We can use this, in tandem with the `not_eof` function, the character traits (provided by the stream) to test whether we've hit the end of the file, and also test against the newline character. While the next character is not `EOF` or the newline character (signifying a blank line), we can continue reading lines into the buffer. Once the condition fails, we can return `true`. (This indicates that processing should commence.)

In the case where the stream error bits are set, we should log and return `false`. The `get_entry` function is defined as follows:

```
static bool get_entry(std::istream& stream, std::u8string& buffer)
{
    using traits = typename std::istream::traits_type;
    const auto endl = traits::to_int_type(stream.widen('\n'));
    buffer.clear();
    for (auto next_char = stream.peek();
        traits::not_eof(next_char) && next_char != endl;
        next_char=stream.peek()) {

        for (auto c=stream.get(); traits::not_eof(c) && c != endl;
             c=stream.get()) {
            buffer.push_back(traits::to_char_type(c));
        }

        if (!stream){
            spdlog::warn("an error occurred when parsing the stream");
            return false;
        }
        buffer.push_back(' '); // replace the \n with a space
    }
    return true;
}
```

At this point, we have gathered enough information to know what our external interface is going to be. Of course, we need to define a new class that derives (and implements the interface of) `FileReader` with one additional function that takes a `std::istream` argument instead of a file path that will actually implement our parsing operation. (This is the same setup as the JSON reader.) The class definition is as follows:

```
namespace duckies {

class FreeTextReader : public FileReader {
public:
    using typename FileReader::Data;
    using typename FileReader::FSPath;
    void read_stream(Data& data, std::istream& view) const;
```

```
    void read_file(Data& data, const FSPath& path) const override;
    std::string_view supported_file_extension() const noexcept override;
};

} // namespace duckies
```

This is placed in free_reader.h alongside the many pattern macros defined earlier. Now we can fill in the body of the read_stream method (in free_reader.cpp). The work will mostly be done in a for loop, whose condition is a call to the get_entry function. In the body of the for loop, it is important that we consume the next character, which is either a blank-line newline character or EOF. If we don't do this, we get stuck in an infinite loop. In any case, we can use this at the end of the loop to test whether we have reached the end of the file and should terminate the loop. With all this in mind, the body of the read_stream function is now as follows:

```
void FreeTextReader::read_stream(Data& data, std::istream& stream) const
{
    using traits = typename std::istream::traits_type;
    std::u8string buffer;

    for (; get_entry(stream, buffer);) {
        auto next_char = stream.get(); // consume the endl we just saw

        if (buffer.empty()) { continue;}

        parse_entry(data, buffer);
        if (!traits::not_eof(next_char)) { break; }
    }
}
```

The remaining undefined functions are the read_file and supported_file_extension required functions for the FileReader interface, which is now simply defined as follows:

```
void FreeTextReader::read_file(Data& data, const FSPath& path) const
{
    std::ifstream stream(path);
    read_stream(data, stream);
}
std::string_view FreeTextReader::supported_file_extension() const noexcept
{
    return "txt";
}
```

This concludes all the logic for reading the free-form text entries, but we are not yet finished. We need to write some tests for our parsing logic, which is the topic of the final section.

Writing tests

Now we need to write some tests to make sure our patterns and `FileReader` interface perform as expected. For this, we create a new file called `test_free_reader.cpp` and add it to the test target. The setup is very similar to before, except we need to also include the regular expressions library (and link this on the CMake target) and re-declare the patterns. At the top of the file, we place these includes and the definition of the static patterns, as follows:

```
#include <gtest/gtest.h>

#include <ctre-unicode.hpp>

#include "free_reader.h"

using namespace duckies;

static constexpr ctll::fixed_string date { RE_DATE };
static constexpr ctll::fixed_string dd_coord { RE_DD };
static constexpr ctll::fixed_string dms_coord { RE_DMS };
```

Next, we can start to write some small tests for each of the patterns. For instance, we can write a test that checks that the full date pattern matches an ISO date string such as `2025-04-21`. If the match is successful, then the match object itself should contain a value, and each of the ISO groups should also contain a value. We can test that this is indeed the case as follows:

```
TEST(Free, TestDateREISO)
{
    std::string s = "2025-04-21";

    auto match = ctre::match<date>(s);
    EXPECT_TRUE(match);
    EXPECT_TRUE(match.get<iso_date_day_group>());
    EXPECT_TRUE(match.get<iso_date_month_group>());
    EXPECT_TRUE(match.get<iso_date_year_group>());
}
```

We can fill in many more tests of this kind for the various other date string formats that we can match. These look more or less identical to the ISO test, so we skip those here. (They are contained in the code folder for this chapter in the repository for this book.) We also need to test the coordinate pattern. These patterns are more complicated, so we've broken them down further. For instance, we've added another test for the decimal-degree format coordinate string, as follows:

```
TEST(Free, TestCoordREDD)
{
    std::u8string s = u8"51.5074, -0.1278";

    auto match = ctre::match<dd_coord>(s);

    EXPECT_TRUE(match);
    EXPECT_TRUE(match.get<ctll::fixed_string("dd_lat")>());
    EXPECT_TRUE(match.get<ctll::fixed_string("dd_lon")>());
}
```

Note that the string needs to be a `std::u8string`, so the `match` function interprets it as a UTF-8 string. This is because our pattern includes Unicode symbols. (This fact was revealed by this very test.) Of course, we also add a selection of tests for the degree-minute-second format strings that are omitted here.

The final set of tests that we need are those that test the `FreeTextReader` class that all the work in this chapter has built toward. Here, we really need to test two things. The first is that we correctly parse individual entries and extract the correct values from the text. The second thing is that the individual entries within a file are correctly disambiguated by the blank-line mechanism. A test for the first case can be constructed as follows:

```
TEST(Free, TestReadOneEntry)
{
 FreeTextReader reader;

 std::string text(
     "June 10 2024: This morning I saw a bright yellow rubber "
     "duck was spotted\n"
     "cruising leisurely on the Thames River in London (51 30' "
```

```
    "26''N, 7' 39''W).\n"
    "It had a tiny blue scarf around its neck.\n");

    std::istringstream ss(text);

    RubberDuckData data;
    reader.read_stream(data, ss);

    auto coords = data.coordinates();
    ASSERT_EQ(coords.size(), 1);

    auto& first_coord = coords[0];
    EXPECT_NEAR(
        first_coord.latitude, 51.0f + 30.f / 60 + 26.f / 3600, 1e-7);
    EXPECT_NEAR(
        first_coord.longitude, -(0.0f + 7.0f / 60 + 39.0f / 3600), 1e-7);
}
```

Indeed, the first time we ran this test, we found an interesting bug in that our decimal-digit pattern didn't require a decimal point and thus matched on the date (`10 202`), leading to a failed test (and a handy logged warning). We changed the pattern to require the decimal point and at least one trailing digit (as would anyway be reasonably expected). For the second test, we can duplicate the same entry twice, separated by the required blank line, and rerun the test to see whether the number of processed entries is now two instead of one. This is given in the following code:

```
TEST(Free, TestReadManyEntries)
{
    FreeTextReader reader;

    std::string text(
        "June 10 2024: This morning I saw a bright yellow rubber "
        "duck was spotted\n"
        "cruising leisurely on the Thames River in London (51 30' "
        "26''N, 7' 39''W).\n"
        "It had a tiny blue scarf around its neck.\n"
        "\n"
        "June 10 2024: This morning I saw a bright yellow rubber "
        "duck was spotted\n"
```

```
        "cruising leisurely on the Thames River in London (51 30' "
        "26''N, 7' 39''W).\n"
        "It had a tiny blue scarf around its neck.\n");

    std::istringstream ss(text);

    RubberDuckData data;
    reader.read_stream(data, ss);

    auto coords = data.coordinates();
    ASSERT_EQ(coords.size(), 2);
}
```

These tests are important for making sure that our program does what we intend. We've already described several examples of bugs and shifts in our approach that have been exposed through these tests. The tests we've included here are a bare minimum of what is required. We should also test all the edge cases and unusual patterns that might arise (some, but not all, of these are included in the code repository). However, with all these tests passing, we've finished our basic implementation of the `FreeTextReader` class.

Summary

In this chapter, we designed a system of functions that extracts various pieces of information from unstructured text using regular expressions. These were combined with some logic to extract blocks of text separated by blank lines that constitute individual entries in the free-text responses. All these features come together to define a new implementation of the `FileReader` class from the previous chapter. This means we can now read in all the data provided by the client ready to be processed, which is the content of the next chapter.

This chapter made use of the ctre library, which is a template-only implementation of Perl-compatible regular expressions. This library is nice because it is fast and doesn't add external library dependencies, but, as we've seen, in testing, it adds some complexity to the task. The tests were essential in designing and writing the code for this chapter, as described at many points in the commentary surrounding the code snippets. In the next chapter, we will explore the *k*-means clustering algorithm to group the ducky sightings to find their origins.

11

Clustering Data

The remaining challenge is to cluster the data that we can now read from files so we can analyze the locality of the data (to find out where the rubber ducks originate). For this task, we're going to implement a k-means clustering, which is a fairly basic data science tool that labels data according to its proximity to other data. The algorithm itself is relatively straightforward, but we will also need lots of supporting structure to embed our geographic data into an appropriate space and to decide on the number of clusters to fit.

The k-means clustering itself is an exercise in implementing a standard algorithm efficiently. However, finding the number of clusters is a different problem entirely. For this, we will need to find an appropriate method of scoring different clusterings that will allow us to choose the best value of k. This will be combined with some kind of search over a range of k values. For this part, we will need us to construct our own algorithm.

In this chapter, we will cover the following basic topics:

- Understanding k-means clustering
- Implementing the clustering algorithm
- Testing our implementation
- Understanding limitations and opportunities to expand

Technical requirements

This chapter shows the third stage of developing our rubber duckies application but only requires the GoogleTest library, which has been used in previous chapters. We have provided a vcpkg manifest file for those who want to use this mechanism for installing dependencies.

The code for this chapter can be found in the `Chapter-11` folder in the repository for this book on GitHub: `https://github.com/PacktPublishing/The-CPP-Programmers-Mindset`.

Understanding *k*-means clustering

Clustering is a very basic problem that appears in many different contexts. It is an example of an **unsupervised learning** problem, meaning that the task is to learn the clusters from the data without the need for additional information. (A linear regression is a classic example of a **supervised learning** problem, since it requires both the underlying data and the corresponding set of outcomes.) There are many algorithms for clustering data, but by far the simplest is k-means clustering. Here, the task is to divide the data into k clusters in such a way that minimizes some kind of objective function, which is usually the distance to the mean of the cluster. (The objective function can be chosen to invoke specific constraints on the clusters that one wishes to find.) An illustration of a set of two-dimensional data clustered using k-means is shown in *Figure 11.1*; the cluster centers are denoted by large X's, and the marker denotes which cluster each point is associated with. The k-means clustering algorithm treats k as a fixed number, so it doesn't quite do what we want. However, we can still use the logic of this algorithm as a starting point for our method.

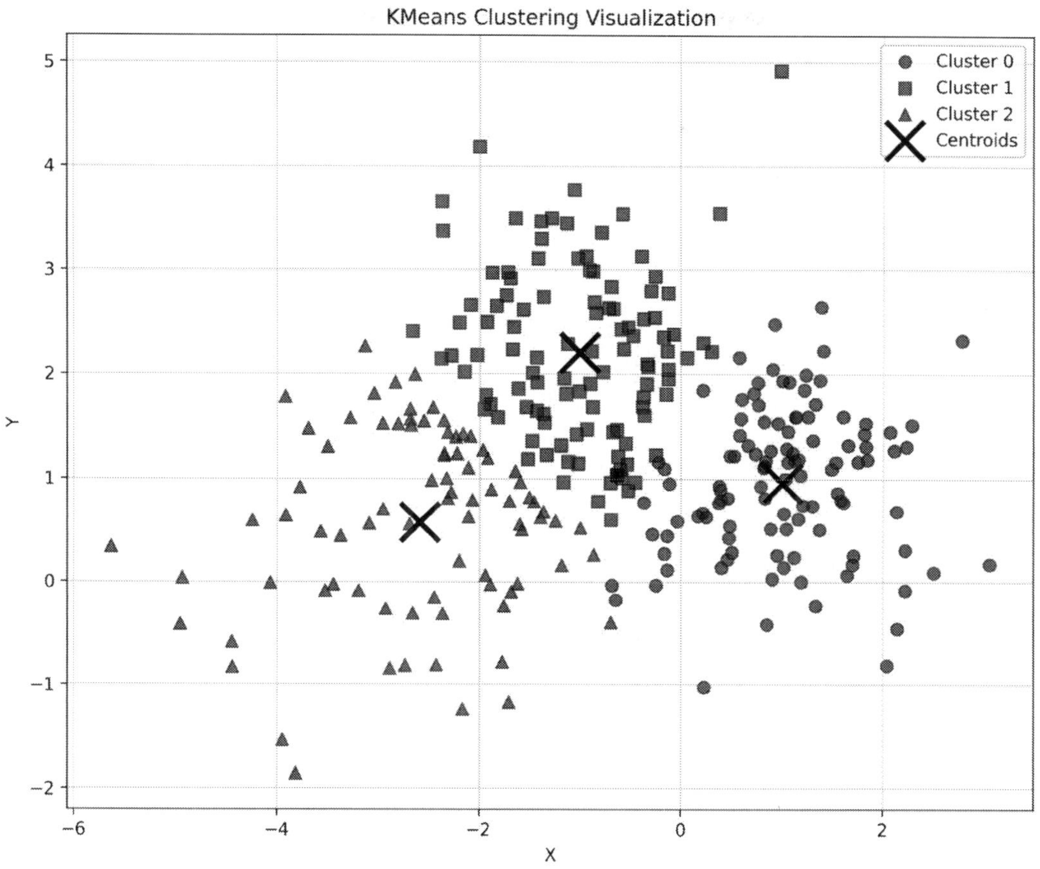

Figure 11.1: A set of two-dimensional data that has been clustered by the k-means algorithm. The mean (centroids) of each cluster is denoted by a large X. The icon shape denotes which cluster each point is associated with. In this case, k = 3 is denoted by square (top), triangle (bottom-left), and circle (bottom-right) markers.

The general problem is as follows. Suppose we are given a set of N observations, x_i, where $i = 0,1, \dots, N-1$, in d-dimensional real space, R^{d}, and some $0 < k < N$. The task is to find a partition, $S_1, \dots, S_k$, of the observations such that the within-cluster sum of squares is minimized; that is, we want to minimize the following sum:

$$\sum_{i=1}^{k} \sum_{x \in S_i} \| x - \mu_i \|^2$$

Here, μ_i denotes the mean of the points in the set S_i. A very simple algorithm for performing k-means clustering runs as follows. First, assign each of the observations randomly to the different cluster sets, S_i. Then, repeat the following two steps in sequence until the sets no longer change:

1. Compute the mean, μ_i, of each cluster, S_i.
2. Assign each point to the cluster whose mean is closest to it.

This algorithm will eventually converge (stop), but it is prone to converge to so-called **local minima**, where local changes no longer make any improvement to the objective function, but the clustering does not achieve the global minimum within-cluster sum of squares. The idea is that by randomly assigning the data at the beginning, you can try multiple different starting configurations with the hope that one of them will converge to the global minimum. There are better algorithms for k-means clustering, but the basic one should be sufficient for our purposes.

Our data consists of individual coordinates, each of which describes a position on the globe (a sphere). In particular, our data does not live in the d-dimensional real space we saw in the discussion of k-means . In order to apply the k-means algorithm, we need to first embed our data (hopefully in a meaningful way) into some real space. The obvious choice is three-dimensional real space, where we take the latitude and longitude and use these to produce a vector (in the mathematical sense) that contains the x, y, and z coordinates in real space. We can then perform clustering in this three-dimensional space, which will still produce relatively meaningful results on the sphere.

Let's talk about some simplifying assumptions. The Earth is approximately spherical, but not exactly. The Earth is slightly compressed in the north-south axis and correspondingly larger in the east-west axis. (The diameter at the equator is larger than the diameter between the north and south poles.) However, this doesn't make any difference in terms of clustering the data. (The difference between the perfectly spherical geodesic distance and sea-level distance on Earth is very small.) For reference, the radius of the Earth is approximately 6,378 km. Moreover, we can scale the sphere so that it has a radius of 1 km. This just makes the computations slightly simpler (and puts the numbers in a range where floating-point numbers have more accuracy).

We can set the center of the Earth to be the origin, with the x-y plane slicing through the equator. (We're ignoring planetary rotation and orbits and all those things as this is not an exercise in orbital mechanics.) The prime meridian (0 degrees longitude) is the positive x direction (coordinate (1,0,0)) and the north pole is in the positive z direction (coordinate (0,0,1)). With this setup, the latitude measures the angle (at the origin) from the x-y plane, and the longitude tells you the rotation around the z axis. With all of this together, the function that takes us from latitude-longitude pairs to x-y-z coordinates is given by the following expression. (Note that we have to convert from degrees to radians by multiplying each angle by $\pi/180$.)

$$(\psi, \lambda) \mapsto \left(\cos\left(\frac{\pi}{180}\psi\right)\cos\left(\frac{\pi}{180}\lambda\right), \cos\left(\frac{\pi}{180}\psi\right)\sin\left(\frac{\pi}{180}\lambda\right), \sin\left(\frac{\pi}{180}\psi\right)\right)$$

One of the first things we will need to implement is taking the input coordinates and expanding them out into these vectors of real numbers (rather than pairs of angles) using this expression. There are other ways of embedding the sphere into some vector space that allow us to capture different properties of the data, but this one should be sufficient for us. The geometry works out so that a spherical cluster in the three-dimensional space corresponds to a "disk" on the surface of the Earth (with a slightly adjusted radius). We will, eventually, need to translate the center of each cluster back onto the surface of the Earth, but this actually just amounts to computing the two angles from the three coordinates given.

Choosing the number of clusters

At this stage, you might be wondering how we chose the number k of clusters to find. This is a complicated question, as there are several different techniques that one might use to select an appropriate k to use. Some of these rely on the statistical properties of the data, while some function more by trial and error. There is no one method that will always give you precisely the right number of clusters to use. Sometimes this number is limited or completely prescribed by the application or context. In our case, the nature of the problem places some limits on the nature of clusters.

Ideally, we want our clusters to be fairly localized to particular places. What this means in practice is that we want the diameter (the maximal distance between any two points within a cluster) to be relatively small compared to the diameter of the sphere, possibly even limited to a fixed size. For instance, a 100 km diameter circle on the surface of the Earth, scaled accordingly to our radius of 1 km, would mean a maximum radius of approximately 0.000137 km in the three-dimensional space. (This is relatively simple geometry, but it is not so important.) Of course, such a restriction can also cause problems, so we need to be careful. We can use this more as an indication that more clusters might be needed rather than a hard constraint on the size of the clusters.

There are many techniques that one can use, depending on the characteristics and nature of the problem. The best thing to do in this case, if you are unfamiliar with the options available, is to consult somebody with data science expertise. (This could be speaking to a colleague, talking to your client, or, with care, consulting online communities such as Stack Overflow.)

Most of the time, if the number of clusters must be found, you will need to construct some kind of search over a range of possible k values where you try to optimize the performance of the clustering (measured by some metric) against the number of clusters. Common metrics include **silhouette** scores or the **Akaike information criterion**, possibly combined with some adjustment to penalize a larger number of clusters. (An optimization of a metric such as these will often favor single-point clusters, so one must modify the metric to favor fewer clusters.)

The silhouette score measures the relative size of each cluster (as measured by the average distance between points within the cluster) compared to the minimum average distance to points in other clusters. The result is a number between -1 and 1, where a score of 1 means the clusters are relatively small and relatively far apart. Unfortunately, computing the silhouette score is very expensive, requiring $O(N^2)$ computations. We can reduce that by using the average distance to the means of clusters rather than computing all the distances within each cluster, giving a reduced complexity of $O(Nk)$. (Our observation about the geometry of the problem might yield an alternative approach here, but we'll endeavor to keep this as standard as possible.) The task is to maximize the average silhouette score over the range of permissible cluster sizes. This seems like a relatively sensible approach.

Dividing the work

We already know that we need to use multithreading to accelerate the computation of these clusters. Here we have two options for how to proceed, depending on our overall strategy for clustering. One is to multithread different independent runs of the algorithm for different random initializations of the algorithm. The alternative is to divide the data itself into multiple batches. This approach requires more coordination and interaction between the different threads to make sure there are no conflicts between assigning observations to different groups from different threads. However, this does mean we have to hold the complete workspace in memory, which might be quite large. Given that we have read in the whole dataset at this point, we aren't too concerned about memory capacity here. But for truly massive datasets, one might have to consider chunking the data into batches that can be processed more readily in memory.

Now that we have discussed some of the theory, it's time to put this together and implement our clustering algorithm. This is the topic of the next section.

Implementing the clustering algorithm

Our implementation has several pieces. The main piece is the implementation of the k-means clustering algorithm. The second piece is the logic to increase (or decrease) the number of clusters until the fit is satisfying. The third piece is to transform the latitude-longitude coordinates into three-dimensional space so that the clustering can be done. This is the first piece that we shall tackle since it is quite straightforward. The logic for setting the number of groups is certainly the hardest part, but we can't test this until we have the k-means algorithm working.

Before we get started, we need to make some changes to our `CMakeLists.txt` and add new files to the `clustering` folder of our project. First, we create `clustering/CMakeLists.txt`, which will define the library target and the tests for this component of the project. This `CMakeLists.txt` should contain the following code:

```
add_library(ducky_clustering
  clustering.h
  clustering.cpp
  coord3.cpp
  coord3.h
  kmeans.cpp
  kmeans.h
)

target_link_libraries(ducky_clustering
  PUBLIC
    duckies_common
    spdlog::spdlog
  )
```

We also need to add `add_subdirectory(clustering)` to the main `CMakeLists.txt` beneath the other directories, and add the target `ducky_clustering` to the list of linked libraries of the main application. We will need this when we tie everything together in the next chapter. With this all set up, let's move on to writing the embedding into three-dimensional space.

Constructing the embedding

The embedding takes our two angles, ψ and λ, denoting the latitude and longitude, respectively, and converts these into vectors in three-dimensional space, (x, y, z). This is a new space, so we need a new data structure to represent it. This will help us make the rest of the computation slightly more readable by abstracting the addition, scalar multiplication, and distance computations on these points. Three dimensions is small enough that we can implement this using a struct with three data members. The definition of this structure is as follows, placed in a new file called `coord3.h`:

```
namespace duckies {

struct Coord3 {
    float x = 0.0f;
    float y = 0.0f;
    float z = 0.0f;
};

// ... functions

} //namespace duckies
```

This is not the only thing we need. We also need two arithmetic operators (more could be implemented, but we only need two), namely the add-in-place operator and multiplication by a scalar (float), defined as `constexpr` functions alongside the struct definition, as follows:

```
constexpr Coord3& operator+=(Coord3& lhs, const Coord3& rhs) noexcept {
    lhs.x += rhs.x;
    lhs.y += rhs.y;
    lhs.z += rhs.z;
    return lhs;
}

constexpr Coord3& operator*=(Coord3& lhs, const float& scalar) noexcept {
    lhs.x *= scalar;
    lhs.y *= scalar;
    lhs.z *= scalar;
    return lhs;
}
```

This will allow us to compute the mean of clusters, which is the main place these operations will be used. (Note that these should be placed inside the namespace alongside the struct definition so they can be found using argument-dependent lookup.)

We also need the distance, and in fact the square difference, between two vectors in this space. These are also easily defined as follows (also as inline functions in the `coord3.h` header inside the `duckies` namespace):

```
constexpr float dist2_squared(const Coord3& lhs, const Coord3& rhs)
noexcept {
    auto x = lhs.x - rhs.x;
    auto y = lhs.y - rhs.y;
    auto z = lhs.z - rhs.z;
    return x * x + y * y + z * z;
}

inline float dist2(const Coord3& lhs, const Coord3& rhs) noexcept {
    return std::hypot(lhs.x - rhs.x, lhs.y - rhs.y, lhs.z - rhs.z);
}
```

The `std::hypot` function computes the square root of the sum of squares of its arguments (it computes the length of the hypotenuse of the three-dimensional triangle whose sides are the arguments). This requires including the `cmath` header.

The final function we need is to convert a batch of angle coordinates into a batch of `Coord3` vectors that we can use in the clustering algorithm. This function is declared here as follows, but we place the definition in a corresponding `.cpp` file:

```
std::vector<Coord3> coord3_embedding(
    std::span<const Coordinate> coords) noexcept;
```

The definition of this function basically makes use of the formula given in the previous section, with a few changes to avoid recomputing expensive trigonometric functions and to perform the conversions from degrees to radians. We can wrap all this in an OpenMP parallel block to do all these (fairly expensive) computations in parallel, which should dramatically improve the time spent computing the embedding. The body of the function is placed in `coord3.cpp`, as follows:

```
std::vector<Coord3> coord3_embedding(std::span<const Coordinate> coords) {
    std::vector<Coord3> result(coords.size());
    const auto N = coords.size();
```

```
#pragma omp parallel for default(none) shared(N, result, coords)
    for (size_t i = 0; i < N; ++i) {
        auto& coords3 = result[i];
        const auto& angles = coords[i];

        auto psi = std::numbers::pi_v<float> * angles.latitude / 180.;
        auto lambda = std::numbers::pi_v<float> * angles.longitude / 180.;

        auto cospsi = std::cosf(psi);

        coords3.x = cospsi * std::cosf(lambda);
        coords3.y = cospsi * std::sinf(lambda);
        coords3.z = std::sinf(psi);
    }

    return result;
}
```

We will also need the function that takes coordinates in three-dimensional space and will convert these to the latitude and longitude. We need to take a little care here because the points that we convert might not lie on the surface of the unit sphere. Rather than producing a batch function like the embedding, we will write a small inline function (in `coord3.h`) that does a single conversion. This function is defined as follows:

```
inline Coordinate to_coordinates(const Coord3& coord) noexcept {
    auto r = std::hypot(coord.x, coord.y, coord.z);
    constexpr auto pi = std::numbers::pi_v<float>;

    auto lat = 180.0f * std::asinf(coord.z / r) / pi;
    auto lon = 180.0f * std::atan2f(coord.y, coord.x) / pi;

    return { lat, lon };
}
```

This function actually contains a small bug, but we'll discuss this in more detail later. To complete this implementation, we just need to add the two files, `coord3.h` and `coord3.cpp`, to the `ducky_clustering` target in the corresponding `CMakeLists.txt`. Now we can move on to implementing the k-means clustering algorithm.

Implementing the clustering algorithm

The k-means algorithm we've chosen is very simple, consisting of one step of setup and then two iterative steps that are repeated until the clusters stop changing (or a maximum number of iterations is reached). In terms of inputs, we need the data itself (in `Coord3` form) and the number of clusters to find. We also need a source for the randomness when we randomly assign labels to initialize the algorithm. We'll also need to keep various pieces of metadata alongside. The most obvious is the set of labels, stored in a vector with the same length as the data. We also need to store the current cluster means (denoted μ_i in the earlier discussion). These are `Coord3` instances, also stored in a vector, one for each possible label. It is also convenient to store a vector containing the size of each of the clusters. Since each of these requires some storage that persists over several iterations, we can use a class to package this up nicely.

The next thing is understanding what methods are needed. The algorithm contains three distinct steps, each of which can be packaged into a single method. This allows us to write a separate driver function that uses each of the three stages to perform the clustering until convergence or until we run out of iterations. This should give us enough to get started. This approach allows us to test the different aspects of the algorithm without needing to run through the whole algorithm.

The first stage is to create the class outline with all the data members and methods as described previously. We're also going to add a `set_labels` method for testing purposes. The class is defined as follows, placed in the new `kmeans.h` header file:

```
namespace duckies {

class KMeans {
    std::vector<int> labels_ {};
    std::vector<Coord3> cluster_means_ {};
    std::vector<size_t> cluster_size_ {};
    std::span<const Coord3> data_ {};
    size_t n_clusters_ = 0;

public:
    KMeans(std::span<const Coord3> data, size_t n_clusters);

    // getter methods ...

    void set_labels(std::vector<int> labels);
```

```
    void assign_random_labels(size_t seed);
    void recompute_means();
    bool update_labels();
};

} // namespace duckies
```

The constructor assigns the named members and sets the size of the other members to be the number of clusters (as in the case of `cluster_means_`, `cluster_size_`) and the length of the data (as for `labels_`). At the moment, these are not initialized with any data or values except setting them to 0. We've omitted the definition to save space here. The `update_labels` function returns `true` if the function changes any of the labels, and `false` otherwise. As usual, we've omitted the getter functions from the definition, since these are all very standard and mostly used for inspecting the state. We might need to add methods to this class later when it comes to implementing our logic for changing the number of clusters.

The next step is to implement these methods. The code for the methods is placed in a new file, `kmeans.cpp`, alongside the header file. Both of these files will need to be added to the `ducky_clustering` target in `CMakeLists.txt`. As usual, at the top of this file, we include the `kmeans.h` header and add `using namespace duckies` to bring all the names into scope.

The simplest method by far is `assign_random_labels`, which only requires assigning a randomly generated number between 0 and `n_clusters_ - 1`. For this, we can use a random number generator (`std::mt19937_64`) in conjunction with a uniform integer distribution and a simple iteration through the vector of labels. This is the code for this process:

```
void KMeans::assign_random_labels(size_t seed) {
    std::mt19937_64 rng(seed);
    std::uniform_int_distribution<int> dist(0, n_clusters_ - 1);

    // clear any lingering cluster sizes
    cluster_size_.assign(n_clusters_, 0);

    for (const auto& label : labels_) {
        label = dist(rng);
        cluster_size_[label] += 1;
    }
}
```

The `set_labels` method is similarly simple, although we want to be careful that the number of clusters and the associated data structures are similarly updated. We defer to the incoming labels to update the value of `n_clusters_`. We should also check that the size of the new labels is the same as the size of the data, but we're just going to use an `assert` rather than something more complex. (This method is primarily for testing.) The code is as follows:

```
void KMeans::set_labels(std::vector<int> labels) {
    assert(labels.size() == data_.size());
    labels_ = std::move(labels);

    cluster_size_.clear();

    for (const auto& label : labels_) {
        if (label >= static_cast<int>(cluster_size_.size())) {
            cluster_size_.resize(label + 1);
        }

        cluster_size_[label] += 1;
    }

    n_clusters_ = cluster_size_.size();
    cluster_means_.assign(n_clusters_, Coord3 { 0.0f, 0.0f, 0.0f });
}
```

Next up is the `recompute_means` method. This function needs to iterate through the data and the corresponding labels and accumulate each vector into the running total for that label. At the end, we have to divide by the amount of data associated with each label, provided the cluster has at least one point. This might not be the best approach: long sums of floating-point numbers can rapidly accumulate errors as one side gets larger and the other stays relatively small. Perhaps a better approach would be to normalize the accumulation by dividing by the cluster size as we go. An even better approach would be to use a divide-and-conquer approach. We haven't tested this, so we don't know if it is a problem that we need to do something about yet. Ignoring this problem for now, here is the code for the `recompute_means` method:

```
void KMeans::recompute_means() {
    const auto N = data_.size();
    cluster_means_.assign(n_clusters_, Coord3 { 0.0f, 0.0f, 0.0f });
```

```
    for (size_t i = 0; i < N; ++i) {
        auto label = labels_[i];
        cluster_means_[label] += data_[i];
    }

    for (size_t i = 0; i < n_clusters_; ++i) {
        if (cluster_size_[i] > 0) {
            cluster_means_[i] *= 1.0f / cluster_size_[i];
        }
    }
}
```

The one remaining method (for now at least) is `update_labels`. This is by far the most complicated since each step involves computing the distance to each of the current means, finding the index of the closest mean, then updating the label accordingly (if appropriate). Let's focus on finding the closest mean for a moment. Here we'd like to use `std::min_element` with a carefully designed comparison operator that computes the distance from the (currently fixed) reference point to each mean and compares these distances. However, this strategy ends up computing the distances for each comparison. This is unnecessary. The distance function here is not too complicated, but it does involve some computations, and avoiding recomputation is never a bad thing. (In fact, `std::transform_reduce` might be more appropriate, but this returns the minimum distance, not the position where it is attained.) Instead, we're going to write our own search function.

The strategy is very simple: we iterate through each of the means, keeping track of the best distance we've seen so far and its position. For each point, we compute the distance and update it if this is less than the current best. This is all very standard. What is not quite standard is that instead of distance, we're going to use the square distance. This doesn't change the mathematics (with this specific choice of distance function). The code for this function is as follows:

```
template <typename It>
static auto min_distance(
    const Coord3& pt, const It& begin, const It& end) noexcept {
    It min_value = begin;
    float current_best = std::numeric_limits<float>::infinity();
    for (auto it = begin; it != end; ++it) {
        auto this_distance = dist2_squared(pt, *it);
        if (this_distance < current_best) {
            min_value = it;
```

```
            current_best = this_distance;
        }
    }
    return min_value;
}
```

With this function, writing the `update_labels` function is quite straightforward. The process is to iterate through each of the points, find the closest mean using the `min_distance` function, and use this to compute the new label. Now, this label might be the same as the old one, in which case we don't need to do anything. However, if the label has changed, we have three things to do:

- We need to update the label to the new label
- We need to decrement the count of the old label in `cluster_size_` and increment the count for the new label
- We need to update the return `bool` to be `true`, indicating that a change has been made

The new label is easy to compute because it is the index of the closest mean point in the `cluster_means_` array. Since we return the iterator from our `min_distance` function, we can obtain this index by taking the difference of the two. With all this in mind, the function is defined as follows:

```
bool KMeans::update_labels() {
    bool has_changed = false;
    const auto N = data_.size();

    const auto means_begin = cluster_means_.begin();
    const auto means_end = cluster_means_.end();

    for (size_t i = 0; i < N; ++i) {
        const auto& pt = data_[i];
        auto min_pos = min_distance(pt, means_begin, means_end);
        auto new_label = static_cast<int>(min_pos - means_begin);
        auto old_label = labels_[i];

        if (new_label != old_label) {
            labels_[i] = new_label;
            --cluster_size_[old_label];
            ++cluster_size_[new_label];
            has_changed = true;
        }
```

```
    }

    return has_changed;
}
```

With this complete, we have finished the implementation of the KMeans class for now. What we have yet to do is implement the k-means algorithm as a whole. We could implement this as a method on the KMeans class, but we actually don't have to since all the operations that are needed to run the algorithm are exposed through the methods we just defined. For this reason, we add a free function, taking a reference to the KMeans driver class, along with the seed and a maximum number of iterations needed to set up the algorithm. The prototype is placed in the kmeans.h header, and the definition, as follows, is placed in the corresponding kmeans.cpp file:

```
bool kmeans_cluster(KMeans& driver, size_t seed, int max_iterations) {
    driver.assign_random_labels(seed);

    int i = 0;
    bool has_changed = true;
    for (; i < max_iterations && has_changed; ++i) {
        driver.recompute_means();
        has_changed = driver.update_labels();
    }

    if (i < max_iterations) {
        spdlog::info("kmeans converged in {} iterations", i);
    } else {
        spdlog::warn(
            "kmeans failed to converge in {} iterations", max_iterations);
    }
    return i < max_iterations;
}
```

We've included some basic logging in this function to provide debugging information about the speed of convergence. Once the algorithm is finished, the driver object contains all the information about the converged clustering, including the mean for each cluster and the size of each cluster. Since each of these objects allocates quite a lot of data, we would like to reuse it if possible, rather than creating a new instance for each new clustering, though this might not be possible. This completes the implementation of the clustering algorithm. Now we come to the tricky part of deciding how many clusters to use.

Deciding on the number of clusters and computing the clustering

We've already seen that finding the most appropriate number of clusters is a difficult problem. We've also seen that a relatively sensible approach for our problem is using (simplified) silhouette scores. Before we can proceed, we need to make the definitions formal here. The silhouette score for the ith data point is a combination of two numbers, $a(i)$ and $b(i)$. The first is the distance from the ith point to the mean of its cluster, μ_j (here, j is the label of point i). The second number, $b(i)$, is the minimum distance from the ith point the other cluster means to μ_s where $s \neq j$.

The silhouette on its own is not sufficient to find the best number of clusters; we also need to penalize clusters of size 0 and, to a lesser extent, clusters of size 1. Otherwise, we can end up in a scenario where the silhouette scores are relatively constant over the range of k values, but, for larger values of k, most of the clusters are empty. A normalized penalty of $-1/k$ for empty clusters and $-1/2\,k$ for clusters of size 1 should be sufficient to discourage this behavior.

Obviously, we need to write a function for computing this modified score. This needs to take a reference to a `KMeans` object and compute both the silhouette score and the penalty, and return the sum of these two as the final score. The `compute_score` function is declared in `kmeans.h` and defined in `kmeans.cpp`, as follows:

```
float duckies::compute_score(const KMeans& driver) {
    const auto& means = driver.cluster_means();
    const auto& labels = driver.labels();
    const auto data = driver.data();
    const auto num_clusters = driver.n_clusters();

    float silhouette = 0.0f;

    for (size_t i = 0; i < data.size(); ++i) {
        float a_i = dist2(data[i], means[labels[i]]);
        float b_i = 1.0f;

        for (size_t cluster_i = 0; cluster_i < num_clusters; ++cluster_i) {
            if (cluster_i != labels[i]) {
                auto dist = dist2(means[cluster_i], data[i]);
                if (dist < b_i) {
                    b_i = dist;
```

```
                }
            }
        }

        silhouette += (b_i - a_i) / std::max(a_i, b_i);
    }

    silhouette /= data.size();

    auto& sizes = driver.cluster_sizes();
    float penalty = 0.0f;
    for (size_t i=0; i<num_clusters; ++i) {
        if (sizes[i] == 0) {
            penalty += 1.0f;
        } else if (sizes[i] == 1) {
            penalty += 0.5f;
        }
    }
    penalty /= num_clusters;

    return silhouette - penalty;
}
```

This function will need to be called on each of the trial clusterings for each test *k* value. The best clustering for each *k* value will be passed on to the global search process to find the best overall clustering. Our process for this will be to create a vector of `KMeans` objects and a vector of scores, which are both populated using multiple threads to improve the throughput. The best clustering is the one whose corresponding score is maximal. The routine should construct these vectors and return a pair of the best clustering and its score; we will need this in further processing. The code is as follows; as before, the function is declared in `kmeans.h` and defined in `kmeans.cpp`:

```
std::pair<KMeans, float> duckies::best_kmeans_cluster(
    std::span<const Coord3> data, size_t k, size_t n_repetitions,
    int max_iterations) {
    std::vector<KMeans> drivers;
    std::vector<float> scores(n_repetitions, -1.0f);
    drivers.reserve(n_repetitions);
    for (size_t i = 0; i < n_repetitions; ++i) {
```

```
        drivers.emplace_back(data, k);
    }

#pragma omp parallel for default(none) shared(drivers, scores)
    for (size_t i = 0; i < n_repetitions; ++i) {
        size_t seed = std::random_device {}();
        if (kmeans_cluster(drivers[i], seed, max_iterations)) {
            scores[i] = compute_score(drivers[i]);
        }
    }

    auto best = std::max_element(scores.begin(), scores.end());
    auto best_idx = static_cast<size_t>(best - scores.begin());

    return { std::move(drivers[best_idx]), *best };
}
```

With this function in place, we can find the best attempt for each different value of k, but we have yet to find the best value of k. For this we need to perform some kind of search (or optimization) over the range of k values. The question then is what strategy to use. The most basic implementation is a simple linear search, but this means computing all of the possible values of k. This might work well if the range of k values is relatively small, but if this range is large, then this becomes prohibitively expensive. On the other hand, something like a binary search would more rapidly reduce the search range, but now we have to decide which half of the data to continue searching at each step.

The binary search seems the most appropriate. Our strategy will be to find the midpoint of the range, and then use the midpoint of the two branches (the quarter values) to pick the branch to continue into. This process terminates when there are no more than three values left in the range, at which point we have to check each one. Our goal with this is to avoid computing any clustering that we don't need. We're going to break this function into multiple parts because it's going to be quite complicated. Let's start by declaring the function (in `clustering.h`) along with a supporting structure for the cluster data, as follows:

```
namespace duckies {

struct Cluster {
    Coordinate position;
```

```
    size_t num_points;
};

[[nodiscard]]
std::vector<Cluster> compute_clusters(const RubberDuckData& data,
    size_t min_clusters, size_t max_clusters, int num_repetitions,
    size_t max_iterations);

} // namespace duckies
```

The first part of the function sets up the data and some additional metadata that will be used in the recursion. The first few lines of the function are as follows:

```
std::vector<Cluster> duckies::compute_clusters(const RubberDuckData& data,
    size_t min_clusters, size_t max_clusters, size_t num_repetitions,
    size_t max_iterations) {
    using ClusterScore = std::pair<KMeans, float>;

    auto embedded_data = coord3_embedding(data.coordinates());

    // snip ...
}
```

Next, we need to create the storage for the result. Since we only need the means and sizes for the results, we're only going to store these in the running best. This means we don't have to make copies of the entire `KMeans` class each iteration. The next piece of code constructs a vector to contain these means and a small lambda function to update them. The following code is placed inside the function body, below the definition of `embedded_data`:

```
    // snip ...
    std::vector<std::pair<Coord3, size_t>> best;
    float best_score;
    auto update_best = [&](ClusterScore& other) {
        if (other.second > best_score) {
            best_score = other.second;
            auto& kmeans = other.first;
            best.clear();
            best.reserve(kmeans.n_clusters());
            for (size_t i=0; i<kmeans.n_clusters(); ++i) {
```

```
                best.emplace_back(
                    kmeans.cluster_means()[i], kmeans.cluster_sizes()[i]);
            }
        }
    };

    // snip...
```

At each iteration, we will need to compute three pairs of clusters and scores (as a `ClusterScore` pair). The values we need are those at the maximum and minimum values of *k* that remain and the midpoint. We can store these in a vector, for convenient searching later. We need to set this up now with the following code, placed below the `update_best` lambda function:

```
    // snip ...
    constexpr size_t working_set_size = 3;
    std::vector<ClusterScore> working_set;
    working_set.reserve(working_set_size);
    for (size_t i=0; i<working_set_size; ++i) {
        working_set.emplace_back(KMeans(embedded_data, 0), -1.0f);
    }
    // snip ...
```

We can also define a small lambda function that returns an iterator to the pair with the best score within the `working_set` vector. This will be useful for updating the best seen score as we go and for finding the final value after we have finished the iteration. We also define a second lambda to extract the score from the working set at each index. These lambda functions are defined as follows:

```
    // snip ...
    auto best_working = [&] {
        return std::max_element(working_set.begin(), working_set.end(),
                    [](const ClusterScore& l, const ClusterScore& r) {
                            return l.second < r.second; });
    };

    auto score = [&](size_t i) { return working_set[i].second; };
    // snip ...
```

We can also add a new function that computes clustering values for an updated *k* value for each of the positions, which does not recompute if the clustering in that position matches the new value of *k*. This is defined as follows:

```
// snip ...
auto update = [&](size_t i, size_t new_k) {
    if (working_set[i].first.n_clusters() != new_k) {
        working_set[i] = best_kmeans_cluster(
            embedded_data, new_k, num_repetitions, max_iterations);
    }
};
```

Next, we need to set up the bisection loop. First, we define `low_k` and `high_k` to be `min_clusters` and `max_clusters`, respectively, and the loop condition is that the high value is greater than the low value. The first step is to compute the clustering for each of the *k* values in question using the `update` lambda function. We can also update the best score (if necessary) using the best of these four current working values. The bisecting logic here is to move into the higher *k* range if the `high_k` score is larger than both other scores; otherwise, we favor moving to the lower *k* range. The final part is to shrink the range according to the size of the three intervals. This is done using the following code:

```
// snip ...
size_t low_k = min_clusters;
size_t high_k = max_clusters;

while (high_k > low_k) {
    auto mid_k = (low_k + high_k) / 2;
    update(0, low_k);
    update(1, mid_k);
    update(2, high_k);

    auto iter_best = best_working();
    update_best(*iter_best);

    if (score(2) >= score(1) && score(2) > score(0)) {
        low_k = mid_k + 1;
    } else {
        high_k = mid_k - 1;
```

```
        }
    }
    // snip ...
```

With the bisection loop finished, we should now have found the best k value and the corresponding set of clusters. The final steps are to construct the vector of `Cluster` objects to return to the user. These are geographical (latitude and longitude) coordinates. At the moment, our clusters are stored in the embedded space (as `Coord3` structures), so we need to perform a conversion. This is handled using the `to_coordinates` function that we declared earlier. The final part of the code is as follows:

```
    // snip ...
    std::vector<Cluster> result;
    result.reserve(best.size());

    for (const auto& cluster : best) {
        result.emplace_back(to_coordinates(cluster.first), cluster.
second);
    }

    return result;
    // end of function
}
```

There are some potential problems with this implementation. The silhouette score function does not need to be **concave**, and thus might have multiple local maxima. We might not attain the best possible number of clusters k using this procedure, but hopefully the geometry of the data will mean that this doesn't happen in practice. A linear search over all the possible values of k would not suffer from this downside, but it would be so expensive and slow as to make it intractable. One might be able to devise some alternate strategy that doesn't suffer from the same problem, but this should work for now. We won't know for sure until we test, which is the topic of the next section.

Testing our implementation

The next step is to write some tests for everything that we have implemented here. Of course, we should be doing this as we go along (and this was the case as we developed the code for this book), but we need to dedicate time to this separately to properly explain the tests that we construct.

As always, the tests have exposed various defects in the implementation that have allowed us to arrive at the solution that we have presented. Most of these are small, such as using the incorrect variables, and others are more significant (such as the logic in the bisection loop). Tests are important for making sure your code works correctly (or, at least, as expected) and that future changes do not break it.

Throughout this challenge, we've placed tests in files prefixed by `test_` followed by the name of the component (see the `Chapter-11` folder in the GitHub repository: `https://github.com/PacktPublishing/The-CPP-Programmers-Mindset` for examples). This section will be no different. We also need to construct a new CMake target called `test_clustering` that will be used to build and run all these tests. This target needs to link the `GTest::gtest_main` target, to define the main function for the test harness, and link the `ducky_clustering` target that defines our clustering code. We have three main parts of this library—`kmeans`, `clustering`, and `coord3`—so our tests should have three files: `test_kmeans.cpp`, `test_clustering.cpp`, and `test_coord3.cpp`. With all these added to the `test_clustering` target in `CMakeLists.txt`, we can start to write the tests themselves, starting with the coordinate embedding in `test_coord3.cpp`.

Testing the embedding

Before we get started, we're actually going to define `operator==` and the stream-out operator for the `Coord3` struct. This will make writing the tests and reading the output significantly simpler. The equality operator can be defined as an inline (actually, `constexpr`) function in the header, but the stream-out operator is defined in the header to avoid including the heavy `<ostream>` header in our interface header file. (Little details such as this can dramatically improve compile times in larger projects, not that it makes a huge difference here.) With these written, we can write the first tests for the arithmetic properties operations on the structure, as follows:

```
TEST(Coord3, TestCoord3Addition) {
    Coord3 origin { 0.0f, 0.0f, 0.0f };

    Coord3 x { 1.0f, 0.0f, 0.0f };
    Coord3 y { 0.0f, 1.0f, 0.0f };
    Coord3 z { 0.0f, 0.0f, 1.0f };

    EXPECT_EQ(origin += x, x);

    Coord3 xy { 1.0f, 1.0f, 0.0f };
```

```
    EXPECT_EQ(origin += y, xy);

    Coord3 xyz { 1.0f, 1.0f, 1.0f };
    EXPECT_EQ(origin += z, xyz);
}

TEST(Coord3, TestScalarMultiplication){
    Coord3 xyz { 1.0f, 1.0f, 1.0f };

    xyz *= 0.5f;

    Coord3 expected { 0.5f, 0.5f, 0.5f };
    EXPECT_EQ(xyz, expected);
}
```

These tests check that each of the components is updated correctly, in both cases. We don't need to randomize the inputs and statistically check that these are always correctly defined because these operators are so simple. Sometimes, something more thorough is needed, particularly if there are special cases to be handled. Moving on, we also need to check that the distance functions perform correctly. Here, we can check both the `dist2` function (which computes the Euclidean distance) and the `dist2_squared` function (which computes the square of this distance) at the same time. The test code is as follows:

```
TEST(Coord3, TestEuclideanDistance) {
    Coord3 x { 1.0f, 0.74f, -0.25f };
    Coord3 y { 1.0f, 0.24f, 0.25f };

    auto expected = std::sqrtf(0.5);
    auto norm = dist2(x, y);

    EXPECT_NEAR(norm, expected, 1e-7);
    EXPECT_NEAR(dist2_squared(x, y), expected * expected, 2e-7f);
}
```

The final pair of functions to test are those that perform the embedding from latitude-longitude pairs to `Coord3` and the map that computes the return direction. For this test, we're going to construct a vector of `Coordinate` (latitude-longitude) objects representing a selection of simple directions. Then we convert these to `Coord3` and check that these are as expected. At the same time, we'll convert these back (using `to_coordinates`) to the `Coordinate` objects. Then we compare the round-trip results with the original coordinates. If all goes well, these should match. The test code is as follows:

```
TEST(Coord3, TestEmbeddingCardinalPositions) {
    std::vector<Coordinate> cardinals { { 0.0f, 0.0f }, { 90.0f, 0.0f },
        { -90.0f, 0.0f }, { 0.0f, 90.0f }, { 0.0f, -90.0f }, { 0.0f,
180.0f } };

    std::vector<Coord3> expected { { 1.0f, 0.0f, 0.0f }, { 0.0f, 0.0f,
1.0f },
        { 0.0f, 0.0f, -1.0f }, { 0.0f, 1.0f, 0.0f }, { 0.0f, -1.0f, 0.0f
},
        { -1.0f, 0.0f, 0.0f } };

    auto transformed = coord3_embedding(cardinals);

    ASSERT_EQ(transformed.size(), cardinals.size());

    for (size_t i = 0; i < expected.size(); ++i) {
        EXPECT_NEAR(dist2(transformed[i], expected[i]), 0.0f, 1e-7f);

        auto rt = to_coordinates(transformed[i]);
        EXPECT_NEAR(rt.latitude, cardinals[i].latitude, 1e-7) << i;
        EXPECT_NEAR(rt.longitude, cardinals[i].longitude, 1e-7) << i;
    }
}
```

This test might actually fail with the code that we've defined so far. The reason is very subtle, and concerns a floating-point error. Let's look at the second case, `{90.0f, 0.0f}`. The embedding converts this latitude and longitude pair into a coordinate that is very close to the desired `{0.0f, 0.0f, 1.0f}`, but not exactly equal. There is a small error in these trigonometric computations in the `x` component of the order `-4e-8`. This is a very small error, but it is a negative value. (Your results may vary slightly, depending on the actual implementation of `sinf` and `cosf`.)

Thus, in the `to_coordinates` function, when we use `atan2f`, the return longitude value is `-180`. This is obviously incorrect. To fix this problem, we're going to clamp values of `coord.x` and `coord.y` that are very close to 0 with actual 0. We can do this by inserting the following lines into the `to_coordinates` function and replacing `coord.x` and `coord.y` with these new `x` and `y` values, respectively, in the call to `atan2f`:

```
constexpr float epsilon = std::numeric_limits<float>::epsilon();
float x = (std::fabs(coord.x) < epsilon) ? 0.0f : coord.x;
float y = (std::fabs(coord.y) < epsilon) ? 0.0f : coord.y;
```

With this fix in place, all the embedding tests pass and we can move on to testing the `KMeans` class and affiliated functions.

Testing the *k*-means clustering logic

The `KMeans` class implements various aspects of the *k*-means clustering algorithm and we should test each of these in tandem. In all of these tests, we're going to need some sample data to work with. For this, we can create a static array of `Coord3` objects that are naturally clustered and simply take spans of this array as our input data in each of the tests. The data is defined as follows:

```
static constexpr Coord3 polar_data[] = {
    { 0.0f, 0.0f, 1.0f },
    { 0.0f, 0.0f, -1.0f },
    { 0.0f, 0.099833417f, 0.995004165 },
    { 0.099833417f, 0.0f, 0.995004165 },
    { -0.099833417f, 0.0f, 0.995004165 },
    { 0.0f, -0.099833417f, 0.995004165 },
    { 0.0f, 0.099833417f, -0.995004165 },
    { 0.099833417f, 0.0f, -0.995004165 },
    { -0.099833417f, 0.0f, -0.995004165 },
    { 0.0f, -0.099833417f, -0.995004165 },
};
```

This data is distributed (evenly) around the north and south poles of the sphere, with one point at each pole and four additional points nearby. Naturally, the data has two clusters, each consisting of the data at one of the poles.

Let's start with the `compute_means` method. This function should add up the points that belong to each cluster (as currently defined) and divide by the size of the clusters. This should be relatively simple to test in ordinary cases, but we should also include a test where there is a cluster with no points. This should give the average as the origin rather than undefined. The first of these cases is as follows:

```
TEST(KMeans, TestComputeMeans) {
    KMeans k_means(std::span<const Coord3>(polar_data, 10), size_t(2));

    k_means.set_labels({ 0, 1, 0, 0, 0, 0, 1, 1, 1, 1 });

    const auto& sizes = k_means.cluster_sizes();
    EXPECT_EQ(sizes[0], 5);
    EXPECT_EQ(sizes[1], 5);

    k_means.recompute_means();

    auto means = k_means.cluster_means();

    Coord3 north_mean { 0.0f, 0.0f, (4 * 0.995004165 + 1.0) / 5.0 };
    Coord3 south_mean { 0.0f, 0.0f, (4 * -0.995004165 + -1.0) / 5.0 };

    EXPECT_NEAR(dist2(north_mean, means[0]), 0.0f, 1e-7);
    EXPECT_NEAR(dist2(south_mean, means[1]), 0.0f, 1e-7);
}
```

For the second case, we need to set labels slightly differently, because the `set_labels` method recomputes the number of clusters based on the largest seen label. Simply changing all the `0` labels to 2 instead has the desired effect, and the label `0` is our zero-sized cluster for testing. Otherwise, the test is very simple, defined as follows:

```
TEST(KMeans, TestMeansEmptyCluster) {
    KMeans k_means(std::span<const Coord3>(polar_data, 10), size_t(3));
    k_means.set_labels({ 2, 1, 2, 2, 2, 2, 1, 1, 1, 1 });
    const auto& sizes = k_means.cluster_sizes();
    ASSERT_EQ(sizes.size(), 3);
    EXPECT_EQ(sizes[0], 0);
```

```
    k_means.recompute_means();
    const auto& means = k_means.cluster_means();
    ASSERT_EQ(means.size(), 3);

    EXPECT_EQ(means[0], Coord3(0.0f, 0.0f, 0.0f));
}
```

We also need to test the random assignment of labels. This is tricky because of the random nature since one might technically randomly assign the same label to all of the points. However, with 10 points in our data set and 2 labels, the probability of assigning all points the same label is 1 in 1,024, which should be sufficiently rare. Besides, seeding the random generator should make this far less likely to happen in practice. (Note that a seeded generation of the same class should produce the same sequence of random bytes on all platforms. However, it is not guaranteed that the distribution is implemented in precisely the same way everywhere, thus giving different numbers on different platforms or with different versions of the standard library.) Technicalities aside, the process is to assign random labels and check that all labels are assigned and within the set range. The code is as follows:

```
TEST(KMeans, TestRandomAssignment) {
    const size_t k = 2;
    KMeans k_means(std::span<const Coord3>(polar_data, 10), k);
    k_means.assign_random_labels(12345);

    std::set<int> seen;
    for (const auto& label : k_means.labels()) {
        EXPECT_GE(label, 0);
        EXPECT_LT(label, k);
        seen.insert(label);
    }

    EXPECT_EQ(seen.size(), k);
}
```

The remaining method for the clustering algorithm is the `update_labels` method, which is probably best tested by running through the algorithm itself and checking the labels. We know that if we run the clustering with $k = 2$, we should end up with one cluster at each pole. Moreover, the algorithm should converge very quickly for such a dataset (usually 1–2 iterations at most).

Let's write a test that exercises the `update_labels` method and tests that the algorithm actually converges as expected. Since we've tested the label assignment and the compute means method, this can really only fail if the `update_labels` method does not function appropriately. The code is as follows:

```
TEST(KMeans, TestConvergeIterations) {
    KMeans k_means(std::span<const Coord3>(polar_data, 10), size_t(2));
    k_means.assign_random_labels(12345);
    int no_iters = 0;
    bool changed = true;
    for (; changed && no_iters < 10; ++no_iters) {
        k_means.recompute_means();
        changed = k_means.update_labels();
    }

    ASSERT_LT(no_iters, 10);
    const auto& labels = k_means.labels();

    EXPECT_EQ(labels[2], labels[0]);
    EXPECT_EQ(labels[3], labels[0]);
    EXPECT_EQ(labels[4], labels[0]);
    EXPECT_EQ(labels[5], labels[0]);
    EXPECT_EQ(labels[6], labels[1]);
    EXPECT_EQ(labels[7], labels[1]);
    EXPECT_EQ(labels[8], labels[1]);
    EXPECT_EQ(labels[9], labels[1]);
}
```

We haven't used our `kmeans_cluster` function here because we want to keep track of the number of iterations used. We've included a test for that function in the repository, but it is almost identical to the test we just wrote, so we won't include it here.

The remaining functions that we need to test involve the computation of scores. We can test that the scoring works appropriately for the two clusters, where both clusters are used to their full capacity, so there should be no penalties applied. In this case, we are essentially testing the implementation of the silhouette score. This test is defined as follows:

```
TEST(KMeans, TestScoreFunctionTwoClusters) {
    KMeans k_means(std::span<const Coord3>(polar_data, 10), size_t(2));
```

```
    k_means.set_labels({ 0, 1, 0, 0, 0, 0, 1, 1, 1, 1 });
    k_means.recompute_means();
    ASSERT_EQ(k_means.n_clusters(), 2);
    auto score = compute_score(k_means);

    EXPECT_GT(score, 0.9f);
}
```

The other cases we need to test are where a penalty is applied for empty clusters. Here we demonstrate one of these cases where we have a single data point and a single cluster, thus incurring a small penalty for having a one-point cluster. The test is defined as follows:

```
TEST(KMeans, TestScoreFunctionSinglePoint) {
    std::vector<Coord3> data { { 0.0f, 0.0f, 0.0f } };
    KMeans kmeans(data, 1);
    kmeans.set_labels({ 0 });
    auto score = compute_score(kmeans);

    EXPECT_NEAR(score, 0.5f, 1.0e-7f);
}
```

We leave out the other tests of this kind for the sake of space and move on to testing the final component, the full clustering algorithm.

Testing the clustering algorithm

The final function we need to test is the `compute_clusters` function. This function performs the bisection combined with the clustering algorithm to find the best clustering for the data. From our point of view, we need to test that, when applied to something such as our `polar_data` from the `KMeans` tests, the method finds $k = 2$ and the appropriate clustering in a reasonable number of steps. We just need to run the function with some data to exercise the code within. Let's see what that might look like:

```
TEST(Clustering, TestClusteringPolarData)
{
    RubberDuckData data;
    data.reserve_additional(10);
    constexpr float km100 = 0.89833485f;

    data.insert(90.f, 0.0f, std::chrono::year_month_day {}, "");
```

```
    data.insert(-90.f, 0.0f, std::chrono::year_month_day {}, "");
    data.insert(90.f - km100, 0.0f, std::chrono::year_month_day {}, "");
    data.insert(90.f - km100, 90.0f, std::chrono::year_month_day {}, "");
    data.insert(90.f - km100, 180.0f, std::chrono::year_month_day {}, "");
    data.insert(90.f - km100, -90.0f, std::chrono::year_month_day {}, "");
    data.insert(-90.f + km100, 0.0f, std::chrono::year_month_day {}, "");
    data.insert(-90.f + km100, 90.0f, std::chrono::year_month_day {}, "");
    data.insert(-90.f + km100, 180.0f, std::chrono::year_month_day {},
"");
    data.insert(-90.f + km100, -90.0f, std::chrono::year_month_day {},
"");

    auto clusters = compute_clusters(data, 1, 10, 5, 100);
    ASSERT_EQ(clusters.size(), 2);

    for (const auto& cluster : clusters) {
        EXPECT_EQ(cluster.num_points, 5);
    }
}
```

The data is essentially constructed from the polar data from the earlier tests, but written in terms of latitude and longitude instead of the three-dimensional coordinates. Since the `compute_clusters` function takes a reference to `RubberDuckData`, we also have to provide the date and description strings, but these are not used so they can essentially be empty. We run the function with this data and some default settings, searching the range of k between 1 and 10 for the best choice, which should hopefully be 2. The other parameters are the number of repetitions to use for finding the clustering, and the maximum number of iterations to use in each k-means fitting process. The function returns a vector of clusters, consisting of the coordinates of the mean and the size of the cluster. For testing, we just check that the number of found clusters is 2 as expected, and that each cluster contains 5 points.

With all this done, we have a working implementation of our algorithm and some tests to ensure that it works correctly. In the next section, we will look at some of the limitations of our approach and what could be done to improve the implementation.

Understanding limitations and opportunities to expand

In this chapter, we've implemented and used the k-means clustering algorithm to find regions where the data is localized. This is by no means the only algorithm for accomplishing this task. In fact, we've faced many challenges with this approach, most notably in finding the appropriate value of k for our clustering. The binary search we use in tandem with our modified silhouette score does work (at least on our test cases) to find such a value, but it is by no means guaranteed to do so. We can afford such shortcuts here because of the nature and geometry of our data (being naturally clustered and distributed over the surface of the sphere). Our approach might not work as well, or at all, if our data were more randomly distributed and loosely clustered. Remember, this chapter is less about how to use k-means as a tool for data science and more about the process of solving the problem.

Ideally, data problems such as this would be subject to a longer period of study where one could properly explore the data and experiment with different methodologies. All problems require trial and error, and it is quite rare that one finds the best solution right away (especially at the beginning). This problem was no different. We tried multiple different methods for finding the value of k, trying to balance complexity (in an intellectual sense), speed, and efficiency. The solution we arrived at uses the silhouette score, which measures the spread of individual clusters against the spread of clusters themselves. There are many other scores and metrics that one could use for finding the value of k. We also experimented with the Calinski-Harabasz index and the Davies-Bouldin index, but these proved to be difficult to work with for our problem. (These might perform better if the underlying geometry of the data were less structured than ours.)

One of the biggest limitations of our approach is the space complexity. Each instance of our `KMeans` class requires the allocation of an array of labels of the same size as the data. Coupling this with the need to perform several clusterings in parallel to find the best clustering for each k, and the need to compute these clusterings for multiple values of k-means we require quite a lot of memory. Now, to keep the project simple, we've made an assumption that the data is small enough to fit into reasonable memory. If this were not the case, we would have to divide the computation into pieces or distribute it across multiple computers in a cluster. Batching the computation might also help further parallelize the computation to achieve better throughput.

In retrospect, the k-means clustering might not be the best choice of algorithm for clustering this data, and a more hierarchical approach might be better. This is why reflecting on solutions is so important, as it allows you to formally make observations about what worked well and what could have been done better and more efficiently in the future. Most of the time, these revelations come too late to be useful for solving the problem at hand, but at least the lessons can be taken forward to the next problem.

Generalizing the implementation

Our implementation of k-means is intrinsically linked to the data that we have; we can only use our functions to cluster data in three-dimensional real space. However, if you dig into the implementation itself, you'll find that we mostly make use of the distance function and the arithmetic operations on the `Coord3` struct. Thus, in theory, we could replace (via a template argument) `Coord3` with any other coordinate-like data structure and an associated distance function. The scoring functions are similar. This would allow us to use the implementation elsewhere in other projects (or just make it available as a standalone library).

We also used the most basic embedding of the geographical data into three-dimensional space, but there are many others, depending on what properties of the data you need to expose. For instance, in some applications, it might be better to embed the data into some n-dimensional space using spherical harmonics (or similar). This would capture more of the spherical structure of the data, allowing a more nuanced clustering than mere location. This goes hand in hand with a generalized driver class with arbitrary coordinate-like structures.

Identifying opportunities to generalize the methodology so that it can potentially be reused is a useful process. It forces you to go back over your code and see what properties are used and how, and for you to better understand the conceptual process and think about the algorithm more abstractly. This does not mean that you should always strive to write the most general code possible; this will quickly lead to confusing code that is hard to read. Remember, you should first solve the problem in front of you.

This concludes the chapter. In the next chapter, we will put everything together and run the complete application on some sample data.

Summary

In this chapter, we implemented an embedding from geographical data into three-dimensional real space, and a k-means clustering algorithm for the embedded data. This was a relatively simple procedure, following a well-known algorithm. The remaining challenge was to devise an algorithm for finding the most appropriate number of clusters to use. This was more involved, and we eventually settled on a binary search over k using a combination of a silhouette score and a penalty for empty and single-point clusters. This approach works correctly on our test data, but is probably not robust enough for more general data. (Remember, this chapter is about solving our specific problem, not about learning how to use k-means clustering more generally.)

In the next chapter, we can put together all the components of the problem that we've built so far and run the application on (a small sample of) real data. At this point, we will have completed the project and can look back over the whole process and reflect on what we have built. This will be a good opportunity to examine what worked well, what didn't work so well, and what we might change if we face a similar problem in the future.

12

Reflecting on What We Have Built

In this chapter, we will put everything together and test our application on some sample data. This is an important part of the process, not only to verify that the pieces have come together correctly and work as expected but also as a morale boost for you. Big projects can be quite exhausting, but nothing restores energy like having a working prototype and seeing the output pop into the terminal for the first time.

In the second half of this chapter, we will reflect on what we have built. We will examine the good parts, the ugly parts, and the things we could have done better. You should always try to set aside some time to reflect, especially if things don't go to plan, so that next time you can do better. Sometimes, formalizing this process by taking notes and keeping records can really help when you encounter similar problems in the future.

In this chapter, we will cover the following basic topics:

- Putting everything together
- Examining the more difficult parts
- Reviewing the techniques we used
- What to take away

Technical requirements

This chapter shows the final stage of developing our rubber duckies application. It does not have additional libraries beyond those that we have used in *Chapters 8* through *11*. We have provided a vcpkg manifest file for those who want to use this mechanism for installing dependencies.

The code for this chapter can be found in the Chapter-12 folder in the repository for this book on GitHub: https://github.com/PacktPublishing/The-CPP-Programmers-Mindset.

Putting everything together

The final step of building our solution is to put all the individual pieces together into a single application. We've already set up most of the framework but we need to complete the run_and_report function in main.cpp with the file reading and clustering components. However, as we have developed these other components, we have encountered several other parameters that we might want to add to the command-line interface as configurable parameters. Certainly, this should be the case with the *k* range for the clustering, the maximum number of iterations to be used in finding the clustering, and the number of repetitions to be used in computing each clustering. Thanks to our careful structuring earlier, we can easily add these parameters to the interface with sensible defaults.

To add new configuration options to the command-line arguments, we just need to add the corresponding lines following the options.add_options() call in the parse_config function. We have four options to add kmin and kmax for determining the range of *k* values to search, max_iter for the number of iterations in each run of the *k*-means algorithm, and num_repetitions for the number of trial clusterings to run to find the best representative for each value of *k*. These options are added to the interface by inserting the following lines after the add_options call:

```
("kmin", po::value<size_t>()->default_value(2),
  "minimum number of clusters to find")
("kmax", po::value<size_t>()->default_value(256),
  "maximum number of clusters to find")
("max_iter", po::value<size_t>()->default_value(100),
  "maximum number of iterations to find each clustering")
("repetitions", po::value<size_t>()->default_value(20),
  "number of trial clusterings for each value of k")
```

Notice that we set the default value for each of these options. This is for two reasons. The first is that the user might not be able to guess a reasonable set of defaults to use for their first set of experiments. By setting these, we take away a barrier to entry for the user and allow them to start experimenting with the data directly. The second is that we had already partly set the interface, so any changes that require new options to be provided would be breaking changes in future versions, which we always want to avoid. Adding a default value allows existing workflows to continue (hypothetically, of course) with the new version with minimal disruption.

The next task is to write the `run_and_report` function. In this case, it makes sense to introduce an additional helper function to read the files one at a time into the `RubberDuckData` structure, ready to be processed by the `compute_clusters` function we wrote in the previous chapter. This new function, which we can call `get_data`, needs to get the map file readers using the `get_readers` function defined in *Chapter 9* and iterate through the paths passed in at the command line. However, we also need to perform a little extra work before we pass the path to the reader itself. For instance, we need to check that the file exists and corresponds to one of our readers (which we can do at the same time as getting the appropriate reader from the map). The skeleton of this new function is as follows:

```
RubberDuckData get_data(const po::variables_map& args) {
    using PathVec = std::vector<std::filesystem::path>;
    const auto readers = get_readers();

    RubberDuckData data;

    for (const auto& path : args["paths"].as<PathVec>()) {
        // to be completed ...
    }

    return data;
}
```

The code that goes in the body of the loop in this function is pretty much as we described. First, we need to check that the path exists, logging and moving on if not. Then we need to extract the extension from the path, logging and moving on if this is empty, and find the appropriate reader if one exists. The one complication here is that the `extension` method on `std::filesystem::path` returns a `path` object that includes the preceding `.` character, but our reader interface does not include the `.` character, so we have to strip this off. Finding the reader from the `readers` map is handled using the `find` method to allow for the possibility that there is no match. The loop code is as follows:

```
    spdlog::info("processing file {}", path.c_str());
    if (!std::filesystem::exists(path)) {
        spdlog::warn(
            "path argument {} does not exist, skipping", path.c_str());
        continue;
    }
```

```
    auto ext = path.extension().string();
    if (ext.empty()) {
        spdlog::warn("path {} does not have an extesion", path.c_str());
        continue;
    }

    auto search = ext.substr(1); // remove the .
    auto reader = readers.find(search);
    if (reader == readers.end()) {
        spdlog::warn(
            "no file reader for files with \"{}\" extension", search);
        continue;
    }

    reader->second->read_file(data, path);
```

Once this loop finishes, we should have fully populated the `RubberDuckData` object data with the data from all the files we have processed ready to be used for clustering. Before we can get there, we have one last thing to fix. In *Chapter 8*, where we set up the command-line interface, we wrote a small amount of placeholder code for printing out the results of the clustering, which at the time we thought would be a `std::vector` containing `Coordinate` objects. However, as we built out the clustering code, we instead introduced a new `Cluster` struct that contains both a `Coordinate` and the number of points that have been assigned to that cluster. We need to modify our original placeholder code to work with these updated details and to print the number of points alongside the position.

The main work that still needs to be done is to call the `compute_clusters` function on the data obtained from `get_data`. For this, we need to extract our four new configuration options from the `variables_map` passed into the `run_and_report` function. Remember too that we need to run all of this inside the `handle_errors` wrapper to catch any unhandled exceptions that might occur in unexpected circumstances. With all this in mind, the final version of the `run_and_report` function is now as follows:

```
void run_and_report(const po::variables_map& args) {
    handle_errors([&] {
      auto data = get_data(args);
```

```
        auto k_min = args["kmin"].as<size_t>();
        auto k_max = args["kmax"].as<size_t>();
        auto num_repetitions = args["repetitions"].as<size_t>();
        auto max_iterations = args["max_iter"].as<size_t>();

        auto results = compute_clusters(
            data, k_min, k_max, num_repetitions, max_iterations);

        for (const auto& cluster : results) {
            std::cout << std::format(
                "{: 7.3f} {: 8.3f} {}\n",
                    cluster.position.latitude,
                    cluster.position.longitude,
                    cluster.num_points);
        }
    });
}
```

This completes the implementation of our solution, and the one remaining task is to run this on the sample data files that we have to make sure it works correctly before turning this over to our client. Let's first compile the application in release mode using the following commands in the terminal (or through your IDE of choice):

```
cmake -B build -S . -GNinja -DCMAKE_BUILD_TYPE=Release
cmake --build build --config=Release
```

Assuming the build continues without error (which it should have), the compiled application (called `duckies` or `duckies.exe` on Windows) in the `build` directory that we can execute on the sample data, is found inside the repository alongside the source code. We can run the sample files of the application using the following command (assuming your working directory is the root of the source):

```
build/duckies samples/test.csv samples/test.json sample/test.txt
```

The command will run for a small amount of time before printing the results to the terminal in the format that we specified. We found 5 clusters in our sample data, each associated with approximately 215 entries. Can you guess the locations?

```
-17.825   31.034 214
 19.076   72.878 215
```

```
-41.287  174.776 214
-23.551  -46.634 212
 51.508   -0.128 217
```

If we use the -v flag on the command line, we will see more verbose logging from the application. Remember that the code repository contains more logging commands than we showed in the code snippets here to reveal the process of the computation. With the implementation complete and working, we can now look back over everything and reflect on what we accomplished.

Examining the more difficult parts

Now is the point at which we look back over what we have done and understand what went well, what went badly, and what we could do better next time. This is a critical part of learning. This problem has many challenges, some very small and others significantly larger. Let's start by listing some of the things that have gone well. One of the aspects of the solution that proceeded especially smoothly was designing and implementing the command-line interface, including updating it with additional options earlier in this chapter. Using a framework such as Boost program options makes this task especially simple by hiding all the details that would otherwise have to be implemented by hand.

The file readers interface that we designed proved to be quite sufficient, although we might have modified the `supported_file_extension` string to include the leading `.` character (which is a very trivial adjustment), and streamlined the process of generating the mapping of readers. Implementing the first two readers (CSV and JSON) was very easy, despite the differences between the two libraries that we used. Implementing the free-text reader was somewhat more involved, and we had some problems with our choice of regular expressions library.

By far the most difficult part was constructing an algorithm to determine the most appropriate value of k for the k-means clustering. This was not entirely unexpected. In the end, we chose a very simple approach that makes use of the (simplified) silhouette scores for each cluster, combined with a slight penalty for clusterings that include empty or single-point clusters. This might not be the most robust approach (we have not proven that the algorithm always produces the desired outcome), but it does seem to work on our sample data. However, this might be a reasonable compromise given the time constraints and the need to keep the code relatively simple; a working solution now is better than a perfect solution never delivered.

Determining the number of clusters to find was a difficult task, but the clustering itself seems to work very effectively. Turning on verbose logging in our application reveals that the clustering algorithm performs fast and efficiently, converging in 2–3 iterations in most cases. This is probably more a statement about the regularity of our data rather than the implementation itself, but it is still nice to see.

The regular expressions used in *Chapter 10* proved to be quite problematic. This is not unusual for regular expressions, but we encountered some additional problems that might be specific to our choice of regular expressions library. The problem, if you recall, was that groups were duplicated in multiple branches of the pattern. This meant that we had to switch to using numbered groups instead. This was not a total disaster, since constructing the fix was not too difficult, but it did cost us time spent debugging. This problem might have arisen with using other libraries too, but we did not have time to experiment. The lesson here is to make sure you're familiar with the libraries that you use and their nuances.

Putting everything together at the end was quite straightforward because we put in the planning work early on and designed the components in such a way that they fit together nicely. This meant that at the end, we had very little work to do except write some very standard code to loop through the input files and produce the results. We made full use of a modular design for this project, allowing us to test each component in isolation without sacrificing performance. This also helped us compartmentalize the dependencies, which might be important if our code has a lot of dependencies. However, you should be careful if there are shared library dependencies, since you will need these to be linked and distributed along with your executable.

Reflecting on our computational thinking

We haven't talked much in the last few chapters about the four elements of computational thinking. This is because we did most of this work up front in *Chapter 8*. That being said, each chapter has presented its own selection of smaller problems that had to be solved. Let's take a moment to recall some of those challenges and the choices we made along the way.

In *Chapter 9*, that challenge was threefold. We had to read data from CSV files and JSON files, for which we used libraries to do the heavy lifting. The remaining part was designing a common interface that allows us to use the libraries externally without repeating the code for using each library. (Each library provided a rather different interface, so there is a fair amount of work hidden in this interface.) This is fundamentally an abstraction problem, understanding precisely the set of functionality required for reading the data into our data structure.

In *Chapter 10*, we dealt with the one remaining type of files: the free-text responses. This was a (multiple) pattern-matching exercise with some additional details. We constructed the patterns in smaller pieces (put together using some ugly preprocessor macros and compiler string literal auto-concatenation). Once each pattern fragment and then each pattern was complete, we then constructed a multi-pass "filtering" system to extract all the necessary information to populate the data. In our very simple example, this amounted to two passes. Here, there was an interesting strategy problem of whether to do everything in one pass or use multiple passes. Since each entry in our data is expected to be quite short, we opted for multiple passes since this is easier to implement. The advantage of a single pass would be more apparent if the cost of traversing each entry were larger.

In *Chapter 11*, we solved the clustering problem. This was the largest challenge we tackled and it had many pieces. At the heart, there are three problems to solve here, which are only revealed after investigating clustering algorithms in general. The first problem we identified was finding an embedding of our geographical coordinate data into an appropriate vector space in which we can actually perform clustering. In the case of spherical coordinates mapped into three-dimensional real space, this is a simple mathematical expression. The second problem was the k-means clustering itself. Here, we implemented a standard algorithm, and it was quite easy once we had organized our data.

The final component of the clustering was to find an appropriate number of clusters. This component itself has two sub-components: scoring the performance of each clustering and searching the range of permissible number of clusters. We opted for a modified (simplified) silhouette score, which was quite easy to implement, followed by a binary search over the range. A binary search is a standard tool in the software engineer's toolkit and it seemed to do the job here. However, in this case, it might not be the most appropriate choice even if it was easy to implement. The problem is that the scoring function might not be concave (it might not have a unique maximum) and simply inspecting the score at the end might not be sufficiently descriptive of the behavior between these values. (For instance, if we search over the range from 2 to 100, we might choose a branch from 51 to 100 because the score at 100 clusters is larger than at 51, but the maximum might appear in the other range, 2–51.)

Also, in this chapter, we made use of an abstract notion of a point in a vector space, via the `Coord3` struct. By defining the `operator+=` and `operator*=` arithmetic operators for the relevant types, we can write the algorithm in such a way that the actual type can be replaced (via template argument) should we wish to generalize the algorithm. (We mentioned this in the discussion at the end of *Chapter 11*.) This is yet another instance of abstraction at work: we have isolated the two latent properties that are required to implement the k-means algorithm, namely those of addition and scalar multiplication. (These two operations are what make it a vector space, when they satisfy a set of conditions.) Not only does this allow for possible generalization, but it also makes our implementation cleaner and easier to read.

In each of these challenges, and in the project more generally, we've used a selection of techniques. Let's take a moment to think back over these techniques in the next section.

Reviewing the techniques we've used

We've used several different algorithmic designs, structural and behavioral patterns, and several other techniques in this project. Starting from the top level of the project, one of the main features of our repository is the modularity. We've mentioned this before several times, but this design (though more of a technique for CMake/repository design than C++) is very useful for several reasons. Helping compartmentalize dependencies and enabling testing are just two. By separating the repository into smaller, descriptive parts that are easy to find, we make it easier for new developers (and us in the future) to find things in the repository. It also reduces the "cognitive overhead" of working with the repository, since one does not need to keep the details of each component in mind, only the broad strokes of each component. This leads us nicely into the next technique.

The file readers component is a realization of the **facade** design pattern, presenting a virtual interface (`FileReader`) that is implemented for various file types. This pattern is very useful for hiding different implementations behind a single unified interface. Note that, in this circumstance, there is no performance penalty to using this pattern since the (tiny) added cost of a virtual interface is dwarfed by the work of reading the files, and we don't expect to perform too many of these calls. That being said, it is always worth considering the performance impact of these virtual functions each time you decide to use them. The only downside of this pattern is that any changes to the interface class demand recompilation of all the individual reader classes and are a breaking API/ABI change. For internal components, this is less of a problem, but it is nonetheless something to consider.

Directly or indirectly, we've made use of templates throughout the project, mostly through libraries. In a few instances, we used template functions to avoid explicitly naming a type, such as iterators or regular expression matches and groups. These small template functions don't carry a large compilation time overhead, but template metaprogramming does. We can see this in the free-text reader class, which takes significantly longer to compile than the other file readers because of the heavy use of templates. This compile-time cost is rewarded with runtime performance, since templates are often inlined and produce code that can be aggressively optimized.

We made heavy use of `std::span` and `std::string_view` (and friends) throughout this project, because it allows us to examine the contents of a contiguous region of memory without copying and without binding the source to a particular memory management mechanism, as would be the case if using a reference to `std::vector` or `std::string`. This allows our interface to be used more widely without necessitating a copy of data. In the same way, we made use of the C++ stream interface in two of our file readers to avoid tying our readers to just files or other kinds of readable objects. This allows us to use `std::stringstream` for testing purposes.

There are, of course, several other minor techniques that we've used throughout, but these are the ones we wish to highlight. In the next section, we look back over the project more broadly and look for things to take away.

What to take away

The first and most important thing to take away from this exercise is that we did indeed solve the problem: we found the sources of the rubber ducks. (At least as far as the sample data we have.) However, this was by no means a smooth process. We had multiple hiccups along the way, numerous bugs that had to be found and fixed, choices about what approach to take, and numerous missteps and backtracks. The few that we documented along the way were genuine bugs that appear when running tests or otherwise running the code. Bugs are a common occurrence in any software development and are to be anticipated. However, we had some other larger problems to solve along the way, too.

We've already talked about the difficulty in developing an algorithm to find the appropriate number of clusters. That is not a simple problem, and the approach depends on the specifics of the problem at hand and the nature of the data. In our case, we consulted with several data scientists and tried several different scoring mechanisms before settling on the silhouette score with the penalty for empty or singleton clusters. This took a good amount of experimentation and testing before we arrived at the best solution we could in the time (and space) available.

In contrast, some aspects of the project went very smoothly. Implementing the command-line interface was very easy (although it could certainly use some polish). This is because we chose a library that we were familiar with and, because of the earlier planning, knew mostly what this interface was to include. Similarly, implementing the JSON and CSV file readers was a fairly smooth process, with only minor bumps. Finally, pulling everything together at the end also went fairly smoothly, although we did have to adjust the default number of repetitions slightly to avoid the problem of "local minima" that we discussed in *Chapter 11*.

Every project will have false starts, dead ends, bugs, and libraries that don't quite deliver what you need. There will be things that take some time to work through. Other parts will go smoothly and be easy to implement. Talking with colleagues and/or experts, as well as consulting documentation, books, and helpful community forums such as Stack Overflow (`https://stackoverflow.com`), can really help if you're stuck. Sometimes, **large language model** (**LLM**)-based coding assistants can be a great help, although beware that these can also lead you down the wrong path on occasion. (In fact, we experienced this exact problem when writing the script to generate the sample data for this chapter!) Sometimes, though, all you need is a jump start to get all the pieces to fit into place.

This concludes our brief reflection on the project that has covered *Chapters 7–12*.

Summary

In this chapter, we put the final touches on the application we have been building over the last few chapters. This involved pulling together the file readers that we developed in *Chapters 9* and *10* into a loop that inspects the extension of each file, provided by the command line, performs a clustering on the resulting records, and prints the results out to the terminal. In doing so, we added a few extra configuration options to the command-line interface with sensible defaults so that the user (the client) can configure the range of k values to search in the clustering.

In the remainder of the chapter, we looked back over the whole process and examined some of the difficult parts, some of the techniques we used, and some points to take away from our efforts. It is important to reflect on what you have done and what you might do if you had more time, more resources, better technologies, or better knowledge. This will aid you well the next time you come across a similar problem. After all, once you've seen enough problems, you start to notice that most of them look quite similar to things you have seen before. In the next chapter, we examine the problems of scaling up code to tackle really large problems.

13

The Problems of Scale

At a certain point, the power of a single computer is insufficient to solve a problem, and one must seek to expand to use multiple computers as part of a cluster. Scaling up computation comes with a new set of problems that must be solved. Managing the work between each of the individual nodes is one part, and distributing data is another. Most importantly, one must manage the number of workers that can access a shared resource at a time or face suboptimal performance or worse.

In this chapter, we examine some of the technical challenges associated with scaling up our code to solve larger and more complex problems, and some of the technologies we need to overcome these challenges. We start with some of the mechanisms for controlling data access (at a thread level), which give us insight into the kind of mechanisms we need at even larger scales. Next, we see how to use the **message passing interface** (**MPI**) to coordinate data and work between many nodes in a large cluster. Then, we discuss some situations that can result in bottlenecks that slow the progress of computations. We conclude with a short discussion about how to migrate large-scale computation to the cloud.

In this chapter, we're going to cover the following main topics:

- Making data safely accessible
- Communicating between processes
- Understanding bottlenecks
- Special considerations for the cloud

Technical requirements

This chapter covers how to make use of multiple threads, multiple processors, or multiple computers to solve problems on a very large scale. The code for this chapter does not rely on any external services, but it might be instructive to run some of the examples in such a scenario. The code for this chapter can be found in the `Chapter-13` folder in the GitHub repository for this book: `https://github.com/PacktPublishing/The-CPP-Programmers-Mindset`.

Making data safely accessible with mutex locks

Any programmer will tell you that one of the first problems one might encounter in a multithreaded program is data races. This is where one thread reads a value that is modified by another thread. Since the order of thread execution is non-deterministic, one cannot know in which order the read and write occur. Thus, the value that is accessed is unknowable. Most programming languages provide mechanisms for preventing data races, such as **mutual exclusion** (**mutex**) locks.

Mutex locks are a very big hammer for preventing data races. The idea is that one thread acquires the lock and then performs work that modifies the data that the lock protects. Each new thread that tries to acquire the lock now blocks (it doesn't proceed any further, yielding to the operating system to allow other processes/threads to run) until the original thread releases the lock. This obviously means that your program cannot do as much work; the purpose of using threads is that one can run them at the same time. However, sometimes they are unavoidable. For example, consider the following function decorator class, which caches the result of the function to avoid rerunning the (expensive) function on arguments we've already seen:

```
#include <memory>
#include <mutex>
#include <string>
#include <unordered_map>

template <typename F>
class CachingFunction
{
    std::recursive_mutex lock_;
    std::unordered_map<std::string, std::unique_ptr<std::string>> cache_;
    F function_;

public:
```

```
    CachingFunction(F&& function) : function_(std::forward<F>(function))
    {}

    const std::string& operator()(const std::string& arg)
    {
        std::lock_guard access(lock_);

        auto& cached = cache_[arg];
        if (!cached) {
            cached = std::make_unique<std::string>(function_(arg));
        }

        return *cached;
    }
};
```

Here, the cache is a simple hash map containing the arguments (a simple string in this case) and a unique pointer to the result of the computation. You might be wondering why the values in this map are pointers to the result type and not just the result type itself. This is, first, to keep the nodes of the map relatively small. The result type of the function might be large (even a `std::string` is quite large), and it is better to keep the nodes relatively small. Second, using a smart pointer allows greater flexibility with the container class and ensures that the pointers (and references taken from them) remain stable regardless of what happens in the cache. Finally, the result of calling the function might be an empty string, and we need to distinguish somehow between an unseen argument and an argument for which the result is empty. (This might not be the best pattern for this, but it is one such option.)

Here, we're using `std::string` as an example to keep the code short; obviously, the return value could be anything. Such a construction is very powerful, particularly in recursive call chains (hence the choice of `recursive_mutex`), for repeatedly performing expensive computations. In an ideal circumstance, the result is already held in the cache, and so the lock is held for a very short amount of time while this value is retrieved from the cache. If we haven't seen this argument before, we have to hold the lock while we perform the computation and insert this into the cache. To make the code a little simpler, we actually store the result inside a `unique_ptr`, which has the added benefit of giving stable references, even if the backing cache data structure does not guarantee such stability.

If this function is to be used in a multithreaded context, then the mutex lock is essential. Ideally, the cost of executing the function outweighs the cost of acquiring the lock and searching the cache. We expect that most calls will result in a cache hit and thus a very fast return path, so the mutex is not held for very long. In the small number of calls that result in a cache miss, the execution time is longer, but not significantly longer than the expensive function ordinarily would have been. The worst case is that two threads try to compute new (different) values at the same time, where the second thread now has to wait for the first to finish before starting its own lengthy computations. There is no remedy for this, at least not without adopting a very different design.

Atomic values are a lighter means of synchronizing values in multithreaded environments, and allow the processor to resolve the order of accesses. We've seen these before when we discussed shared pointers in *Chapter 5*. These carry a much smaller penalty in terms of access time, but are limited in type and scope. Of course, such things are only necessary where data is to be mutated in one of the threads in question. If all threads only read data, then no locking mechanisms are necessary. Similarly, if different threads write to different locations in memory (even if these are managed by the same vector, for instance), then again, there is no need to lock these accesses.

Other synchronizing mechanisms

Managing data accesses is one instance where programmers must be proactive in synchronizing operations among different threads of execution. For instance, one might want to cause threads to wait until a particular time (condition variables and barriers) or limit the number of threads that can run at a given time (semaphores). Semaphores are useful for creating **back pressure** in a multithreaded (or otherwise asynchronous) environment, and thus prevent overloading system resources. For instance, consider the following code:

```
void write_data(Writer& writer, const Data& data)
{
    static std::counting_semaphore<2> writers_control;

    writers_control.acquire();

    writer.write(data);

    writers_control.release();
}
```

This function ensures that at most two threads can write to the `Writer` instance passed as an argument. This `Writer` instance might be a database connection or the filesystem, where multiple threads all trying to write at once might overload the mechanism (e.g., by causing thrashing). The semaphore itself carries a counter, in this case, initialized to 2. Each new thread that tries to acquire the semaphore decrements the counter by 1, unless the counter is already at `0`, in which case the thread blocks until the counter is incremented again (on release from another thread).

Condition variables allow for communication between threads at a finer-grained level. A thread can wait for a condition variable to be set by some other thread. A condition variable has a method that waits, based on a mutex lock, until a predicate, determined by the associated condition, is satisfied. At this time, the thread is allowed to progress. Threads waiting on the condition variable can be notified one at a time, or all at once when the condition is updated. This mechanism can be used, for instance, to signal that data is ready to be processed or that a task has finished executing. Consider, for instance, the following very crude asynchronous task class:

```
#include <thread>
#include <mutex>
#include <condition_variable>

class Task {
    std::mutex lock_;
    std::condition_variable condition_;
    std::thread worker_;
    bool is_finished_ = false;

public:

    template <typename F>
    Task(F&& func)
        : worker_([f=std::forward<F>(func), this]() {
            f();
            std::unique_lock lk(lock_);
            is_finished_ = true;
            lk.unlock();
            condition_.notify_all();
        })
    {}
```

```
    ~Task() { worker_.join(); }

    bool is_finished() {
        std::lock_guard lk(lock_);
        return is_finished_;
    }

    void wait() {
        std::unique_lock lk(lock_);
        condition_.wait(lk, [this] { return is_finished_; })
    }
};
```

This isn't a perfect use case for a condition variable, but it does illustrate the mechanics. The mutex is used to control access to the variables themselves. The `is_finished` method simply checks whether the flag is set, but will not block (at least not for long). The `wait` method blocks execution until the condition is set. In this very simple example, the class owns the thread that executes the function, but generally, with such a setup, one would submit to a thread pool.

Barriers are synchronization points that prevent threads from progressing until the other threads reach the same point. This is useful, for instance, if your computation makes use of an iterative process where multiple threads use the previous set of results from all threads to create the next step. Here is a simple example:

```
#include <barrier>
#include <vector>

void do_work(std::span<double> my_results, std::span<const double> prev_
result);


int main(int argc, char** argv) {
    int no_iterations = 5;
    int no_workers = 5;
    int no_points = 1000;
    int pts_per_worker = no_points / no_workers;

    std::barrier sync(no_workers);
```

```
    std::vector<std::thread> threads;
    std::vector<double> work_even(no_points);
    std::vector<double> work_odd(no_points);

    int worker_id = 0;
    for (int worker_id = 0; worker_id < no_workers; ++worker_id) {
        threads.emplace_back(
        [&, id=worker_id]() {
            double* results_base_ptr = nullptr;
            const double* data_base_ptr = nullptr;
            size_t offset = id*pts_per_worker;

            for (int i=0; i<no_iterations; ++i) {

                // the worker will wait here until all results
                // are complete.
                sync.arrive_and_wait();

                if (i % 2 == 0) {
                    results_base_ptr = work_even.data();
                    data_base_ptr = work_odd.data();
                } else {
                    results_base_ptr = work_odd.data();
                    data_base_ptr = work_even.data();
                }

                do_work(
                    {results_base_ptr + offset, pts_per_worker},
                    {data_base_ptr, no_points}
                );
            }
        });
    }

    return 0;
}
```

In this example, each worker thread populates part of the result based on the whole of the previous result array, including the bits computed by other workers. In order for this to work, all the threads must finish a given iteration before the next iteration is allowed to begin; otherwise, we create a race condition. This, like other examples in this section, is only a demonstration of how these mechanisms can be used, and so the data access patterns shown might not be optimal. Be careful before you copy this kind of code.

Multithreading might not be sufficient to distribute your large problems over enough cores to finish them in a reasonable amount of time. In this case, one might need to communicate between multiple processes on the same host or between multiple host machines, which is the topic of the next section.

Communicating between processes

The main mechanism for communicating between processes is **message passing**. Here, small packets of data are passed between the processes via a separate channel: a network socket, a UNIX socket, or otherwise. Passing messages should be regarded as a fairly expensive operation, and the amount of information passed between processes should be fairly minimal. In the (somewhat rare) circumstance that all processes are running on the same computer, **shared memory** can be used as a very high-speed interchange for data. The same restrictions for accesses among many threads apply here; data accesses to shared memory must be synchronized using process-level synchronization mechanisms, such as mutexes and locks discussed earlier.

The standard tool for passing messages between processes as part of a larger system of distributed work is the **MPI**. This is a standard interface, implemented by various vendors such as Microsoft and the open source OpenMPI, that provides functions for communicating between processes via shared memory or networks, or any number of other methods. MPI has been around for a long time, and most of the standard job scheduler systems on high-performance compute clusters (e.g., Slurm) have support for messages passed via this interface.

The basic functions in MPI are `MPI_Send` and `MPI_Recv`, which, as the names suggest, send or receive packets of information between different processes that are part of the distributed system (more on how this distributed system is set up shortly). Each node in the system has a **rank**, which is a unique identifier for the process. This is used to identify the target of a sent message, or to identify the block of work that the node is responsible for. The rank itself is an integer in the range from `0` to the total number of nodes in the network. A very basic MPI application has the following structure:

```
#include <mpi.h>

void do_work(std::span<int, 2> out, int arg, int divisor) {
    out[0] = arg / divisor;
    out[1] = arg % divisor;
}

int main(int argc, char** argv) {
    MPI_Init(&argc, &argv); // Initialize the runtime

    int n_nodes = 0;
    int rank = 0;

    // get the pool info
    MPI_Comm_size(MPI_COMM_WORLD, &n_nodes);
    MPI_Comm_rank(MPI_COMM_WORLD, &rank);

    // Distribute data/work to each of the nodes
    int arg = 0;
    if (rank == 0) {
        for (int other_node=1; other_node<n_nodes; other_node++) {
            MPI_Send(&other_node, 1, MPI_INT,
                     other_node, 0, MPI_COMM_WORLD);
        }
    } else {
        MPI_Recv(&arg, 1, MPI_INT, 0, 0,
                 MPI_COMM_WORLD, MPI_STATUS_IGNORE);
    }

    // Do the work
    std::array<int, 2> out{};
    std::mt19937 gen(0xABBA ^ (rank + n_nodes));
    int my_divisor = std::uniform_int_distribution(2, 25)(gen);
    do_work(out, arg, my_divisor);

    // Retrieve the results from the other nodes
    if (rank == 0) {
```

```
        std::array<int, 2> other_out {};
        for (int other_node=1; other_node<n_nodes; other_node++) {
            MPI_Recv(other_out.data(), 2,
                     MPI_INT, other_node, 0,
                     MPI_COMM_WORLD, MPI_STATUS_IGNORE);
            out[0] += other_out[0];
            out[1] += other_out[1];
        }
    } else {
        MPI_Send(out.data(), 2, MPI_INT, 0, 0, MPI_COMM_WORLD);
    }

    // Report/postprocess/etc
    std::cout << out[0] << " " << out[1] << std::endl;

    MPI_Finalize(); // Close the runtime
    return 0;
}
```

This shows the basics of using the MPI C interface. Unfortunately, there isn't a standardized C++ interface that takes care of some of the more complex mechanics of transferring data between nodes. To compile an MPI program, one must use the `mpic++` compiler wrapper. If you're using CMake, this is handled by finding the MPI package and linking it to your application. MPI applications should be started using the `mpirun` launcher, which takes care of setting up the MPI runtime prior to executing your specific application.

In this very simple example, we used the basic send and receive functions, but these are rather limited in scope. MPI provides many other mechanisms for distributing data among the different processes. For instance, the `MPI_Bcast` broadcast function sends an entire array from one process to all other processes. The related `MPI_Scatter` function breaks an array into chunks that are distributed across the various processes. This allows you to spread the total work effectively between all the processes. The opposite of the scatter function is `MPI_Gather`, which collects data from arrays on each of the processes and uses the data to fill an array on the invoking process.

Also, in our example, we retrieved the processed numbers from each of the processes and summed the integers together. This kind of gather-and-reduce operation could actually have been handled (more efficiently) by the MPI runtime by making use of the `MPI_Reduce` function instead. Here is the command we could have used instead of the entire second `if-else` block:

```
std::array<int, 2> reduced {};
MPI_Reduce(
    out.data(), /* send data */
    reduced.data(), /* place to put result on root */
    out.size(), /* number of elements */
    MPI_INT, /* data type */
    MPI_SUM, /* operation to reduce with */
    0, /* root that should get the reduced value */
    MPI_COMM_WORLD /* the communicator handle */
);
```

All processes run the same command, but only the process with the rank equal to root needs a valid receive array (`reduced.data()`, in our example). There are, of course, several other reduction operations and other variants of this function.

It's quite easy to see how one could communicate relatively simple structures containing only fundamental values or array-like types (containing fundamental types) might be transmitted without difficulty, but objects that have an opaque representation (e.g., a class with a pointer-to implementation) will require more work to send. In these cases, some kind of **serialization** is necessary to turn your complex objects into a more basic representation as raw bytes or text that can then be transmitted and deserialized on the other end.

Boost has a wrapper for MPI that takes care of this additional complexity using its own serialization framework. This greatly simplifies the process of communicating objects over the channels exposed by MPI, but is not necessarily the most efficient means of doing so. Depending on the situation, it might be a good idea to replace Boost serialization with a (more modern) serialization framework that can achieve better performance than Boost.

Serialization

Serialization is the process of transforming a complex object into a self-contained block of data, usually raw bytes or text, so it can be transmitted across a network or stored on disk to be reconstituted later. For simple integers or floating-point numbers, this is relatively easy, since we can just dump their binary representation or write out their digits in some base (e.g., base 10). Of course, it isn't quite this simple because of **byte ordering**. Most processors are **little-endian**, which means they are stored in order with the least significant byte first. We can see this by constructing a multi-byte integer and printing out the bytes, as shown here:

```
int num = 0x1A'2B'3C'4D;
std::array<std::byte, sizeof(int)> byte_array {};
std::memcpy(byte_array.data(), &num, sizeof(int));

std::cout << "0x";
for (auto byte : byte_array) {
    std::cout << std::setw(2) << std::hex
              << static_cast<unsigned>(byte);
}
std::cout << std::endl;
```

The number, `num`, presented on line 1 is written out in the usual order (at least for English), where the digits to the left are the most significant; when we write the number *13*, the *1* refers to the number of 10s and the *3* to the number of units, so this is $1 \times 10 + 3$. Here, there is a small complication because the "digits" are bytes (i.e., pairs of hexadecimal digits). We might say that `num` is defined using a **big-endian** representation. Running the preceding block of code (see the main function in `byte_order.cpp` in the code repository) prints out the true byte representation of the `num` integer as `0x4d3c2b1a` rather than the order that was used to define it. Notice that each byte still appears in the same order; the least significant byte is `0x4A` rather than being swapped to be `0xA4`.

As we said, most modern processors use little-endian ordering internally, but big-endian ordering is widely used for network transmissions, for instance. Depending on the use, one might want to serialize an object (such as an integer) in either byte ordering or at least mark binary data as either little-endian or big-endian. Most serialization frameworks provide this facility.

Text formats such as JSON are very common for storing or transmitting hierarchical data in a semi-readable format. This was popularized for communicating between browser and server, hence the name "JavaScript Object Notation." Text representations are typically larger than binary formats, but serve a different purpose and are generally more portable.

Boost.Serialization is a general-purpose serialization framework that does not require external tools to compile. This library makes use of templates to add serialization support to your classes by implementing either a `serialize` method or separate `load` and `save` methods. (These can also be implemented externally if the class cannot be modified.) A very basic example is as follows:

```
class SerializableAddressbookEntry {
    std::string name;
    std::string address;
    std::string email;

public:
    // methods...

    template <typename Archive>
    void serialize(Archive& ar, const unsigned /* version */)
    {
        ar & name;
        ar & address;
        ar & email;
    }

};
```

This function is used to implement both the serialization and deserialization processes. The library itself can customize the construction of the class during the deserialization process, which might be important for classes that do not have public constructors or contain hidden implementation details. Once the `serialize` function is defined, one can serialize into one of the several binary formats provided by the library. For instance, this class can be serialized into a portable binary file and written to a file as follows:

```
#include <boost/serialization/string.hpp>
#include <boost/archive/binary_oarchive.hpp>
#include <fstream>

int main() {
    SerializableAddressbookEntry entry {
        std::string("Darth Vadar"),
        std::string("Galaxy far far away"),
        std::string("Vadar@darth.sith")
```

```
    };

    std::ofstream os("out.bin", std::ios::binary);
    boost::archive::binary_oarchive archive(os);

    archive << entry;

    return 0;
};
```

Deserialization is handled in much the same way. This approach is quite flexible, but has some severe limitations. Since the `serialize` methods are templates, they need to be exposed in the header files if they are on the boundary of your library. This can be particularly problematic if your library has compiled components containing implementations that need to be serialized. There is a mechanism to make this work, but it is rather troublesome to make it work in practice. Moreover, each serialization function invokes many templates, meaning that complex class hierarchies and classes with many different data members can quickly add up to additional minutes of compile time.

Other serialization frameworks abandon the expensive template mechanisms in favor of an external compilation tool. For example, for the **protocol buffer (protobuf)** framework, you write a schema for your classes that describes the data members that are required to serialize the class (note that this need not be all of them). A separate tool then transpiles this to a new `.h`/`.cpp` file pair that contains the code necessary to serialize and deserialize the messages. This code does not contain any complicated templates and thus does not inflate the compile time as much (at the cost of an external step!). The protobuf documentation (`https://protobuf.dev`) is generally very easy to follow and gives a very similar example to the preceding one.

Now, we understand some of the practicalities of implementing distributed systems for solving large-scale problems on clusters of computers. Next, we look at some of the bottlenecks we might encounter in such systems.

Understanding bottlenecks

Many bottlenecks occur from moving data around. We saw this in *Chapter 4*, with the CPU, where moving data from RAM into the CPU registers is a relatively slow operation compared to operations within the CPU itself, and moving data over a network is many times slower than this. Moving data between different processes on different computers is something that needs to be considered quite carefully.

The MPI framework forces one to be explicit about moving data, which makes it easier to understand where these kinds of transfer bottlenecks occur. However, these are not the only kind of bottlenecks. Of course, there are computation bottlenecks too, where long computations hold up the progress of the whole system, and there are external bottlenecks, such as loading data from disk or communicating with external services.

Long computations and loading latency are less of a problem if they don't hold up the whole system. (Here, *system* refers to the whole computer or cluster that is performing the global operation.) One of the advantages of a multi-headed system is that each node can make progress even if any given node is held up by a particular operation. This relies on the fact that each of the nodes is performing largely independent computations and requires relatively little communication with the other nodes. There is still, however, a problem with contention whenever there are shared resources (including the network connecting the nodes). It is this contention that one must understand in order to find and mitigate bottlenecks.

Of course, the type and number of bottlenecks you might encounter depend heavily on the problem, the nature and storage of the data, and the number of external services (or devices) that you must interact with in solving the problem. In the remainder of this section, we give some specific examples from different categories and what kind of mitigations can be put in place (if any).

Computation bottlenecks

The specific kind of computational bottleneck we want to highlight here occurs when one has a sequential calculation in which each step is divided into small and non-uniform packages of work that are distributed among the nodes in a cluster. The problem arises when one package of work takes longer than the others, causing the whole process to stall until the longer task is completed.

To make this more concrete, suppose one is an aircraft engineer testing the stresses of an airframe at various points of a flight. Such a test involves simulating the various forces at play on different parts of the aircraft, which are obviously extremely complex. Indeed, for each tick of the simulation, there will be a large system of partial differential equations that must be solved to find the forces that are acting on various parts of the aircraft. The time increments themselves must be done sequentially; the previous state of all the various forces contributes to the next step. These kinds of computations are often performed on large-scale compute clusters.

The thing that makes this kind of simulation complicated is that the geometry determines how quickly one can produce force information to the desired accuracy, which obviously varies greatly over the different parts of the plane. This means that one can end up with different parts of the plane taking longer to compute than others. This could lead to a situation where many nodes are idle while the tricky parts of the geometry are computed. Now, hopefully, with a problem this large, there is enough work in the rest of the problem to keep all the workers busy until the long computations are finished. Nevertheless, it might be wise to start those particular calculations as early as possible so there is as much opportunity for this to happen as possible.

Bottlenecks from accessing shared resources

Shared resources will always prove problematic for distributed systems. At best, a limited number of nodes can access the resource at a given time, and at worst, the nodes compete directly for the resource and cause the resource itself to become non-responsive. It is always better to limit the number of nodes that can access the resource at a given time so the resource is able to operate at optimal efficiency the whole time, rather than allowing the different nodes to thrash the resource, causing it to slow down or stop entirely.

Let's consider the following scenario. Say you're processing a large number of video files, and one of the preprocessing steps involves sending each frame to an external machine learning model (via a REST API) to extract certain information from each image in sequence. The external API has rate limiting in place, so a single host (or cluster) can only send 1,000 requests per minute; otherwise, requests from that host are blocked for several minutes. Once the preprocessing is done, your system performs a complicated stitching together of all the data and produces some kind of output. All this must be written back to permanent storage for later analysis.

It is not difficult to completely saturate the REST API rate limiting, even with a handful of threads running on a single machine. A large number of workers, each running multiple threads, will very quickly saturate the bandwidth. (We've deliberately chosen small numbers here to emphasize the issue.) Understanding the workload here is quite important. Sending frames to the external service is one of the early steps of the work, and is usually followed by a large amount of computation work. If we can arrange so that each frame (or batch of frames) that is sent to the service is followed by at least 60 seconds of computation, then it should be possible to keep all the workers busy and avoid a timeout on the service. Of course, it might not be possible to split the work up in this way.

A very simple means of handling the rate limiting is to use some kind of semaphore that keeps track of the number of requests that have been submitted in the past 60 seconds. However, one quickly realizes that this is easier said than done. A better approach is to use a pair of queues that keep track of requests waiting to be sent and requests that are "cooling down." If we give each request a completion time, we know when to remove them from the cooling-down queue and allow new requests to be sent. We're not going to engineer a solution here because this would require a much greater dive into MPI and synchronization.

There is another shared resource in this scenario: the disks from which we are reading the video files. Shared storage pools are a situation that you are much more likely to encounter. When we access the same storage pool from multiple different nodes (and the cluster does not have protections for this), we can overload the capability of the storage pool to read and write data. For this reason, it is generally a good idea to stagger the reads and writes wherever possible. Writing large contiguous files rather than lots of smaller files can also have a dramatic effect on performance. (Spinning disks have a great deal of "seek time" that adds latency to the writing process, which is amortized if the writes occur to sequential blocks.) One can also make use of local caches to store temporary files before they are written back to the main storage array. For instance, in **Slurm**, one can get the location of the local scratch disks from the `SLURM_TMPDIR` environment variable. (Be aware that data stored here will probably be cleared once the job expires.)

Now that we understand the kinds of bottlenecks that can appear when working in large-scale computation systems, we should look at some of the special considerations for setting up these systems in the cloud.

Special considerations for the cloud

The cloud provides flexible, scalable compute resources that make computation accessible to those who cannot afford or warrant a large compute cluster for their own use. This can be a very powerful tool if deployed correctly, and can also be very cost-effective, but achieving the correct level of orchestration can be rather tricky. In this section, we outline some of the nuances that make the cloud especially powerful and some of the tips for avoiding problems.

The biggest problem with setting up compute infrastructure in the cloud to run high-performance compute workflows is in setting up each of the nodes with the required software, such as making sure that all the nodes have compatible versions of MPI and all the other library dependencies necessary for the work. One must also do all the orchestration that is usually handled by cluster administrators on other HPC clusters. This makes it sound like a difficult task, but it is not; see `https://cluster-in-the-cloud.readthedocs.io/en/latest/index.html` for some detailed instructions on how to get started.

One of the great strengths of using the cloud is that one can allocate precisely the resources necessary for a job, and quickly deallocate them once your work is finished. For sporadic workloads that would leave in-house equipment unused, this kind of flexibility is tremendously powerful. That being said, it is important that you deallocate the resources that are not being used since cloud resources can have substantial running costs.

The key point for using cloud computing is to ensure that as much of the problem is run on cloud resources (hopefully in the same data center). For instance, the data used in the problem should be stored in cloud storage, which benefits from low-latency, high-speed access over all the nodes in the cluster. Obtaining data from other sources will not usually be as fast. Links between virtual machines that live in the same data center are very fast and have very high capacity, which can reduce the effect of communication bottlenecks in your workflows.

Summary

Problems that are too large for a single computer with a handful of threads require a larger and better coordinated effort from a cluster of computers. To coordinate work among a large number of nodes in a cluster requires a message passing infrastructure, such as the numerous implementations of MPI. These can be deployed on in-house compute clusters, externally managed clusters, or in the cloud. In all cases, the programming is the same, and it is for the MPI implementation to enable the work to proceed. However, this does not mean you shouldn't think carefully about the organization of the cluster and the work being performed.

When multiple nodes are involved, one must be careful about the way that one accesses data and other resources. Multiple simultaneous accesses to a shared resource can create congestion and, in extreme cases, severely degrade performance. In the cloud, one must take care to consider where data and the compute nodes are located. The best performance will come when the data is also stored in the same cloud to maximize the bandwidth with the compute resources and minimize the latency of inter-node communication. In the next chapter, we will see how to use specialized computation devices such as GPUs to accelerate some computation tasks.

14

Dealing with GPUs and Specialized Hardware

CPUs are immensely complicated and capable of processing vast quantities of data, but because of their general-purpose nature, they sometimes cannot provide the throughput necessary for some problems. For instance, real-time, low-latency computations are not well-suited to running on a CPU that is also running a full operating system. In these instances, one might turn to specialized accelerator hardware or coprocessors. **Graphics processing units** (**GPUs**) offer very high throughput compute and high bandwidth memory, and are perfect for problems that require vast number-crunching capabilities. **Field programmable gate arrays** (**FPGAs**) can be configured for very low latency and low power computation, which makes them good for time-critical or embedded applications. Programming for these devices often requires a different approach from general CPU programming.

This chapter has two parts and mostly focuses on GPU programming. In the first part of the chapter (the first two sections), we discuss the architecture of GPUs and some of the nuances that one needs to be aware of when programming these devices. In the second part of the chapter, we discuss the various means of writing code for specialized devices, focusing on NVIDIA GPUs and CUDA, since this seems to be the most commonly employed means. This chapter is not intended to be a fully informative discussion of how to program a GPU or FPGA (or some other accelerator or coprocessor), but instead, a taste of what programming these devices involves and where to get started.

In this chapter, we're going to cover the following main topics:

- Understanding GPU architecture
- Using Thrust algorithms and OpenMP offloading
- Writing algorithms for GPU using CUDA C++
- Coordinating between GPU threads
- Using SYCL to write code for many devices

Technical requirements

This chapter covers writing code for computation devices such as GPUs, and thus requires additional library support to run. For CUDA programming, you will need to install the CUDA toolkit (`https://developer.nvidia.com/cuda-toolkit`). When configuring CMake, you may need to provide an environment variable or CMake variable to instruct CMake where to find this installed toolkit. You will not need an NVIDIA GPU to build the software, but you won't be able to run the code as is. For AMD GPUs, one can use the `hipify` tool to convert CUDA-specific source to ROCm-HIP source, but this is not necessarily an error-free or complete process.

In the final section, we look at using SYCL to homogenize the process of writing code for various devices. The Intel OneAPI base toolkit includes a complete SYCL and the data-parallel C++ compiler (DPC++), but there are other distributions available.

The code for this chapter can be found in the `Chapter-14` folder in the GitHub repository for this book: `https://github.com/PacktPublishing/The-CPP-Programmers-Mindset`.

Understanding GPU architecture

Over the past 20 years, general-purpose GPU programming has exploded into the mainstream, especially in the context of machine learning. GPUs excel at high-throughput, massively parallel number crunching on a large scale; they were originally designed to compute coordinate transforms of voxels and textures in 3D graphics applications at very high speed. Now, they have been expanded to a very flexible computation tool that can be a huge asset for solving problems.

Programming with GPUs splits the code into two parts: the **host code** that runs on the main computer, and the **device code** that runs on the GPU. One cannot simply take ordinary functions and run them on a GPU. Instead, one must instruct the compiler to produce device functions by marking them with the `__device__` attribute. Moreover, one cannot just call these from the host, and they must be scheduled by the runtime library and driver by launching a **kernel**. A kernel is a special function that executes on the device but is launched from the host. (Note that we use the term *launch* here because this is not quite a simple function call, as we shall see later.)

The architecture of a GPU is very different from that of a CPU. GPU cores are very much simpler than CPU cores and do not operate independently. The phrase that is usually used to describe these is **single instruction, multiple threads** (**SIMT**). (Compare this with the SIMD instructions that we discussed in *Chapter 4*, but note that these are not the same.) The premise is that each thread within a group operates in lock-step with the other threads of that group, but the data that they operate upon can be determined independently by the thread, usually based on each thread's index within the larger group.

Threads on a GPU are extremely lightweight, and context switches between one group of threads and another are very cheap. Indeed, the idea is that many thousands of threads will be active at any given time, and that when one group of threads stalls (for instance, loading data from memory), another group can take its place and make progress. This allows memory latency to be "hidden" by the massive parallelism.

GPU threads might not be as capable as general-purpose CPU threads, such as those provided through the operating system, but they are still capable of complex code paths. They can execute branching instructions, such as conditionals or loops, and interact with memory in a non-linear way (unlike SIMD instructions, for instance). However, their lock-step execution patterns make taking different branches within a group of threads problematic. In effect, this forces the GPU to execute both branches sequentially, with the threads that did not take the relevant branch temporarily disabled. The performance impact of this might be negligible, or it could be catastrophic, depending on the nature of the branch.

Blocks, grids, and warps

Work on a GPU is arranged hierarchically, with individual threads arranged into **blocks**, and many blocks arranged into a **grid**. The threads within a block work together to solve an instance of a problem, while the grid as a whole solves many such copies of this problem. Threads within a block can communicate with one another (more on this later). The threads within a block will be distributed among one or more **warps**, which are groups of threads that are executed in lock-step as described before. On NVIDIA GPUs, a warp consists of 32 threads, and generally, the computation potential is maximized when the block size is a multiple of the warp size. A (simplified) schematic diagram for how threads (arranged into wards) are organized into blocks and then grouped into a grid, and the mapping of the grid onto the hardware resources is shown in *Figure 14.1*.

The blocks themselves are executed on one of several **streaming multiprocessors** (**SMs**), which are clusters of a (fairly large) number of compute cores, a register page, various banks of memory, and other supporting hardware. The maximum number of blocks that can be executed on an SM at any given time is called the **occupancy**, and this is one of the indicators of how effective a kernel will be at processing data as fast as possible. (Of course, this is not a definitive measure.) The maximum occupancy is determined by the amount of resources required by a block: the number of threads in the block, the number of registers used by each thread, and the usage of shared memory.

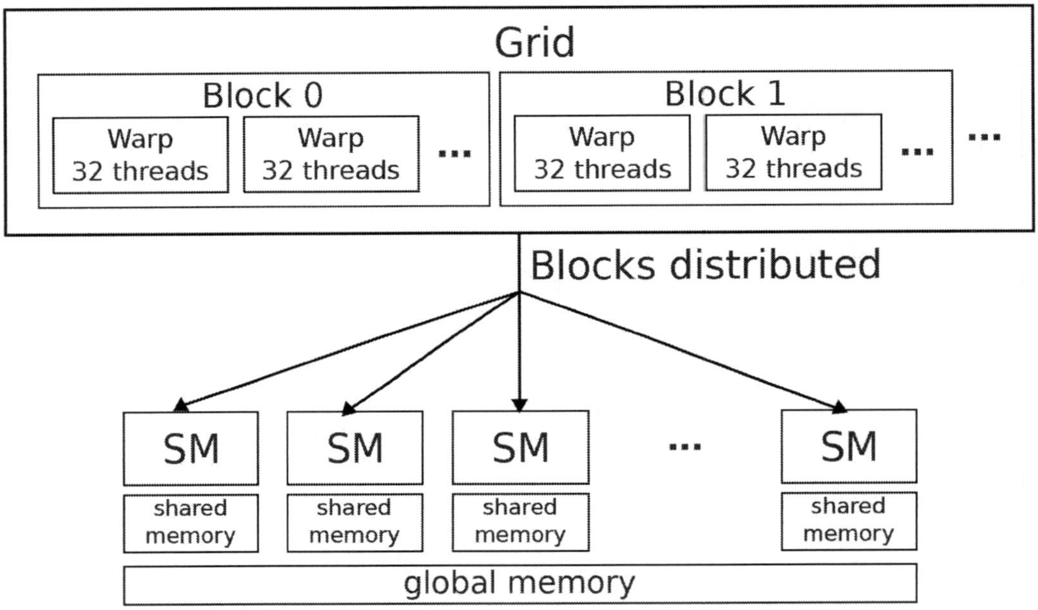

Figure 14.1: A block diagram showing the hardware components of the GPU (bottom half) and the logical layout of a CUDA kernel (top half), and the distribution of the blocks in the grid over the different SMs of the GPU

Defining the grid configuration can be a somewhat tricky task and depends heavily on the task to be performed. Arranging it so the size of the block matches elements of the computation can be very convenient and make programming easier, but it might not be optimal, especially if the block size is not an integral multiple of the warp size. For very small problems, one might need to divide the work among smaller groups of threads (16, 8, 4, 2, or even 1 thread per unit of work), but this might have consequences for other resources such as registers and shared memory.

Each thread has access to at most 255 registers, but this is not the only constraint. Each SM has a fixed-size register page that is shared by all the threads that are active on that SM. For most NVIDIA GPUs, there are 64K 4-byte registers available, which must be divided among the active threads. With 16 active warps on the SM, this would mean each thread can use at most 128 registers. Exceeding this number simply limits the number of warps that can be active on the SM. This, in turn, may limit the throughput substantially in memory-bound workflows, but less so in compute-bound workflows.

The CUDA toolkit includes an excellent profiler and performance tuning tool called **Nsight Compute**. This can provide extremely detailed runtime information about your kernels and report bottlenecks and problematic patterns. This software also includes an occupancy calculator that will tell you, given a specific configuration of block size, number of registers, and shared memory usage, exactly how many blocks can be active on an SM at a given time.

GPU memory

Like the execution model, GPU memory is also hierarchical. The **global memory** is the large pool of memory that functions like system RAM. It is typically allocated from the host and made available to specific kernels by passing a pointer to the kernel itself. Global memory is accessible to all of the SMs on the device, and thus by each of the threads that execute on the GPU. Each SM also has access to a relatively small pool of **shared memory**, which is divided among the blocks that execute on that SM (look again at *Figure 14.1*). On many GPUs, the maximum amount of shared memory that can be allocated for a specific block is 48 KiB, while the total amount of shared memory available might be 64 KiB or up to 228 KiB on an H100. The CUDA samples repository (`https://github.com/NVIDIA/cuda-samples`) contains a sample executable (`1_Utilities/deviceQuery`) that will print out information such as the shared memory configuration and other details, should you need it.

Each thread also has access to a relatively small amount of local cache memory, which is primarily used for function stack frames and for storing local variables when there aren't enough registers available. Physically, this is located within the global memory and thus might not provide any performance benefits. This local memory can only be allocated by the compiler.

Memory locality is far less important on GPUs than on a CPU. (Recall that the GPU model allows massive parallelism to hide memory latency.) However, some patterns of access are more optimal than others. Global memory is optimized for accessing memory in a thread-sequential ordering within warps; 32 sequential loads per warp (on newer hardware, this number may be lower). Such loads can be **coalesced** into a single transaction between the SM and global memory, rather than 32 smaller transactions, and reduce bandwidth pressure. Strided memory accesses by threads are likely to break this coalescing process, thus requiring more memory transactions and decreasing the memory bandwidth usage. In these cases, it might be best to use the shared memory as an intermediary between the global memory and the threads since shared memory does not suffer the same penalties for strided access.

GPU memory is very fast and has a very fast interconnect with the GPU itself. Maximizing bandwidth usage is a balance between loading data in coalesced chunks, making use of shared memory, and, for their most recent chips, making use of asynchronous memory operations. (NVIDIA H100 GPUs added a memory manager that can be asynchronously loaded from global memory to shared memory.) The best approach is often to use these memory structures in a hierarchical pattern alongside the *grid-block-thread* hierarchy: grids interacting primarily with global memory, blocks interacting primarily with shared memory, and threads interacting primarily with registers.

Now that we have a theoretical understanding of how GPUs are organized and how they operate, we can think about how to write code that operates on a GPU. We will start with how to use Thrust and OpenMP to do just that.

Using Thrust algorithms and OpenMP offloading

Thrust is NVIDIA's C++ library for parallel and device-aware containers and algorithms. It (mostly) replicates the standard library interface but allows for the data to be stored on a device (GPU) and for algorithms to be implemented by kernels. Thrust is distributed as part of the CUDA toolkit, so it is generally very easy to use as part of CUDA projects. (AMD ROCm also provides a similar library.)

The backbone containers provided by Thrust are the various vector classes. A Thrust `host_vector` operates very much like `std::vector`, with data stored in linear memory that grows geometrically when it runs out of space. On the other hand, a `device_vector` is entirely contained in GPU memory, with data allocated by `cudaMalloc` (or equivalent). A third `universal_vector` is a vector based on unified memory spaces, whereby the transfer of data from host memory to device memory is handled transparently at runtime based on where the data is accessed. This obviously incurs a transportation along the host-device interconnect (PCIe in many configurations), but on devices with an integrated GPU and CPU, no transfer needs to occur since both the GPU and CPU share the same physical memory.

The abstractions in Thrust go beyond the simple data structures. For instance, one can interact with the contents of `thrust::device_vector` using iterators. Dereferencing such an iterator on the host will incur a transfer of the referenced data so it can be used as normal. This can make it easier to write code that interacts with device memory and moves data to and from the device. However, generally, it is best to avoid such movements whenever possible; a PCIe bus is fairly fast, but not nearly as fast as the memory bus on either the CPU or GPU, and limited in capacity. One should always try to operate on the data where it resides. (Obviously, some transfers are necessary, but these should be as minimal as possible.) The following snippet of code shows how to construct data on the host, move it to the device, and then use the iterator abstractions of `device_vector` to print out the values:

```
#include <thrust/host_vector.h>
#include <thrust/device_vector.h>
// ...

thrust::host_vector<float> h_data { 1.f, 2.f, 3.f };

// transfer from host to device
thrust::device_vector d_data(h_data);

// ... operate on the data on GPU

// inspect some of the values
for (const auto& val : d_data) {
    std::cout << val << '\n';
}

h_data = d_data; // move all the data back
```

Of course, the code shown here is like the bookends of the operation. First, we set up data on the host, move it to the device, perform some operations on it (using kernels), and then move the final results back to the host. (Printing the values out like this is very useful for debugging.) The next question is how to operate on the data between these bookends.

Thrust algorithms

In many ways, Thrust algorithms are similar to the standard library algorithms except that they will use the device to do the work when the data is stored on the device. This allows one to write code that executes on a GPU with very little effort and no additional knowledge of how to program the GPUs themselves. This is also one of the reasons we advocated for reducing your problems to a set of relatively standard operations provided by the standard library. This is a very easy way to fully exploit the hardware you have available. (Thrust algorithms may also have some performance benefits over standard algorithms, even if these are not implemented on the device!)

The first set of algorithms we want to highlight is those that move or create data from one place to another. Copying data to and from a device is best done using the vector-level operations described previously, but they can also be done with the `thrust::copy` algorithm function. The advantage is that this algorithm can also copy from device to device, and allows for more fine-tuned copies than the full-vector operations. Alongside the copy operations are the `thrust::fill` and `thrust::generate` algorithms, which are used to fill memory with values (a single value in the case of `fill` and dynamically generated values in the case of `generate`).

The Thrust sort functions work the same way as their standard library cousins. In the basic configuration, one provides the begin and end iterators to the range to be sorted, and values are compared by a less-than operator. There is a second overload that accepts an alternative ordering, such as a `thrust::greater` instance to sort in reverse order. This would also allow one to sort paired values by comparing the first element with a custom comparison functor (more on this shortly). Thrust also provides a `sort_by_key` function, which sorts one range according to keys in another range. This is logically equivalent to sorting pairs by the first value, but where the first and second values of the pairs are stored in separate vectors. This might be the case, for instance, when working with sparsely stored vectors.

The most flexible set of functions comes in the form of `thrust::transform`, of which there are several overloads. The first takes a pair of input iterators, a single output iterator (as is usual for standard algorithm functions), and a unary operation to apply to the input range to generate the results stored in the output range. A second overload takes a second input iterator and a binary operation to apply to the two input ranges. The combination of these two can already be quite powerful. The CUDA standard library implements device-compatible functors in the `cuda/std/functional` header (a direct parallel of the `functional` header in the standard library).

However, one can easily create new functors using lambda functions. For instance, we can implement a SAXPY-like function in Thrust as follows:

```
#include <thrust/host_vector.h>
#include <thrust/device_vector.h>
#include <thrust/transform.h>
// ...

void saxpy(float a,
           const thrust::device_vector<float>& x,
           const thrust::device_vector<float>& y,
           thrust::device_vector<float>& out
           )
{
    thrust::transform(
            x.begin(), x.end(),
            y.begin(),
            out.begin(),
            [a] __device__ (float xe, float ye) {
                return a * xe + ye;
            }
        );
}
```

This implementation takes the x values from the vector called x (via the iterator-defined range of `x.begin()` to `x.end()`), and the y values from the iterator-defined range of `y.begin()` to `y.begin() + x.size()`, and writes the results of `a*x+y` into the `out.begin()` to `out.begin() + x.size()` range. The assumption is that the `y` and `out` vectors contain as many elements as `x`, which, of course, should be checked in the wrapping function. Using the `__device__` attribute on a lambda function requires the `-extended-lambda` compiler option to be set in CMake. The alternative is to declare a function object with an appropriately attributed `operator()` and use that in place of the lambda.

These algorithms are very powerful in what they can accomplish, but ultimately, one cannot achieve everything through such functions. However, some functions require more control than is offered through this interface. In this case, one might have to turn to direct CUDA programming, which we shall discuss later. In the meantime, we will discuss an alternative method of writing GPU-accelerated code directly in the C++ source.

OpenMP device offloading

Thrust is an NVIDIA library and doesn't help if you're using a GPU from a different vendor. (AMD does have its own version of Thrust in its standard library, but there are many GPU vendors beyond NVIDIA and AMD.) Those looking for a more general-purpose tool for writing code for GPU programming might also turn to the OpenMP device offloading capability. This was introduced in the OpenMP 4.0 specification to offload computation to accelerators and coprocessors. This includes devices such as GPUs, but also **tensor processing units (TPUs)** that are starting to appear on mainstream processors. For those who are already familiar with the OpenMP model, this might be a low-effort way of engaging with accelerator devices without making large-scale changes to your code base. However, later in this chapter, we will look at a more flexible way of writing device-agnostic code using SYCL.

OpenMP is very easy to use in general, and the device offload is no different. For offloading, we need to use the `target` directive of the OpenMP `pragma` construct. We also need to specify the memory regions that must be transferred to and from the device prior to and following the computation itself. With very little effort, we can implement the `saxpy` function as follows:

```
void openmp_saxpy(float a, const float* x, float* y, int N) {


#pragma omp target teams distribute parallel for \
        map(to:x[0:N]) \
        map(tofrom:y[0:N])
    for (int i=0; i<N; ++i) {
        y[i] += a * x[i];
    }
}
```

The first part of the `omp` declaration specifies to use the offload functionality (`target`) using distributed teams to parallelize the following `for` loop. The `map` clauses describe the data movement that needs to happen between the host and device in order to allow the computation to occur. The `to` statement in the first case indicates that the `x` value is only transferred to the device, but not back; the `tofrom` statement indicates that the data also needs to be copied back to the host.

Once this is done, one must specify the target architecture that should be compiled on the command line. Of course, since we're using OpenMP, we must add the equivalent of `-fopenmp`, but we also need to include an offload architecture. On Clang/LLVM, this is done with the `-fopenmp-targets=` argument, followed by a list of architecture triplets. Other compilers have some limited (experimental) support for non-CPU targets.

If the high-level approach using Thrust algorithms or OpenMP offload fails, you might have to write kernels by hand in CUDA (or ROCm/HIP for AMD GPUs). In the next section, we will see what is involved in translating an algorithm into CUDA C++.

Writing algorithms for GPU using CUDA C++

One of the hardest parts of learning to program GPUs is the massively parallel model of computation. This is radically different from the programming we're used to on CPUs. One must think about the distribution of work up front and how to organize data movement between different elements of the kernel. Once you get used to some of these concepts, then some of the quirks of the architecture start to become apparent (usually once one starts to profile your kernels). This is not going to be a comprehensive introduction to CUDA programming, but it should give enough to get you started.

The first thing we want to do is define a kernel. A CUDA kernel is defined using the `__global__` attribute applied to a function that returns `void`. There are, of course, restrictions on the arguments that can be passed to a kernel (since these must be copied over to the GPU). We cannot pass data by reference, and any pointer values we pass should point to data that is already on the device. You can pass data in standard layout structures and classes, so `std::span` is probably safe to pass in an argument, but `std::vector` is not. A very basic kernel is defined as follows:

```
__global__ void saxpy(float a,
                      const float* __restrict__ x,
                      float* __restrict__ y,
                      int N)
{
    int thread_rank = blockIdx.x * blockDim.x + threadIdx.x;
    int stride = blockDim.x * gridDim.x
    for (int i=thread_rank; i < N; i += stride) {
        y[i] = a*x[i] + y[i];
    }
}
```

This first attempt demonstrates several techniques. First is computing the thread's rank within the block and grid, and using this information to find the work to be done. This is done using the `threadIdx`, `blockIdx`, `blockDim`, and `gridDim` thread variables. In this case, all the threads within all the blocks are working on a single large problem, but it is not uncommon for each block to work on different smaller problems of the same kind in parallel.

The built-in variables such as threadIdx are actually dim3 structures that contain three integers (x, y, and z), which give the thread's assigned position within the block. The blockIdx variable gives the block's position within the grid, and blockDim and gridDim give the overall shape of the blocks and grid (more on this in a moment).

The second technique uses the loop to cover all the elements of the input arrays. Notice that each thread initializes the for loop with its thread rank, so each thread starts this loop in a different place, and the update operation for the loop increments the position by the total size of the grid. Ideally, one launches kernels with a very large grid with many thousands of threads. However, there are limits to the number of threads that can be deployed. Adding a loop like this to your own kernels allows the grid to be smaller (or larger) than the problem size, which gives you a great degree of flexibility.

The use of __restrict__ serves the same purpose as in the CPU programming world. It is an indication to the compiler that the points do not alias; they point to non-overlapping regions of memory. This allows the compiler to optimize the access more aggressively and produce faster code. This is not necessary (and indeed, shouldn't be used if the ranges do overlap for whatever reason) but does lead to a small performance improvement whenever correctly used.

Launching a kernel requires several steps. First, one must ensure that all data is transferred to the device (if necessary), and otherwise arrange the data. Next, one must decide on the shape of the grid. In many cases, the block shape is somewhat decided by the type of the problem and the grid is used to get the coverage (as far as possible) over the whole problem space. The actual kernel launch is done by means of the triple-chevron notation, <<<grid, block>>>, as shown:

```
const int N = 1000;

// Dummy data
thrust::device_vector<float> x_data(N);
thrust::device_vector<float> y_data(N);

float a = 1.0f;

dim3 block { 256 };

dim3 grid {
  (N + block.x - 1) / block.x, // ceil_div

};
```

```
// remove the wrapper around thrust pointers
const float * x = thrust::raw_pointer_cast(x_data.data());
float* y = thrust::raw_pointer_cast(y_data.data());

// launch the kernel
saxpy<<<grid, block>>>(a, x, y, N);

cudaDeviceSynchronize();
```

CUDA kernel launches are asynchronous, so the call to `saxpy` in the preceding code returns immediately, regardless of whether the operation has finished. The following call to `cudaDeviceSynchronize` blocks until the device has finished executing. What doesn't appear here is any check that the kernel finished without errors. This is achieved using `cudaGetLastError`, which returns a `cudaError_t` enumerator that contains an error code; `cudaGetErrorString` can be used to get a meaningful error message from this code, but it won't tell you where it occurred.

In the example, we set the block size with 256 threads in a linear configuration and derived the number of blocks by dividing (with a round up) the size of the work, `N`, by the size of the block. For this operation, a simple 1D block and grid layout is appropriate. We've chosen 256 threads per block somewhat arbitrarily; we can make this larger or smaller, but it should usually be a multiple of the warp size (32 on NVIDIA GPUs). With a 32-bit size type and this block size, we aren't at risk of overflowing the maximum grid size either. To be completely safe, we should really check whether the value would overflow. Also, in this example, we use the `raw_pointer_cast` function to unwrap the tagged pointers that are used in `thrust::device_vector`. This is essential because the kernel expects raw pointers.

At this point, you might be wondering how the performance of this kernel compares to a similar CPU-based implementation. Fortunately, we've already written such functions back in *Chapter 4*. *Figure 14.2* shows the results of benchmarking our CPU kernel (AVX2 variant and a multithreaded version) against the CUDA kernel we defined earlier. The results paint an interesting picture. For very small vector sizes, the cost of launching a CUDA kernel is too large to see any benefit, especially since these small vectors fit into the low-level cache. Notice that the multithreaded implementation eventually fails to outperform the single-threaded code; this is likely due to memory bandwidth saturation. The CPU execution times grow linearly with vector size, which is what we expect given the linear complexity of the `axpy` operation.

The GPU execution times remain constant until the grid size required is large enough to saturate the GPU (an RTX 5070Ti in this instance), and then the execution time grows linearly. The growth rate appears similar to the CPU, but the execution times are significantly smaller.

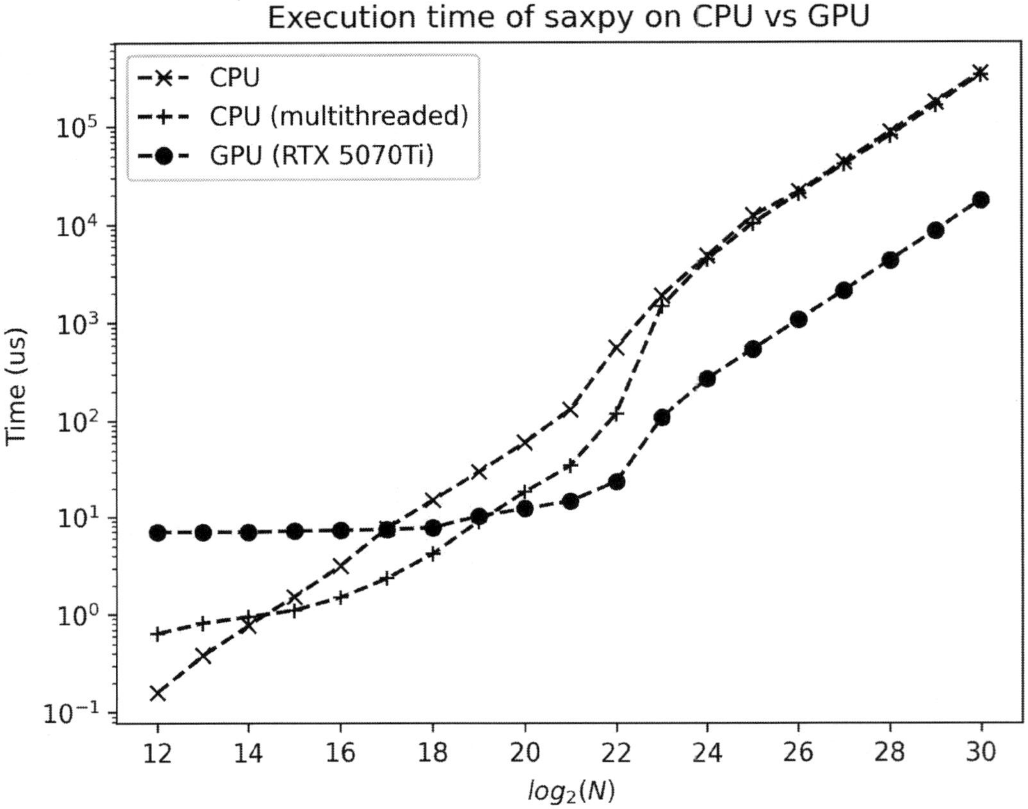

Figure 14.2: A plot of execution times for the saxpy operation implemented on a CPU, multithreaded CPU, and GPU. The x axis shows the vector size (on a log scale) and the y axis the execution time (also on a log scale) in microseconds

CUDA kernels can be templates, too, although this can be a little unwieldy as a function template. Ideally, one might want to encapsulate the actual operation of the kernel into a template class that contains additional metadata about the kernel itself and other supporting functions. This approach is used to great effect in the NVIDIA CUTLASS library (`https://github.com/NVIDIA/cutlass`). A kernel here is a class with numerous template arguments, combined with a template kernel function that provides a universal entry point to such class-based kernels. (Note that member functions, even static ones, cannot be declared `__global__`.)

This is defined as something like the following:

```
template <typename Kernel>
__global__ kernel(typename Kernel::Params params)
{
    Kernel kernel;
    kernel(params);
}
```

The CUTLASS implementation contains some additional setup for shared memory, which we omit here. Once this function is available, one can define the kernel again as follows:

```
template <typename Scalar>
class AxpyKernel {
public:

    struct Params {
        const Scalar* x;
        Scalar* y;
        Scalar a;
        int N;
    };

    __device__ __forceinline__
    void operator()(const Params& params)
    {
        int thread_rank = blockIdx.x * blockDim.x + threadIdx.x;
        int stride = blockDim.x * gridDim.x
        for (int i=thread_rank; i < params.N; i += stride) {
            params.y[i] = params.a*params.x[i] + params.y[i];
        }
    }
};
```

The entry point to this function is `operator()`, which takes a reference to the `Params` struct. Notice that we have annotated this with the `__device__` property, which signals to the compiler that this should be compiled as a device function, and the `__forceinline__` attribute forces this function to be inlined, which avoids the overhead of device function calls. Leaving this out can greatly increase the local memory usage on the GPU, which can be problematic.

This is huge overkill for such a simple kernel, but what this allows is for device-level aggregation of kernels. These kernel objects can be collected together into small clusters of operations that are performed together in a single kernel launch. This eliminates some overhead from launching kernels and allows one to optimize data flow between separate operations. Such a class could also provide functions to get the most appropriate block and grid size for a given problem, allowing the kernel launch process to be streamlined somewhat for users who don't know how to find optimal grid configurations. Launching this kernel is very similar to what we had before:

```
using Kernel = AxpyKernel<float>;

typename Kernels::Params params{
    thrust::raw_pointer_cast(x_data.data()),
    thrust::raw_pointer_cast(y_data.data()),
    a,
    N
};

kernel<Kernel><<<grid, block>>>(params);
```

Where this pattern really shines is when shared memory becomes involved and the complexity of the kernel grows beyond a single function. This is covered in the next section, where we look at the mechanisms for communicating between threads.

Coordinating between GPU threads

Within a single warp or thread block, there are methods of communicating and synchronizing threads. The main mechanisms are the synchronization primitives, such as `__syncthreads`, which block progress until all active threads in the block reach the same point, and shared memory. Shared memory is shared between all the threads in a block, so it can be used as a fast interchange for data, usually as a store for temporary values that are sequentially updated by all the threads in the block. Using only these two mechanisms, one can implement a fairly efficient matrix multiplication kernel with relatively little effort:

```
__global__ void matrix_mul(
    float* __restrict__ C, // m by n matrix, row major
    const float* __restrict__ A, // m by k matrix, row major
    const float* __restrict__ B, // k by n matrix, row major
    int m, int n, int k) {
    constexpr int tile_size = 16; // block is tile_size by tile_size
```

```
    int tx = threadIdx.x;
    int ty = threadIdx.y;

    __shared__ float A_tile[tile_size][tile_size];
    __shared__ float B_tile[tile_size][tile_size];

    // Tiles move across rows of A
    const float* sub_A = A + (blockIdx.y * tile_size * k);
    // Tiles move down columns of B
    const float* sub_B = B + (blockIdx.x * tile_size);
    float* sub_C = C + (blockIdx.y*tile_size)*n + blockIdx.x*tile_size;

    float accumulator = 0.0f;
    for (int tile_k=0; tile_k < gridDim.x; ++tile_k) {
        // read into shared memory tiles
        // move A_tile over by tile_size rows
        auto A_offset = tile_k * tile_size;
        // move B_tile down by tile_size cols
        auto B_offset = tile_k * tile_size * n;

        A_tile[ty][tx] = sub_A[A_offset + ty*k + tx];
        B_tile[ty][tx] = sub_B[B_offset + ty*n + tx];

        // Do not proceed until the memory is copied
        __syncthreads();
        for (int i=0; i<tile_size; ++i) {
            accumulator += A_tile[ty][i] * B_tile[i][tx];
        }
        __syncthreads();
    }
    // write out the result
    sub_C[ty*n + tx] = accumulator;
}
```

In this example, the block must be 2-dimensional with 16 threads in the x and y components. To keep this code short, we've made the assumption that all the matrix dimensions are a multiple of 16. The grid size for this kernel should thus be m/16 by n/16 (by 1). The elements of the multiplication should look rather similar to the example in *Chapter 4*. Here, though, each thread handles the computation of one element of the output matrix. Each block, by reading a tile of A (offset by blockIdx.y*tile_size rows) and a tile of B (offset by blockIdx.x*tile_size columns), accumulates the contribution of those tiles into accumulator. The A tile is then shifted across by tile_size columns, and the B tile is shifted down by tile_size rows (so that the new tile does not overlap the previous one), and the process repeats until we have exhausted all the rows of A and columns of B (the same number). At this point, the result in accumulator is written to the unique position for the given thread in the given block.

Needless to say, this implementation of matrix multiplication performs quite badly compared to cuBLAS. For even relatively small m=n=k=256 matrices, the cuBLAS implementation does better with 16.1 microseconds per iteration with our implementation versus 12.7 microseconds with cuBLAS. (It's also worth pointing out that this seems to be the minimum time for a cuBLAS call; it is not smaller for smaller matrices.) For a larger matrix with m=n=k=4096, our implementation struggles with a time of almost 35 milliseconds per computation, where cuBLAS computes this in just over 4 milliseconds. However, chasing performance was not the purpose of this exercise; that was to show how to use shared memory and coordinate between threads. Still, it is worth remembering that in *Chapter 4*, we benchmarked CPU implementations of matrix multiplication (GEMM), and by comparison, those numbers look rather large!

In the matrix multiplication example, the shared memory is statically allocated by the compiler, like one would allocate a static array, but in CUDA, you can also have dynamic shared memory. This can be useful if the shared memory requirement depends on the shape of the thread block. For instance, one might process a tuple of four floats in each thread and, assuming that each of these tuples is stored contiguously in global memory, moving these into a shared memory buffer prior to processing helps coalesce the global memory accesses. In this case, one would need to allocate 4*sizeof(scalar)*block.x bytes of shared memory at the kernel launch. Let's see what this might look like:

```
__global__ void process_4_tuples_kernel(const float* data_in,
                                        float* data_out,
                                        unsigned num_tuples)
{
    // declare the shared memory
```

```
    extern __shared__ float smem[]; // 1

    // steps (detail omitted)
    // Copy from input to smem
    __syncthreads();
    // Process
}

template <typename DataIn, DataOut>
void process_4_tuples(const DataIn& data_in, DataOut& data_out, unsigned
                      n_tuples)
{
    // block size is fixed, but could also be an argument
    dim3 block { 256, 1, 1 };
    dim3 grid { (n_tuples + 255) / 256, 1, 1 };

    size_t smem_bytes = 4 * sizeof(float) * block.x;

    process_4_tuples_kernel<<<grid, block, smem_bytes>>>( // 2
        raw_pointer_cast(data_in.data()),
        raw_pointer_cast(data_out.data()),
        n_tuples
    );

    auto err = cudaGetLastError();
    if (err != cudaSuccess) {
        throw std::runtime_error();
    }
}
```

There are two parts to this. The first is the definition of the kernel itself, which is mostly omitted here. The critical line is the declaration of the shared memory array, `smem`, marked by the `// 1` comment. This declares an array in shared memory that is to be dynamically allocated by the runtime when the kernel is launched. Later, the number of bytes to be allocated is passed to the kernel launch as `smem_bytes` on the line marked `// 2`. The array can then be used as usual in the kernel itself. The additional steps of the kernel are to copy the data into the shared memory prior to computing. Depending on what computation is performed, a copy of the results back into global memory might also be necessary.

The most important code is contained in the second part. Here, we've wrapped up our kernel launch into a convenient wrapper function (templated so it can take either `thrust::device_vector` or `thrust::universal_vector`), which computes the size of the block and grid as before, and then computes the number of bytes of shared memory required per block. In this case, it has around 4 KiB of shared memory per block, which, in theory, would allow up to 16 concurrent blocks per SM.

Notice that we have to insert a synchronization point between the movement of data and the processing of data. We need to make sure that all of the threads have finished writing to shared memory before we start the computation because this is a cooperative effort among the thread block (each thread touches data that is used by another thread's computation). In some cases, one can avoid calls to the heavy `__syncthreads` synchronization and instead utilize the warp-local synchronize functions to align memory accesses.

Warp-level synchronization and cooperative groups

Sometimes it is necessary to divide up the work so that groups of threads (possibly smaller than a warp in size) cooperate on a single problem. For instance, let's consider the problem of computing the Euclidean norm (the square root of the sum of squares of the elements) of a vector in 32 dimensions (i.e., a vector whose length is exactly the same as a single warp). In order to compute this norm, each thread will have to load its value and square it, but then we have to aggregate the squared values to obtain the full result. This requires the threads in the warp to share their values with an adjacent thread. This is a good opportunity to introduce **cooperative groups**, rather than using the primitive CUDA functions. (Actually, in practice, one should not implement the Euclidean norm in this way, and you should instead use the `thrust::transform_reduce` algorithm. This is just to demonstrate the technique.)

Cooperative groups were introduced in CUDA 9.0 as an interface for organizing and synchronizing threads within the grid, block, individual warps, or smaller groups of threads. We create objects (from the `cooperative_groups` namespace in the `cooperative_groups.h` header) using factory functions as follows:

```
#include "cooperative_groups.h"
namespace cg = cooperative-groups;
// ...

auto grid = cg::this_grid();
auto block = cg::this_thread_block();
auto warp = cg::tiled_partition<32>(block);
```

The first function creates an object that represents the entire grid of threads, the second represents the threads within the block to which the current thread belongs, and the final object represents the warp within the block to which the current thread belongs. We can use these group objects to get the number of threads (size) and the rank of the current thread within each level of the hierarchy. We can also use the warp object in this case to perform the shuffle down operation required for our norm calculation. Putting this all together, our compute functions are as follows:

```
__global__ void compute_2norm(const float* vectors,
                              float* norms,
                              unsigned n_vectors)
{
    constexpr unsigned vector_size = 32;

    auto grid = cg::this_grid();
    auto block = cg::this_thread_block();
    auto warp = cg::tiled_partition<32>(block);

    // For simplicity, assume that a block is 32 threads
    const unsigned my_vector_offset = grid.block_rank()*vector_size;

    float my_value = vectors[my_vector_offset + warp.thread_rank()];

    float my_norm = my_value * my_value;

    for (int offset=16; offset > 0; offset >>= 1) {
        my_norm += warp.shfl_down(my_norm, offset);
    }

    // only thread 0 writes to memory
    if (threadIdx.x == 0) {
        norms[blockIdx.x] = sqrtf(my_norm);
    }
}
```

This process systematically reduces the initial collection of 32 squared numbers down to the first half of the "active" threads until the final result is held in the thread at index `0`. At this point, we take the square root to get the final value and write the result to the output vector. (Actually, it is probably better to write the square value without the square, and let the host decide whether the square norm is sufficient or the true norm is needed.) The cooperative groups give access to several such shuffle functions on warps. In this example, we performed a down shuffle, where each thread copies a value from a thread whose index is `threadIdx.x + offset`. The effect of this is to pass the values from higher index threads down to lower index threads (hence the name). The `shfl_up` function performs the opposite, moving data from lower index threads to higher index threads. The remaining functions copy data from one thread to another based on absolute index (`shfl_up` and `shfl_down` use relative indexing). The `shfl` function copies from a given thread index, while `shfl_xor` copies the value from the threads whose index is the result of `xor` between a mask (given to the function) and the current thread index.

The cooperative groups interface also allows us to synchronize at various levels. Calling the `sync` method on the `thread_block` object (we called this *block* in the previous code example) is equivalent to `__syncthreads`. On `warp`, the `sync` method is more lightweight (utilizing something more akin to `shfl`) to achieve the desired synchronization.

Now we have seen some of the techniques involved in writing CUDA code for NVIDIA GPUs. This is certainly not exhaustive, but it should serve as a reasonable point from which you can get started with GPU programming. (Of course, the most important thing is to understand the very different architectures employed by GPUs compared to CPUs.) Now, we will switch gears and look at SYCL, which can be used to program many different kinds of devices (not only GPUs).

Using SYCL to write code for many devices

SYCL is a C++ abstraction layer for heterogeneous computing. It makes writing code for a range of devices, including GPUs and other accelerators such as FPGAs, fairly simple by abstracting the core concepts. There are two parts to a SYCL application: the first being the source code, which is written in standard C++, with the help of the SYCL library. During compilation, the code that might be executed on devices is written into the binary in a form that allows it to be runtime-compiled for the requested device. (For instance, it might be compiled into an intermediate representation such as **SPIR-V** and placed in the binary for the device driver to compile further for the specific device.) The second component of a SYCL application is the runtime and device drivers. For instance, OpenCL can be used as a backend for SYCL applications. Intel provides its own backend called **Level Zero**.

SYCL applications need to be compiled using a SYCL-compatible compiler, such as Intel's DPC++ compiler. However, the code itself is standard C++, making use of C++ templates and classes to abstract away the device-specific nuances. Of course, there are some restrictions on what can be done inside kernel functions; accessing runtime type information (such as in a `dynamic_cast` of a polymorphic cast or using a virtual function call) is not allowed, for example. Implementing our basic `saxpy` function in SYCL is now very easy:

```
#include <sycl/sycl.hpp>

void sycl_saxpy(float a, const float* x, float* y, int N) {
    sycl::queue queue;
    sycl::range<1> vec_range(N);

    sycl::buffer xbuf(x, vec_range);
    sycl::buffer ybuf(y, vec_range);

    auto event = queue.submit([&](sycl::handler& handle) {
        sycl::accessor x_access(x_buf, handle, sycl::read_only);
        sycl::accessor y_access(y_buf, handle, sycl::read_write);

        handle.parallel_for(vec_range, [=](auto i) {
            y_access[i] = a*x_access[i] + y_access[i];
        });
    });
    event.wait_and_throw();
}
```

The critical objects, from the host's point of view, are the queue and buffers. The queue maintains a sequence of operations to be executed on a single device. We submit a job using the `submit` method. In this case, we pass a lambda function that accepts a `handler` object and, using the `handler` methods, performs the work. The only complication is accessing the data, which is where the `accessor` objects come in. Here, we created them using the `get_access` method on the buffers, passing the handler as an argument. This returns a device-specific means of accessing the data so that it can be used in computations, such as the `parallel_for` operation in this example. Accessors have several different modes; `read_write` and `read_only` are demonstrated here. There is also `write_only`. These signal to the compiler and SYCL runtime what movements need to occur before the data can be used and what accesses are permitted. Note this function is designed to be similar to the other `saxpy` functions from this chapter, and not to be idiomatic SYCL code.

In SYCL, some of the nuances of programming on specific architectures are hidden from the programmer, at least at the highest level, which is desirable for beginners but less so for people who want to push the performance envelope. The SYCL specification does allow for some customization of kernel execution and customizing the data access, but this requires one to dig far deeper than we have time for here. For most tasks, the basic interface that we have shown here should be sufficient to attain the performance needed. (It really isn't possible to optimize `saxpy` much more than what we have written here.) SYCL does offer the same kind of thread-group style as CUDA by providing a two- or three-dimensional range as the first argument to `parallel_for` rather than the one-dimensional (integer) range given here.

One of the best resources for learning about SYCL is the official documentation from the Khronos group: `https://www.khronos.org/sycl/`. This is very comprehensive documentation for the specification itself, accompanied by many other resources. In terms of compilers and implementations, we suggest looking at the Intel oneAPI SYCL implementation and their DPC++ compiler, which is shipped with the oneAPI base toolkit. This concludes our discussion of SYCL and device programming.

Summary

Programming accelerators and coprocessors, such as GPUs, can greatly improve the computational throughput and expand your capabilities for solving problems. However, the programming model for these devices varies greatly, and usually requires a very different approach to programming to make use of the massive parallelism. Understanding the architecture of the target device and the nature of the problem itself is critical to producing fast and efficient code. When it comes to programming these devices, one can either make use of indirect programming using libraries such as NVIDIA Thrust (or equivalent) and OpenMP device offload, or directly using CUDA or SYCL.

One of the early problems one will encounter with using specialized hardware is the movement of data. Sending large amounts of data to and from a GPU, for instance, is expensive and needs to be managed carefully. This can be done automatically, as is the case for OpenMP offload or SYCL, or it can be a manual process. The advantage of a manual approach is that it allows one to be explicit about when memory copies occur. Once data movement is understood, one operates on this by means of kernels. Writing kernels takes some practice and, depending on how complex the operation is, might take several iterations before one arrives at an effective computation. In the next (and final) chapter, we look at how to profile C++ code to identify exactly what factors are slowing down your code.

15

Profiling Your Code

Performance is important in code. A solution to a problem is only useful if it executes in a timely fashion and delivers results quickly enough. One of the main reasons for selecting C++ as a language for implementing solutions is that you want to maximize the speed and throughput of your code. Before performing any kind of optimization, one must always measure carefully and focus only on the functions and sections that need to be fast; prematurely optimizing can introduce a lot of complications without doing anything to improve the performance.

In this chapter, we look at one of the tools one can use to inspect the runtime characteristics of a program and identify the parts of the code that need to be as fast as possible. This tool also helps to identify potential reasons why our code is not performing as well as needed, such as a high percentage of cache misses, branch mispredictions, or problems decoding and enqueuing instructions. The basic tool we use on Linux for this task is `perf`, which performs both sample-based profiling and acts as an interface for the kernel performance counters. We discuss two different kinds of problems that can hinder performance and what this might look like within the profiler.

In this chapter, we're going to cover the following main topics:

- Introducing `perf`
- Identifying memory bottlenecks
- Identifying slow computation
- Monitoring in production

Technical requirements

In this chapter, we use some of the binaries built in the `Chapter-04` folder of the GitHub repository. We will make extensive use of the Google benchmark library here and the `perf` tool that is available in any Linux distribution; you will need to check your distribution's documentation for instructions on how to install this tool if it is not already installed. Users on Windows or macOS will need to check with their operating system vendor for instructions on how to use their profilers, or use a Linux virtual machine.

The code for this chapter can be found in the `Chapter-15` folder in the GitHub repository for this book at `https://github.com/PacktPublishing/The-CPP-Programmers-Mindset`.

Introducing perf

Profiling is the process of recording information about the execution of a program in order to understand its performance characteristics. This can be very crude, such as simply timing the time spent in particular functions or performing particular tasks. This is often the first step in identifying which parts of your program are the most computationally intensive and where you need to focus your performance tuning attention. Remember, you should only spend time optimizing components that need to be fast, and you should always measure (at least) twice before you jump in and make the cut. Performance tuning is time-consuming and difficult to get right, and should not be done at the expense of mission-critical components.

Once you've identified the parts of your program that actually consume the most amount of time (by measuring), you need to dig deeper to understand exactly what, if any, pieces of code aren't maximizing their performance. Now, it's important to understand that performance is a trade-off between many different factors: the movement of data, the speed and capability of the CPU, and the nature of the task. Improving the movement of data characteristics might alleviate some memory bottlenecks, only to expose a computation bottleneck. This is a careful balancing act, and one needs to properly explore the characteristics in order to understand where to find performance.

Most operating systems provide a facility for obtaining very detailed information about the execution of an application. This includes statistics such as the number of data accesses that were serviced by the various layers of cache, the number of memory pages that were accessed using a lookup in the **translational lookaside buffer** or **TLB** (more on this later), whether a page walk was needed, the number of speculative branches that were executed, and the number of those that were actually taken. A page walk is the process of searching through the operating system page table to find the referenced page. These statistics provide a picture (though not necessarily the whole picture) of how well your code is utilizing the resources available.

On Linux, the perf tool is the entry point to accessing this kind of information. This is a command-line tool that periodically samples the execution of a particular application in order to obtain information about which instructions are being executed from the kernel. This information is then processed, usually requiring information about the source code itself, to put together a profile of the execution. Of course, in order to obtain targeted information about particular parts of the application, one must isolate those and profile them separately.

Since most profiling is sample-based, the best strategy is to observe the code running for a long period of time in order to gather enough samples to see any detail. This usually means running the same piece of code many times. One can write the code to do this by hand, but it is much more convenient to use a framework such as Google's benchmark library (which we used in *Chapter 4*) to organize this for us. This also provides other benefits, such as warm-up cycles to prime caches and tools for ensuring the optimizer does not optimize away critical parts of the code. There is, of course, a time for writing simpler applications or simply profiling your executable directly. Microbenchmarking allows you to focus on very small fragments of the bigger picture, but sometimes this can make you miss details elsewhere. For simplicity, we will show mostly profile code written in benchmark form written using the Google benchmark library.

Setting up the repository is easy in this case. First, one needs to find (or otherwise import) the benchmark library. We can just use the CMake find_package mechanism for this. Then, just like the Google Test framework, one needs to link the benchmark framework. Just like the Test framework, the benchmark package provides two linkable targets: benchmark::benchmark, where one must define the main function yourself (possibly via a macro), and the benchmark::benchmark_main target, which includes the standard main function predefined. This is achieved as follows:

```
find_package(benchmark CONFIG REQUIRED)

add_executable(bench_saxpy bench_saxpy.cpp)
target_link_libraries(bench_saxpy PRIVATE benchmark::benchmark_main)
```

Once this is done, you can write the benchmarks as functions that are "registered" using a macro. Benchmark functions accept a State benchmark by reference as arguments, and run the code to be benchmarked within the body of a range-based for loop over the state. There is some scope for setting up the environment for the benchmark prior to running the loop, such as creating vectors that one would operate upon using saxpy. For example, a typical benchmark function might look like this:

```
#include <benchmark/benchmark.h>
// ...
inline constexpr size_t N = 5 * 1024;
```

```
static void bench_saxpy(benchmark::State& state) {
    std::vector<float> x(N, 1.0);
    std::vector<float> y(N, -1.0);
    float a = 2.0;

    for (auto _: state) {
        ct::saxpy_avx512f(a, x, y);
        auto *data = y.data();
        benchmark::DoNotOptimize(data);
        benchmark::ClobberMemory();
    }
}

BENCHMARK(bench_saxpy);
```

Here, we use the block before the start of the `for` loop to construct `x` and `y`. In this case, we're benchmarking the `saxpy` function, which has a memory read component. This has some rather interesting consequences for the benchmark. The fact that the memory location never changes will mean the memory pages associated with these two vectors will likely be within the TLB cache the whole time, which will mean there are fewer TLB misses that will slow the retrieval of memory significantly. This might be realistic since many workflows will operate on the same memory locations repeatedly, and the real question is about the cache performance and compute rather than the management of the data in memory. However, sometimes, this kind of detail might well be a characteristic of the code being benchmarked (for instance, what if one were testing the performance of `push_back` on a `std::vector`, where the allocation is very important?).

The two functions we call inside the benchmark loop are quite important here. The first (aptly named `DoNotOptimize`) contains some inline assembly that causes the optimizer to retain all of the local variables and data and not optimize them away because of non-use, but doesn't actually add any instructions or performance penalty. This is important because we always want to benchmark our code with all of the optimizations turned on. The second function, `ClobberMemory`, inserts a fence that causes all pending writes to memory to complete. This can sometimes be delayed because of the cache, which might materially change the characteristics of a function that, say, operates on small blocks of memory.

Perf the program

Once we have an executable, we can start to run benchmarks. Most IDEs include a profiler option, which usually just offers the sampling-based interface to the actual profiler (depending on your operating system and IDE). On Linux, the best choice for most systems will be the `perf` executable, which is developed alongside the kernel and offers very fine-grained details about every aspect of the application. Using `perf` directly can be a little intimidating, especially from the command line, but this is actually one of its greatest strengths. Before you get started, you might need to adjust your kernel parameters to give you access to the performance counters within the kernel. This can be done within a session using the following `sysctl` call:

```
sudo sysctl -w kernel.perf_event_paranoid=2
```

This allows users to access most of the kernel-level performance counters within the session, but it will reset when the user logs out (or shuts down, etc.). Some functionality might still be disallowed with this setting, in which case you might need to change it again to `1`, `0`, or even `-1`. You should check the documentation before you change anything.

Once this is done, we can invoke the profiler from the terminal. The `perf` application has many different modes in which it can run; each has a different function. The three that we will focus on in this chapter are the `stat`, `record`, and `report` modes. This should be sufficient for most purposes. For far more information about these and other modes, you can read the `perf` wiki here: `https://perfwiki.github.io`.

Perf stat

The `stat` mode runs the executable target application, our benchmark, and gathers statistics from the kernel about this process, then dumps these into the terminal. These statistics are useful for gathering a quick overview of the kinds of issues to be on the lookout for when we dig down. The output of profiling our saxpy implementation from *Chapter 4* might look like this:

```
$ perf stat -d ./bench_saxpy --benchmark_filter="avx512"

Performance counter stats for './bench_saxpy --benchmark_filter=avx512':

            991.62 msec task-clock:u
                  #    1.000 CPUs utilized
                 0      context-switches:u
                  #    0.000 /sec
                 0      cpu-migrations:u
                  #    0.000 /sec                           176
```

```
    page-faults:u
                    #    177.487 /sec
  6,864,233,543        instructions:u
                    #    1.35  insn per cycle
                    #    0.00  stalled cycles per insn      (71.26%)
  5,090,245,103        cycles:u
                    #    5.133 GHz                         (71.37%)
      2,099,158        stalled-cycles-frontend:u
                    #    0.04% frontend cycles idle        (71.42%)
  1,149,926,794        branches:u
                    #    1.160 G/sec                       (71.52%)
         36,981        branch-misses:u
                    #    0.00% of all branches             (71.57%)
  6,742,275,759        L1-dcache-loads:u
                    #    6.799 G/sec                       (71.54%)
  2,266,383,351        L1-dcache-load-misses:u
                    #   33.61% of all L1-dcache accesses   (71.33%)

    0.992075594 seconds time elapsed

    0.982478000 seconds user
    0.001990000 seconds sys
```

(We've adjusted the lines to fit neatly in the space; yours will look slightly different.) The raw numbers (far left column) are actually not that important. The numbers presented after the # symbol are the things to look at here. We can see in this example that we're executing around 1.35 instructions per cycle (which is actually quite low, 2–3 is pretty typical), and 33% of our L1 data accesses are misses. This latter figure is alarmingly high, but not unexpected for the kind of work we're doing (more on this later). We can also see the number of branches and branch misses, and the number of page faults. A page fault occurs when the processor needs data from a page that it has not yet loaded into RAM; these are not really a result of our `saxpy` implementation.

In this case, we requested detailed output (with the `-d` option), but there are more levels of detail that can be provided. The `perf` documentation explains what is included in each level. One can also specify a list of events that one would like reported from a very large list (run `perf list` to obtain the full list available on your system). For instance, we could retrieve (only) the `L1-dcache-loads` and `L1-dcache-load-misses` counts by passing the following option at the command line:

```
-e "L1-dcache-loads,L1-dcache-load-misses"
```

Invoking `perf stat` with this option will cause it to report only these two counter values. This is very useful for targeting specific events, such as cache-related events. When the number of events to record is large, the kernel (and CPU) cannot count these values all the time, so the total counts are actually estimated based on a smaller amount of time spent observing these values. When this happens, the percentage of actual runtime where the values are recorded is displayed as a percentage at the end of the line (see the previous example output).

Perf record

The `record` mode performs sample-based profiling on the application. This means `perf` periodically inspects the execution and records the instructions and functions being used. This is written into a file that can be ingested and interpreted later (using `perf report`) to give very detailed information about where in your code time the processor is spending the most time, and how it is spending its time. This is very useful for identifying which branches are taken, and which parts of the code are "hot." The `record` mode can also record other events, just like the `stat` mode, rather than the default `cycle` event samples.

Sampling and interrupt-based sampling are not precise processes. There is a gap between an event that causes the kernel to record information about the program state and the point at which that information is actually captured. These discrepancies are called **skids**. The position of the program counter can advance by several instructions, possibly far more than you might initially think, especially if the code contains branches. For this reason, one must be quite careful in reading and interpreting the sample profile.

There are a few things to be aware of when invoking the `record` mode of `perf`. The main thing one needs to do is to specify the method for reconstructing the call stack. This is done by adding the `-g` option. In the user-space, this uses the frame pointer to reconstruct the call stack in order to figure out how much time the process spends in each function, and by what means it got there. Later, we will revisit the settings required for this from the target executable. We can actually customize the method used to reconstruct the call graph by instead specifying the `--call-graph <method>` option. (Using the `dwarf` call graph reconstruction method is also common.) Thus, a typical invocation will look like this:

```
$ perf record -g ./bench_saxpy --benchmark_filter=avx512
[ perf record: Woken up 124 times to write data ]
[ perf record: Captured and wrote 32.108 MB perf.data (3988 samples) ]
```

This will write the data into a file called `perf.data`, unless another filename is provided using the `-o <filename>` option. If you do write the data to another file besides `perf.data`, you will need to specify it as an argument when you invoke `perf report`, which we talk about next.

Perf report

The `report` mode consumes a dump of data produced by a previous `perf record` and opens a terminal interface to inspect the data. This is a view of the functions and the proportion of samples that were recorded within each function. Once again, we will usually want to use an additional option to arrange the functions according to their call graph, again using the `-g` option. This will arrange the function calls into the hierarchical view. We also like to be a little more specific and customize the appearance of this graph using the expanded option `-g 'graph,0.5,caller`. The first parameter is the type of display to use, the second is a threshold for filtering, and the final one determines the direction in which one observes the call stack. We've set this to `caller`, so the entries listed as children under each main entry are the functions that are called inside that function. Once we run this mode, we'll get a terminal interface that looks something like this:

```
Samples: 3K of event 'cycles:Pu', Event count (approx.): 4973934526
  Children      Self  Command       Shared Object
        Symbol
+   99.94%     0.00%  bench_saxpy  libbenchmark.so.1.9.1
        [.] 0x00007f3cf7ec6ed1
+   99.94%     0.00%  bench_saxpy  libbenchmark.so.1.9.1
        [.] 0x00007f3cf7edfa81
+   99.94%     0.00%  bench_saxpy  libbenchmark.so.1.9.1
        [.] 0x00007f3cf7edf6b6
+   99.94%     0.13%  bench_saxpy  bench_saxpy
        [.] benchmark::internal::LambdaBenchmark<main::{lambda(benchmark::S
+   99.81%    99.81%  bench_saxpy  bench_saxpy
        [.] ct::saxpy_avx512f(float,
                std::span<float const, 18446744073709551615ul>,
                std::span<float, 18446744073709551615ul>)
```

(We've split up the long lines to help them fit on the page.) You can move up and down using the arrow keys, and expand (or collapse) entries using the *e* key. (You can press *?* for keybinding help.) Once you expand an entry, say the `bench_saxpy` function on line 2 (the entry with 99.81% in the `Self` column), we can see the functions called inside this function. In this case, there is one child function, `ct::saxpy_avx512f`, as shown in the following snippet:

```
-   99.68%    99.68%  bench_saxpy  bench_saxpy
        [.] ct::saxpy_avx512f(float,
                                      std::span<float const,
18446744073709551615ul>,
                                      std::span<float, 18446744073709551615ul>)
      99.68% 0
        ct::saxpy_avx512f(float,
                                   std::span<float const, 18446744073709551615ul>,
                                   std::span<float, 18446744073709551615ul>)
```

This gives a breakdown of how long is spent in each child function. In this case, almost all the time is spent in the function that does all the work of `saxpy`, which really isn't surprising. Moving the cursor down to this line and pressing the *a* (for annotate) key opens a view of the assembly that looks something like this:

```
       │ 60:   vmovups      (%rdi,%rax), %zmm1
  3.92 │       vfmadd213ps  (%rdx,%rax), %zmm2, %zmm1
  6.82 │       vmovups      %zmm1, (%rdx,%rax)
 88.60 │       addq         $0x40,%rax
  0.43 │       cmpq         %rsi,%rax
       │     ↑ jne          60
```

This is the body of the main `for` loop contained in the `saxpy_avx512f` function body. As expected, we're making use of the AVX512 fused-multiply-add instruction, `vfmadd213ps`. In the left-hand margin, we can see the percentage of samples observed at a given instruction. Interestingly, despite the multiply-add instruction being the "heaviest" shown in this block, only 3.92% of samples are attributed to this instruction. This is the skid we described earlier in action. It looks like most of the samples that might be attributed to `vfmadd213ps` have instead been attributed to the `addq` instruction, which is a simple integer addition and thus the cheapest operation here by far. We'll come back to how to read these profiles later in the *Identifying slow computation* section.

Setting up your applications for profiling

So far, we've seen how to launch and run an application under `perf` in various modes and how to access the results (in the case of `record`), but we have not described what we must do in the target application itself to facilitate good profiling. It turns out that very little is needed from the target executable. As we have already mentioned, one should always profile code with all of the optimizations that you would deploy in production (CMake's `Release` configuration, for instance). In order to reconstruct the call graph, such as those we used in the `perf record` and `perf report` programs, we also need to make sure the frame pointer is preserved.

Most optimizing compilers, on most architectures, will repurpose the frame pointer register as another general-purpose register. This prevents `perf` from using this register to obtain the frame information to reconstruct the call graph. To prevent the compiler from doing this, we need to use `-fno-omit-frame-pointer` on GCC and Clang, or its equivalent on other compilers, to prevent the compiler from making this particular optimization. This won't hurt performance in most cases; it just means there is one fewer general-purpose register for the assembler to use. You need to make sure this happens anywhere you want to see detail in the profiler output, including static or shared libraries, if your functionality is broken up into smaller components. A very simple way to achieve this is to turn off the CMake option and set the global `add_compile_options` as follows:

```
option(PROFILING "are we building for profiling" OFF)
if (PROFILING)
    add_compile_options(-fno-omit-frame-pointer)
endif()
```

For a portable library, you should modify this to set the correct flags for each of the compilers that you support. Once this is done, you can build for profiling by simply adding `-DPROFILING=ON` to the CMake configuration step either on the command line or within your IDE, and then you'll be set up for profiling with `perf`.

Writing benchmark functions

We showed how to write a very basic benchmark function earlier in this chapter, but realistically, you probably want to benchmark different configurations of data and test different implementations. Remember, performance is relative. It does not make sense to say something is performant; it only makes sense to say it performs better or worse than some other implementation in certain circumstances. As such, one always needs to benchmark your improvements against what was there before, or the best known alternative. For this reason, one often wants to parameterize benchmarks based on data and implementation.

The benchmark framework offers some options here. The first is the ability to pass in (integer) values into the benchmark function via the state function. This is achieved at the point of registration of the benchmark function. In our example earlier, we used the `BENCHMARK` macro, which is the usual way of declaring benchmarks. To pass arguments to the benchmark itself, we use the `Arg` method on the object created by this macro invocation as follows:

```
//.. snip
BENCHMARK(bench_saxpy)->Arg(1000);
```

This will pass the value (`1000`) in the state, accessed via `state.range(0)` inside the benchmark function itself. We could use this as the length of the vector to use, for instance, but we must still generate those vectors ourselves. The modified benchmark function might be defined as follows:

```
static void bench_saxpy(benchmark::State& state) {
    auto N = state.range(0);
    std::vector<float> x(N, 1.0);
    std::vector<float> y(N, -1.0);
    float a = 2.0;

    for (auto _: state) {
        ct::saxpy_avx512f(a, x, y);
        auto *data = y.data();
        benchmark::DoNotOptimize(data);
        benchmark::ClobberMemory();
    }
}
```

We can specify as many arguments as we like by chaining the `->Arg()` calls together, or we can use the `Range` method to specify a whole range of values at once. One can also pass several arguments at once using `->Args({val1, val2})`, which are then accessed via `state.range(0)`, `state.range(1)`, and so on. The benchmark framework also allows one to build grids of arguments (using `ArgsProduct`) or a custom argument build (using `Apply` and a separate function). See the benchmark user guide for instructions: `https://github.com/google/benchmark`. Benchmark functions can be templates, which is useful for testing the performance of different types within algorithms.

Now that we understand the tools, let's see how we can use them, starting with looking for memory bottlenecks.

Identifying memory bottlenecks

Most code is limited in speed by the rate at which data can be moved around. This can manifest in various ways, including TLB misses (recall that the **TLB** or **translational lookaside buffer** is a cache of pages that have been accessed recently), misses in the various levels of cache, or bad branch predictions and prefetch operations. `perf` will sometimes report these kinds of issues as being **backend-bound**.

To demonstrate the use of these tools, we need an example problem to work on. The example we're going to look at in this section is the problem of computing the outer product of two vectors, which is an entirely memory-bound operation, and there is very little compute involved. The basic function is defined as follows, and we can adjust the lengths of the vectors to see different problematic behaviors:

```
inline void outer_product(float* z,
                          const float* x,
                          const float* y,
                          size_t left_size,
                          size_t right_size) noexcept {
    for (size_t i=0; i<left_size; ++i) {
        for (size_t j=0; j<right_size; ++j) {
            z[i*right_size + j] += x[i] * y[j];
        }
    }
}
```

In theory, when `right_size` is small enough to fit in the cache, this operation will be fast and result in fewer cache misses. (There will still be some cache misses because of the access to the z data.) However, if `right_size` is large, we will start to see larger numbers of cache misses. To test out our theory, we need to write a benchmark, which is done as follows:

```
static void bench_outer_product(benchmark::State& state) {
    auto left_size = static_cast<size_t>(state.range(0));
    auto right_size = static_cast<size_t>(state.range(1));

    std::vector<float> x(left_size, 1.0f);
    std::vector<float> y(right_size, 1.0f);
    std::vector<float> z(left_size * right_size, 0.0f);

```

```
    for (auto _ : state) {
        outer_product(z.data(), x.data(), y.data(), left_size, right_
size);
        benchmark::DoNotOptimize(z.data());
        benchmark::ClobberMemory();
    }
}

BENCHMARK(bench_outer_product)->Args({512, 4096})->Args({128, 16384});
```

Our benchmark uses the state to pass the size of the two vectors, and to get started, we've set up two test cases. In both cases, we've made sure the total number of elements is the same. In the first pair, the right-hand vector (y) has a length of `4096`, which, since we're using `float` scalars (a total of 16 KiB), will comfortably fit in the L1 cache (32 KiB) on many machines. This means we expect a relatively small number of cache misses, generated mostly from reading and writing the output vector, `z`. The second set of arguments has 16,384 elements in the right-hand vector, which is 48 KiB and thus too large to fit in the L1 cache, but probably fits in the L2 or L3 cache (generally this has several megabytes of capacity). Thus, we expect more L1 cache misses resulting from loading smaller pieces of the `y` vector (along with those still arising from the `z` vector reads and writes).

To confirm our suspicions about the cache performance, we need to run the profiler. We can use the `filter` functionality to isolate each of the test cases. The results for the first test case are as follows:

```
$ perf stat -dd ./bench_outer_product --benchmark_filter=4096

Performance counter stats for './bench_weighted_average
                   -benchmark_filter=4096':
            860.95 msec task-clock:u
                   #    0.988 CPUs utilized
                 0      context-switches:u
                   #    0.000 /sec
                 0      cpu-migrations:u
                   #    0.000 /sec
             4,402      page-faults:u
                   #    5.113 K/sec
    22,293,952,664      instructions:u
                   #    5.06  insn per cycle
```

```
                    #    0.00  stalled cycles per insn     (38.36%)
     4,407,209,885       cycles:u
                    #    5.119 GHz                         (38.53%)
        32,855,577       stalled-cycles-frontend:u
                    #    0.75% frontend cycles idle        (38.63%)
     2,774,199,582       branches:u
                    #    3.222 G/sec                       (38.70%)
         2,802,360       branch-misses:u
                    #    0.10% of all branches             (38.70%)
     8,269,491,162       L1-dcache-loads:u
                    #    9.605 G/sec                       (38.66%)
       934,600,184       L1-dcache-load-misses:u
                    #   11.30% of all L1-dcache accesses   (38.50%)
         2,454,223       L1-icache-loads:u
                    #    2.851 M/sec                       (38.38%)
             2,399       L1-icache-load-misses:u
                    #    0.10% of all L1-icache accesses   (38.30%)
        10,852,314       dTLB-loads:u
                    #   12.605 M/sec                       (38.31%)
            95,182       dTLB-load-misses:u
                    #    0.88% of all dTLB cache accesses  (38.31%)
                31       iTLB-loads:u
                    #   36.007 /sec                        (38.31%)
                18       iTLB-load-misses:u
                    #   58.06% of all iTLB cache accesses  (38.31%)

       0.870968145 seconds time elapsed


       0.846629000 seconds user
       0.006944000 seconds sys
```

We can see that roughly one in eight of the L1 data cache loads are misses, which is somewhere in the realm of what we expect from loading and storing data from the z vector. (If anything, this performance is better than we might expect.) Now, we rerun this with the second test case, where the right-hand vector length is 16,384 elements:

```
$ perf stat -dd ./bench_outer_product --benchmark_filter=16384


 Performance counter stats for './bench_outer_product
```

```
--benchmark_filter=16384':

         862.92 msec task-clock:u
                  #    0.998 CPUs utilized
              0      context-switches:u
                  #    0.000 /sec
              0      cpu-migrations:u
                  #    0.000 /sec
          4,416      page-faults:u
                  #    5.118 K/sec
 21,816,256,596      instructions:u
                  #    4.89  insn per cycle
                  #    0.00  stalled cycles per insn     (38.27%)
  4,463,291,768      cycles:u
                  #    5.172 GHz                         (38.37%)
     66,637,294      stalled-cycles-frontend:u
                  #    1.49% frontend cycles idle        (38.49%)
  2,720,367,710      branches:u
                  #    3.153 G/sec                       (38.61%)
        767,549      branch-misses:u
                  #    0.03% of all branches             (38.72%)
  8,265,605,760      L1-dcache-loads:u
                  #    9.579 G/sec                       (38.78%)
  1,393,295,103      L1-dcache-load-misses:u
                  #   16.86% of all L1-dcache accesses   (38.68%)
      5,235,485      L1-icache-loads:u
                  #    6.067 M/sec                       (38.57%)
          1,575      L1-icache-load-misses:u
                  #    0.03% of all L1-icache accesses   (38.46%)
     10,776,135      dTLB-loads:u
                  #   12.488 M/sec                       (38.36%)
        174,783      dTLB-load-misses:u
                  #    1.62% of all dTLB cache accesses  (38.24%)
             70      iTLB-loads:u
                  #   81.120 /sec                        (38.23%)
             47      iTLB-load-misses:u
                  #   67.14% of all iTLB cache accesses  (38.22%)
```

```
        0.864693796 seconds time elapsed

        0.851188000 seconds user
        0.004941000 seconds sys
```

Here, we can see that the proportion of L1 data cache misses is larger than that of the previous test case (about one in six here). Again, the cache performance is perhaps not as bad as we might expect it to be. (Modern processors are incredible.) In both test cases, we're not seeing a great amount of strain on the TLB. This is not surprising because the number of pages covering the whole problem is relatively small, and all the data is contiguous. If your data is more fragmented, you might start to see TLB contention during large-scale computation. (This performance is highly system-dependent, so the numbers can vary quite significantly. However, in several tests on different machines, the cache performance reported here is approximately consistent.)

One of the reasons that the cache performance is this good is that the access pattern is very predictable for the processor. The data within each vector is contiguous, as are the writes. If we disrupt this access pattern, we can expect this performance to drop quickly.

The actual counters reported here don't give us overall information about the performance of the higher-level caches or the RAM bandwidth, but such information might be available. Check `perf list` to explore the kind of counters that are available for your processor vendor. The preceding benchmarks were produced on a Ryzen 7900X desktop processor. For instance, rerunning on an Intel-based laptop gives slightly more information. (Note that most of the information is available on both processors, but one has to dig into the actual hardware event information provided via `perf list` and figure out which ones match the numbers you need.) `perf` gives similar statistics for the Intel chip, but also provides some additional numbers:

```
 Performance counter stats for './bench_outer_product
   --benchmark_filter=4096':


        6,850,563      LLC-loads
                  #    5.770 M/sec                        (66.75%)
        5,222,775      LLC-load-misses
                  #   76.24% of all LL-cache accesses     (59.97%)

 Performance counter stats for './bench_outer_product
   --benchmark_filter=16384':
```

```
      12,466,422      LLC-loads
                 #    9.927 M/sec                        (66.78%)
      11,364,224      LLC-load-misses
                 #   91.16% of all LL-cache accesses     (60.16%)
```

These numbers reflect the number of loads from the **last layer of cache** (**LLC**), which is the L3 cache in this case. The processor that generated these numbers has an 8 MiB L3 cache, which is the same size as the result matrix in both cases. Even if we could fully populate the L3 cache with just the output data, we'd expect there to be a reasonably large number of L3 cache misses for some of the input accesses. However, these numbers are very high (76% and 91%, respectively). These numbers might be slightly inflated by the benchmarking framework or the measurement process itself. Remember that profiler metrics are not an exact picture of only your code, but a messier view of the entire process containing your code.

> In writing this section, the author discovered that it is actually very difficult to write code that forces specific memory load problems. Modern CPUs are extremely sophisticated, so modifying code in some way to try and tease out some particular behavior causes the processor to react differently than how you might expect. Thus, inducing specific behavior is very difficult.

Identifying slow computation

There are many reasons why a particular piece of code might be slower than expected. Most of the time, this is because of memory bottlenecks and suboptimal cache performance. However, one can also run into other problems, such as instruction cache overflows and branch prediction failures. Instruction cache overflows occur when your program contains too many instructions for the processor to keep in cache at any given time. For instance, this might occur if one unrolls a loop into too many steps. Each time the outer loop returns to the beginning, this will cause an instruction cache miss and greatly reduce the ability of the instruction decode to feed instructions to the core itself. `perf` sometimes refers to issues involving instruction decoding and branching as being **frontend-bound**.

In *Chapter 4*, we discussed in detail how speculative execution is one of the reasons modern processors can perform so well, and gave an example of where speculative execution can dramatically improve performance under very specific circumstances. Here, we will dig into this example and examine the `perf` output to see how we can identify some of the indicators of where speculative execution might improve performance. In that example, we gave two implementations of a clamp loop, one which resulted in a conditional move instruction, `cmov`, and one that branched using a conditional and only wrote to memory if the condition was true. This allowed the processor to pipeline the instructions better, resulting in faster execution. If we run these two different modes under `perf`, we can see this fact reflected in the number of branches taken in each case:

```
 Performance counter stats for './bench_clamp_loop --benchmark_
filter=min':

     4,307,035,448      branches:u       #    1.536 G/sec
        14,065,281      branch-misses:u #    0.33% of all branches

 Performance counter stats for './bench_clamp_loop --benchmark_
filter=conditional':

     6,517,490,923      branches:u       #    2.073 G/sec
        23,171,519      branch-misses:u #    0.36% of all branches
```

The raw counter values don't really reflect the difference in performance here. This is partly an artifact of the benchmark framework. The framework runs benchmarks for a given amount of time, so code that runs faster has more iterations and thus the raw counter values might be higher because of this. Moreover, the other code within the benchmark code also affects the counters. If one wants a clearer picture, one needs to look instead at the recorded profiles. Let's start with the implementation that uses the `min` function:

```
perf record -g ./bench_clamp_loop --benchmark_filter=min
perf report -g "graph,0.5,caller"

          |20:   movzwl (%rdi),%eax
   0.46 |        movl   $0xff,%edx
  28.05 |        cmpw   %dx,%ax
   1.69 |        cmoval %edx, %eax
  63.79 |        addq   $0x2,%rdi
        |        movw   %ax,-0x2(%rdi)
   6.00 |        cmpq   %rcx,%rdi
```

Here, we see a large spike in samples just after the cmov instruction (this is likely a sample skid, which we talked about before). If we instead look at the implementation that makes use of the conditional, we see that more samples are just after the comparison instruction instead:

```
perf record -g ./bench_clamp_loop --benchmark_filter=conditional

            |20:    cmpw $0xff,(%rdi)
   62.54 |      ↓ jbe  2f
            |        movl $0xff,%edx
    0.37 |        movw %dx,(%rdi)
   33.55 |2f:    addq $0x2,%rdi
    3.54 |        cmpq %rax,%rdi
            |      ↑ jne  20
```

Perhaps in these cases, the effect would be clearer if instead we allowed the compiler to unroll these loops. (Recall that in *Chapter 4*, we prevented the compiler from performing this optimization to keep the assembly code simple.) In reality, this allows the compiler to vectorize the loops, at which point the distinction between these implementations becomes moot. (This example was constructed somewhat unnaturally to exhibit this precise behavior.)

It's worth mentioning here that we can give hints to the compiler to indicate which branch of a conditional is more likely to be taken, which hopefully will reduce the number of mispredicted branches. This is by tagging conditional statements with the `[[likely]]` or `[[unlikely]]` C++ attributes to indicate that a branch is likely (or unlikely) to be taken during execution. This allows the compiler to organize the code in a way that is more optimal for the likely branch. Another option is to use profile-guided optimization, which somewhat automates this process.

So far, we've only discussed how we examine the performance characteristics in a pre-release setting. However, we shouldn't stop there and should continue to monitor the performance long-term during the deployment. In the next section, we discuss how to monitor our deployed software in the production environment.

Monitoring in production

One thing that we don't discuss often is how to monitor the performance of code in the production environment. Here, the objective is different. We're not trying to optimize the speed at which the code itself runs. Instead, we're watching for changes in which parts of the code are utilized. Our optimized code will always operate very well, but this is only useful if it is actually used.

Suppose, for a moment, that you write some code that solves a particular problem that contains two paths. At the time of writing the code, one path is taken far more frequently than the other, and so most of the time is spent optimizing this path. However, once this code enters production, over time, the balance between the two paths changes, and the unoptimized path is taken more frequently. In this case, it might be worth revisiting the other pathway and spending some time optimizing for the new workflow that has emerged.

One of the ways to achieve this is to add logging to the software that allows you to track which branches are taken so you can monitor whether there are shifts in the data flow. Obviously, there are limits to this; one does not want to interrupt high-performance code with logging, even if most of the work is done in a background thread. However, having logging calls at the point of dispatch to the parts of the software that do the number crunching work can really help the programmer understand the program flow. You can see this kind of logging in lots of high-performance libraries, such as Intel MKL, and these give very valuable insights into how the data is processed internally and why certain routines are used rather than others.

Summary

This chapter looked at how to analyze the way that your code behaves and understand why it might be underperforming compared to expectations. The main tool we use for this is the Linux `perf` tool for examining the performance counters within the Linux kernel. These give very fine-grained information about the way that your program is running, and help find places where performance might be hindered. We gave a couple of examples that illustrated the kind of issues that might appear in real code. There are many factors to consider here, including the way that the CPU decodes and schedules individual micro operations, the cache performance and branch predictions, and the global movement of data between various forms on the system.

Performance is a moving target. Altering code to address a specific issue can expose other issues that mean the performance does not improve as expected; unrolling a loop to improve cache performance might cause the instruction cache to overflow. This is a balance, and one must find the one point within the space of behaviors that you can influence that yields the best performance for the problem that you have. The only way to do this is to measure, using `perf` or something equivalent, and identify the places where there are gains to be made.

This is the final chapter of this book, which, in some way, describes the final stages of developing software: final performance tuning and monitoring the software performance after deployment.

This book is not a precise set of instructions for solving any problem, but instead, a framework and examples of things to consider as you solve ever more complex problems.

16

Unlock Your Exclusive Benefits

Your copy of this book includes the following exclusive benefits:

- Next-gen Packt Reader
- DRM-free PDF/ePub downloads

Follow the guide below to unlock them. The process takes only a few minutes and needs to be completed once.

Unlock this book's free benefits in 3 easy steps

Step 1

Keep your purchase invoice ready for *Step 3*. If you have a physical copy, scan it using your phone and save it as a PDF, JPG, or PNG.

For more help on finding your invoice, visit `https://www.packtpub.com/unlock-benefits/help`.

> **Note:** If you bought this book directly from Packt, no invoice is required. After *Step 2*, you can access your exclusive content right away.

Step 2

Scan the QR code or go to `packtpub.com/unlock`.

On the page that opens (similar to *Figure 16.1* on desktop), search for this book by name and select the correct edition.

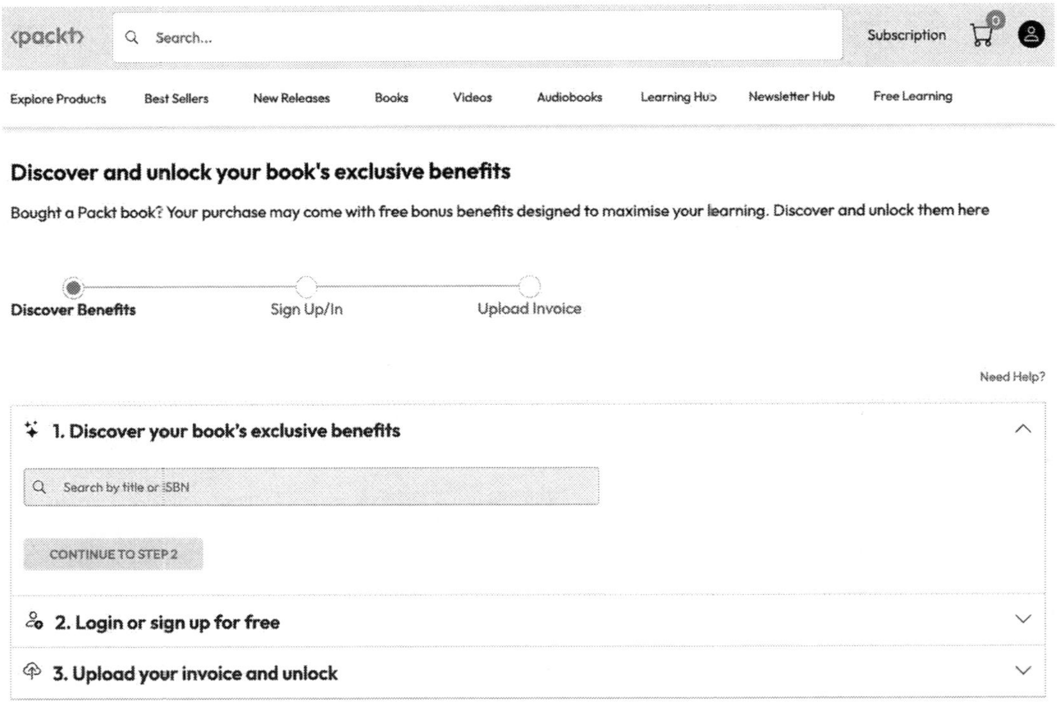

Figure 16.1: Packt unlock landing page on desktop

Step 3

After selecting your book, sign in to your Packt account or create one for free. Then upload your invoice (PDF, PNG, or JPG, up to 10 MB). Follow the on-screen instructions to finish the process.

Other Books You May Enjoy

If you enjoyed this book, you may be interested in these other books by Packt:

C++ Memory Management

Patrice Roy

ISBN: 9781805129806

- Master the C++ object model to write more efficient and maintainable code
- Automate resource management to reduce manual errors and improve safety
- Customize memory allocation operators to optimize performance for specific applications
- Develop your own smart pointers to manage dynamic memory with greater control
- Adapt allocation behavior to meet the unique needs of different data types
- Create safe and fast containers to ensure optimal data handling in your programs
- Utilize standard allocators to streamline memory management in your containers

LLVM Code Generation

Quentin Colombet

ISBN: 9781835462577

- Understand essential compiler concepts, such as SSA, dominance, and ABI
- Build and extend LLVM backends for creating custom compiler features
- Optimize code by manipulating LLVM's Intermediate Representation
- Contribute effectively to LLVM open-source projects and development
- Develop debugging skills for LLVM optimizations and passes
- Grasp how encoding and (dis)assembling work in the context of compilers
- Utilize LLVM's TableGen DSL for creating custom compiler models

GPU Programming with C++ and CUDA

Paulo Motta

ISBN: 9781805128823

- Manage GPU devices and accelerate your applications
- Apply parallelism effectively using CUDA and C++
- Choose between existing libraries and custom GPU solutions
- Package GPU code into libraries for use with Python
- Explore advanced topics such as CUDA streams
- Implement optimization strategies for resource-efficient execution

Packt is searching for authors like you

If you're interested in becoming an author for Packt, please visit `authors.packt.com` and apply today. We have worked with thousands of developers and tech professionals, just like you, to help them share their insight with the global tech community. You can make a general application, apply for a specific hot topic that we are recruiting an author for, or submit your own idea.

Share your thoughts

Now you've finished *The C++ Programmer's Mindset*, we'd love to hear your thoughts! Scan the QR code below to go straight to the Amazon review page for this book and share your feedback or leave a review on the site that you purchased it from.

`https://packt.link/r/1835888437`

Your review is important to us and the tech community and will help us make sure we're delivering excellent quality content.

Subscribe to Deep Engineering

Join thousands of developers and architects who want to understand how software is changing, deepen their expertise, and build systems that last.

Deep Engineering is a weekly expert-led newsletter for experienced practitioners, featuring original analysis, technical interviews, and curated insights on architecture, system design, and modern programming practice.

Scan the QR or visit the link to subscribe for free.

`https://packt.link/deep-engineering-newsletter`

Index

D

E

F

G

H

I

N

O

P

T

U

V

W

Made in United States
Orlando, FL
04 November 2026

90206074R00219